DEBATING DROPOUTS

Critical Policy and
Research Perspectives
on School Leaving

DEBATING DROPOUTS
Critical Policy and
Research Perspectives
on School Leaving

Deirdre Kelly
Jane Gaskell
EDITORS

Teachers College, Columbia University
New York and London

Published by Teachers College Press, 1234 Amsterdam Avenue, New York, NY 10027

A revised version of Chapter 6, "Safety net or safety valve: How choice is constructed in an urban dropout program," by Deirdre M. Kelly, appeared in N. P. Stromquist (Ed.), *Education in Urban Areas* (1994), pp. 63–82, Praeger Publishers, an imprint of Greenwood Publishing Group, Inc., Westport, CT.

Chapter 8 by Leslie G. Roman is adapted from her article "Spectacle in the Dark: Youth as Transgression, Display, and Repression," *Educational Theory,* Winter 1996, vol. 46 (1), pp. 1–22.

Library of Congress Cataloging-in-Publication Data

Debating dropouts : critical policy and research perspectives on
   school leaving / Deirdre Kelly and Jane Gaskell, editors.
      p.   cm.
   Includes bibliographical references and index.
   ISBN 0-8077-3542-6 (cloth).—ISBN 0-8077-3541-8 (pbk.)
    1. School dropouts—United States. 2. School dropouts—Canada.
  3. School dropouts—Research. I. Kelly, Deirdre M. II. Gaskell,
Jane S. (Jane Stobo)
  LC143.D33 1996
  371.2'913'097—dc20   96-12596

ISBN 0-8077-3541-8 (paper)
ISBN 0-8077-3542-6 (cloth)
Printed on acid-free paper
Manufactured in the United States of America
03 02 01 00 99 98 97 96   8 7 6 5 4 3 2 1

To Nora
who dropped into the world when this book was being made

Contents

Acknowledgments

We would like to thank the Social Sciences and Humanities Research Council of Canada without whose support this book could not have been written. SSHRC funded a research network which brought together scholars across Canada to think and write about educational policy in relation to the changing workplace. The conference on which this book was based grew out of the activities of that network.

Conference participants came from across the United States and Canada. We would like to thank them all for the lively discussion and presentations which stimulated everyone to think more clearly.

We would also like to thank Blanche Christensen for her tireless secretarial efforts, Robin Van Heck for her usual careful editing job, Teachers College Press (particularly Brian Ellerbeck and Sarah Biondello) for its interest and editing, and David Beers for editorial suggestions. Our families supported the work in all kinds of ways, and for that we remain grateful.

Foreword

To tell the truth, I worry whenever scholars, practitioners, and/or activists decide to focus on the question of "school dropouts." School-leavers are typically portrayed as young people who "choose" to exit an institution, cognizant or not of the presumed benefits of staying. Whitewashing policies, ideologies, and practices *produce* dropping out as widespread practice and *obscure* the very differentiated benefits of a degree. Such texts often narrate a fable in which staying in school allows a flight from poverty and an escape from racism, as if schooling were fine and leaving were irrational; as if school dropouts were the primary cause of economic and social ills that bedevil our nations.

Even those who have written about school-leavers as agents of resistance, raising their "critical voices" to "reframe dropping out," have left relatively unexamined the global economic relations (Apple, 1981), racial formations (Omi & Winant, 1986), and educational institutions and ideologies (Fine, 1991; see also Chapter 9 in this volume) that purge and alienate poor and working-class youth—both dropouts and graduates. Institutional and structural accountability seems to evaporate whenever rebellious or tragic individuals rise to the foreground in stories of school dropouts.

This introduction travels through a biography of my worries about research on school-staying and school-leaving, particularly about the role of an itchy, activist academic weary of stubborn social conditions that eat the young. I write awed by the task of saying something meaningful about public institutions at a moment in history when trust is so deservedly low and when purveyors of privatization hover, vulture-like, over the decaying body politic of urban America.

In the early 1980s, I tripped, unexpectedly, into my first study of school dropouts. I was the evaluation researcher of a school improvement program, funded by W. Clement Stone, a Chicago insurance entrepreneur, who had given vast sums of money to a small alternative school in the South Bronx. Stone had invented Positive Mental Attitude (PMA) in his corporate workplace and presumed that if only these students, many of whom were on probation or parole and in poverty, could mimic a Positive Mental Attitude by reciting, "I can be wealthy, healthy, and successful," then they too could achieve economic and social well-being. The school took the money. I did the evaluation.

Students answered questions for me in September 1980. By the following June, when the time for a "post-test" had arrived, 30% of the students were gone. They had dropped out, disappeared, returned to the streets, died, or been incarcerated. Turning methodological problem into research opportunity, I retrieved the September data to tease out differences between those who, by year's end, remained and those who had left. As I have reported elsewhere (1991), what emerged was an alarming comparison between dropouts and those students who stayed in school.

As it turned out, school-leavers were significantly *less* depressed, more resilient, and more critical of their constrained economic opportunities. In contrast, students who stayed in school were significantly more depressed, self-blaming, and politically conservative (Fine, 1991).

I wrote then, perhaps too glibly, about dropouts as critics. These young women and men, I contended, were clever analysts of the economy, vigilante critics of the questionable value of a high school credential in the urban economy of the early 1980s. I imputed far too much consciousness to their acts of resistance. After a year of storytelling about those who fled high school too early, I decided to move into a neighborhood with a high school that at the time produced dropout rates in excess of 50%. It was not hard to find one in New York City (Fine, 1991).

Entering a school I will call C.H.S., I was trying to figure out how so many students could pour out of a high school prior to graduation as if it were "natural." I knew well that a high school diploma reaped very different economic benefits according to its holder's class, race/ethnicity, and gender; that students' folk knowledge, gathered on streets and in neighborhoods, indicated little or no correlation between high earnings and number of years spent in school; that in this high school, like others "serving" low-income, minority children, most kids left prior to graduation and most adults presumed this to be "inevitable."

Nevertheless, it took close to a year of ethnographic "hanging out" for me to understand that the question was not *why* so many students would leave, but how the process of dropping out had become so thoroughly seamless. I started to understand that school-leaving was a fundamental part of schooling in low-income communities, not an aberration. Only 20% of C.H.S.'s 9th grade class graduated over a 6-year period: the vast majority disappeared. Further, within U.S. (and now Canadian) policy circles, school-leaving, like teen pregnancy, had become one of Nancy Fraser's (1989) "runaway" social problems, on which declining international competitiveness, crime, social inequities, family "collapse," and individual difficulties could be artificially hung.

By the time I completed my work at C.H.S., it was clear to me that public high schools could release easily the bodies of many school-leavers, disproportionately those brown, black, and/or poor, and at the same time hollow the spirits of many school-stayers. Eager to work with schools and communities, I was quite sure that this critique was not going to be warmly received. Holding a mirror up to a public institution, beleaguered and faltering, filled with good intentions and bad outcomes, was no way to incite social change. The study of dropouts could be a political decoy deflecting our attention away from structural conditions that purge students from schools, and poor and working-class adults from the economy.

Flip channels for a moment and consider another piece of work where Lani Guinier, colleagues, students, and I launched a critical analysis of schooling as it affects *not* those who drop out, but those who *stay*—law students at our home institution, the University of Pennsylvania. I fast-forward to this more recent project where, unlike C.H.S., no one drops out (Fine, Guinier, Balin, Bartow, & Satchel, 1994). Within this elite professional school, incidents of school failure could not be attributed to an individual's low capacity or poor motivation. Qualified men and women of all colors have "equal access" to Penn's law school. All enter with spectacular credentials. Almost everyone graduates. Although our study of the Law School is far too detailed to elaborate here, you may review all the evidence in Fine et al. (1994).

Initially we—actually Ann Bartow, then a law student—conducted a student survey about gender politics at the law school. Ann learned that men and women students were attending psychologically different law schools. Men reported that they were comfortable with faculty, peers, and the adversarial method; clear and unwavering about their interests in bankruptcy, tax law, and litigation; determined to compete and win; satisfied with their participation, engagement, and academic achievements. Women, in contrast, felt alienated from faculty and peers; disliked the adversarial method; expressed an early interest in public-interest laws. But then we noticed that *only* in their first year did women significantly differ from all other students. Gender "differences" disappeared; by their third year, women were indistinguishable from men.

Although women's politics bumped to the right over time, we were curious about how their academic work survived over 3 years of law school. Here we found evidence of a reverse course. Whereas on political items women came to look more like men, on academic indicators men and women grew further apart. Women entered law school with credentials identical to men's, in terms of undergraduate GPA, LSAT, class rank, and quality of undergraduate institution. However, the second year cumulatively to graduation, women collected "deficient" credentials, whereas

White males thrived as a group. By the third year, women were twice as likely to be in the bottom half of the class; six times less likely than men to be in the top 10. Women embarked upon law school as competent, feminist, and engaged, but they left depressed, conservative, and carrying relatively unimpressive academic credentials. The law school data should alarm readers about the very differentiated *costs* of *school-staying* in particular for those who carry scars of what is considered professional socialization.

True to class-based politics, poor high school critics from C.H.S. left, while conformists stayed. Equally true to class-based politics, Penn's elite critics conformed. Pierre Bourdieu wrote on the "rites of institution" in *Language and Symbolic Power* (1991) as if he were writing on either of these schools—C.H.S. or Penn's law school. He explained that the word *institution* should be read as a verb, not a noun, and goes on to describe the "social magic" by which institutions *produce* stratification and embodied identities: "One can see that the process of *institution* consists of assigning properties of a social nature in a way that makes them seem like properties of a physical nature . . . and woman as women . . ." (p. 118).

The act of institution is thus an act of communication, but of a particular kind: It signifies to someone what his identity is, but in a way that both expresses it to him and impresses it on him by expressing it in front of everyone (p. 121). Students who refuse to be institutionalized resist this "social magic." They may leave, as did the dropouts from C.H.S., or they may drown, as women students did at law school. Either way, schools are structured so that critics pay a price (academic, economic, or mental health) *and* their analyses melt into self-blame over time. To study dropouts *per se,* we may lose sight of the critique.

From interviews with C.H.S. school-leavers at ages 17 and 21, and from interviews with first-, second-, and third-year law students, we tracked the *biographies* of critique—these students' and dropouts' *social consciousnesses.* At 17, high school-leavers, like first-year women at the law school, were filled with lively commentary on the economy, labor, schooling, race relations, gender politics, and community life. Critical but hopeful, their personal visions were the fantasies of "what could be." Inspired, they saw few limits. But for both high school dropouts and women law students, in only a short time, their deep social critique turned inward. By their early twenties, both groups of young men and women from very different social positions narrated loyalty to their schools and serious self-castigation for past actions. For the high school-leavers, their expansive social analyses shrunk by age 21. "Successfully" socialized into an adulthood of poverty, the 21-year-old school-leavers withdrew their critique of schools and the economy and offered only embarrassed regrets. They sounded much like the "successfully" socialized third-year women at the law school who had, as one professor had implored them to do, "become gentlemen."

These young adults seem all too willing, ultimately, to blame themselves for their misfortune. Although dropouts, like first-year women at the law school, would flirt with political critique during their late and "wild" teen years, by young adulthood (or year three of law school) they "matured" into self-blame. The psychological project of late capitalism—getting the poor (and school "failures") to hold themselves accountable for their own miserable outcomes—has been a brilliant success. Acts of resistance are well appropriated; personal responsibility for social inequities is well internalized. Critique slides from *institution* to *individual,* inverting over time in the name of "maturity" or "professional socialization."

A note on class: It is important to recognize the obvious. The safety net sitting under and around elite students, those at Penn, for instance, is substantial, woven by a culture ready to catch and promote these elite students. Social institutions, networks, and expectations for the elite are designed to support and resuscitate even those who fall through the cracks. The net sitting under the C.H.S. students, in contrast, has always been torn but was ravaged by the Reagan–Bush administration in the United States, as is similar net fraying in Canada today. For these students, too, there are social institutions, networks, and expectations waiting for them, but these are more likely to be within juvenile justice, probation, jail, mental health institutions, social service programs, or unemployment—waiting to catch these produced failures.

Again—what role exists for intellectuals? If we write on school failure or success abstracted from social and economic conditions, we collude in the self-blame that eventually riddles dropouts, and legitimate the fixed gaze that blames them for social and economic ills. In contrast, public intellectuals may be able to document and perhaps interrupt this perverse reversal of critique. If relentlessly attentive to macrostructural accountability *and* the contradictions of people's lives, we can reveal how smoothly social arrangements and public institutions scaffold class, racial, and gendered trajectories; how they naturalize academic and economic demise; how they are embodied. We can document how social ideologies, dominant discourses, public policies, and youth-related programs produce stratified social relations as they pummel the souls of those gutsy enough to question.

Many have argued that intellectuals bear an obligation to speak aloud and to interrupt the drift to individual blame. As a social psychologist, I feel particularly obligated to dam the rush of "self-esteem" explanations flooding the literature on school failure.

The essays in this volume, *Debating Dropouts,* serve us a delicious feast to feed our intellectual hunger and to incite our political mobilizing. Filled with passion and distance, stories of the micro and analyses of the macro import interdisciplinary and critical perspectives to questions of school-leaving. These essays cross the borders of the United States and Canada, entering urban villages, rural villages, and Navajo reservations. They take as their narrow starting point the "problem" of school dropouts and demonstrate elegantly how this issue has been exploited as a virus which destroyed the moral fabric of otherwise wholesome communities, schools, economies, and nations.

I learned a lot reading these chapters. Both separately and together, they pry open structural, economic, racial, and gendered scenes in which school-leavers have been condemned as the culprits behind the problems of late capitalism (see Chapters 1, 3, 4, and 5), oppressive racial/ethnic formations (Chapter 9), and gender inequities (Chapter 10). Although many of these writers offer important postmodern insights about the absurdity of the binary oppositions sculpted into policy and practice, they also refuse to remain distant theorists. They engage, on the ground, the effects of school leaving. Troubled by the price that young people pay, poor and working class in particular (see Chapter 2), these writers offer important empirical confirmation of the deadly consequences of tracking (Chapter 5), the contradictory effects of alternative schools (Chapter 6), the devastating impact on teachers and students of alienation and disempowerment (Chapter 7), and the sheer meaninglessness of schools expressed by Black youth in Canadian schools (Chapter 9).

When reading across these chapters I was conscious of my own metaphors and fantasies. First, I couldn't help but feel a leper-like quality crawling over the bodies of school-leavers. Perhaps because I was writing this introduction when I was quarantined for chicken pox, contracted from my seven-year-old son, images of contaminating others leapt off the pages of the manuscript. These essays do a terrific job of repositioning school-leavers as a symptom, not the cause, of social inequities.

I was delighted that so many scholars from such diverse intellectual traditions landed on school-leaving as the site from which to launch important theoretical and empirical work. Because dropping out sits at the knotty nexus of economics, racism, public institutions, and questions of individual agency, it is ripe for deep intellectual work. It has rarely been treated that way.

These authors, all in the best tradition of postmodernism, write as critics of categories, advocates for students, and participants in debates about how to make schools better. So many colleagues in the academy *either* situate themselves at the postmodern critical margins, daring not to enter the fray of real problems lest they get dragged into the swamp of material reality, or, like others, particularly in education, situate themselves inside what Roberto Unger (1987) would call structure fetishism, so they can not imagine anything outside the "formative contexts . . . that impose on our practical, passionate and cognitive relations a script we cannot easily rewrite" (p. 201). Struggling with the role of public intellectuals—indeed, education intellectuals at the end of the twentieth century—I only wished that these writers engaged each other in critical talk about the "spaces between" theory, academic research, policy, and activism. Leslie Roman in Chapter 8 dares readers to consider our role as researchers in reproducing as well as interrupting the moral panic surrounding dropouts. She writes: "Are we, as researchers, prepared to think and act against the grain? Will we join with progressive social government activists to make some counterhegemonic noise in contexts that reach broad audiences of policy makers and official agents of the state?"

In this spirit, I tried to invent a conversation among the policy bureaucrats that Paul Anisef and Lesley Andres cite, the students that George Sefa Dei interviewed, and the theorist Kari Dehli.

We learn, early in this book, that "The central purpose of the Stay-in-School Initiative . . . was to respond to the serious threat that the secondary school dropout rates pose to the future productivity of the Canadian economy" (see Chapter 5). You can almost see Kari Dehli snicker as she writes, "Aside from those who live the underside of 'restructuring,' there are many who question whether there is any straightforward link between skills training and the more high-quality, high-wage employment which current policies promise."

To which Leah, one of Dei's most impressive dropout-informants, might explain differently, all the while rolling her eyes:

All I will tell you is that as a Black student it [the school system] kills your character, your innate strengths, it kills certain abilities in order to reincarnate you, to turn you into something totally different. It either leaves you with a complex, or a chip on your shoulder, or a mental or physical disorder or emotional disorder. It literally takes what used to exist and terminates. It takes a strong Black person with inner strength to see what the current education system does to you and to leave it.

Readers of this book will have the opportunity to decide whom to believe, what we all might do to interrupt toxic categories and hold accountable public institutions, and how we can help heal the daily trauma that we ask young people to endure. You will be inspired as you read provocative interruptions of old frames and theoretically enticing new ones. Enjoy the book and get outraged.

—Michelle Fine

REFERENCES

Apple, M. (Ed.). (1981). *Cultural and economic reproduction in education.* London: Routledge & Kegan Paul.

Bourdieu, P. (1991). *Language and symbolic power.* Cambridge: Harvard University Press.

Fine, M., & Guinier, L., Balin, J., Bartow, A., & Satchel, D. (1994). Becoming gentlemen: The education of women at the University of Pennsylvania. *University of Pennsylvania Law Review, 143* (1), 1–110.

Fine, M. (1991). *Framing dropouts: Notes on the politics of an urban high school.* Albany: State University of New York Press.

Fraser, N. (1989). *Unruly practices.* University of Minnesota Press.

Omi, M., & Winant, H. (1986). *Racial formation in the United States.* Boston: Routledge & Kegan Paul.

Unger, R. (1987). *Social theory: Its situation and its task.* Cambridge: Cambridge University Press.

PART I

CURRENT POLICY FRAMES IN NORTH AMERICA: EXPLORING THE DOMINANT STANCE

A new, prevailing wisdom is guiding the thinking of policy makers and policy shapers throughout North America; its watchwords are "global competitiveness" and "economic restructuring." Few are disputing that the increased use of new technologies and the shift toward "knowledge" work will require well-honed math, reading, and writing abilities. But the preoccupation with viewing schooling and its role in society through the single lens of global economic competitiveness closes off other, valid ways of looking at, speaking about, and imagining policies for dropouts. In the dominant policy framework, leaving school before graduating from 12th grade is no longer perceived as just individual tragedy or mistaken judgment but as a threat to economic prosperity and "national security." Not only is there renewed concern about dropouts, but a wave of policy measures geared to addressing the problem have been proposed; politicians from Ottawa to Washington, D.C. have recently set the goal of cutting the dropout rate to 10%.

This book examines the debate in the United States and in Canada—countries which have closely linked economies. They are each other's most important trading partner and are linked by the North American Free Trade Agreement (NAFTA). There are, however, some important differences between the two countries in history, political and social structures, and beliefs. Americans tend to view Canada as enough like the U.S. to make policy comparisons useful. The most striking and recent example of this, of course, has been in the area of health care; the Congressional Budget Office reported that a Canadian-style, single-payer system would be the least costly way to provide health care for all Americans.

Canadians are more aware of differences. The Canadian economy includes more public ownership and a wider net of social services. The school system is constitutionally assigned to the provinces, and teachers' salaries are higher. The individualism of U.S. ideology is mixed with more communitarian traditions. What is striking, however, is the way the debate about schooling and the economy transcends borders, even though the particular forms and reports in which it is expressed are distinct. The global economy leads to global educational rhetoric, a phenomenon which countries as disparate as Mexico, Korea, and Germany also note.

The dominant discourse, and the dominant economy, is that of the United States. U.S. Secretary of Labor Robert Reich, for example, argues in his influential book, *The Work of Nations: Preparing Ourselves for 21st Century Capitalism,* that the fostering of education must now rise to the top of any national government's priority list. The days of nationalist protection of home-based corporations, once a tool government used to secure employment for its citizens, has been eclipsed by the new economic order. Now that a single product might be conceived in one country, designed in another, tested in still another, and manufactured in several more, the purpose of government shifts to readying its citizenry to grab the best paying spots within such "global webs" of production. This means, for Reich, an imperative emphasis on education and training. Every child should have the educational opportunities to become a "symbolic analyst," a term used to describe those who occupy the highly educated top one-fifth of the work force and who Reich estimates are engaged in problem-solving, problem-identifying, and strategic-brokering activities. This means that, because global competition is pushing down the wages of low-skilled workers, students who drop out face grim prospects individually and deter national economic growth more than ever.

Reich heralds only the latest instance where international economic competition and new technologies have raised alarms about out-of-school youth in Canada and the United States (Houston, 1993; see also Chapter 6). The preoccupation with school attendance is far from new. The problem of school attendance is created during times of economic and social restructuring, when people want public policy solutions. Houston describes how out-of-school, self-employed street children in Toronto became defined as a threat to societal values and interests in policy discourse in late 19th-century Canada, at a time when compulsory school attendance laws were being considered, passed, and sometimes enforced. The difficulties in documenting attendance rates at the turn of the century are similar to the difficulties of arriving at a dropout rate today.

Today we are in the middle of another moral panic about dropouts. People across a range of ideological positions cite "alarmingly high" dropout rates to marshal support for various schooling reforms, some at direct odds with each other. Sophisticated public relations campaigns are being waged to convince middle-class suburbanites that dropouts are not just an inner city (read: poor, racial minority) problem and that inadequate education and training are strongly linked to declining economic competitiveness and a lower standard of living for their children. Advertising campaigns that urge young people to stay in school, as illustrated in Figure 1.1, have the ironic effect of further convincing employers and others that dropouts are irrational and deviant. Too much emphasis is being placed on the amount of schooling people receive without an attendant concern

FIGURE I.1. Part of an ad campaign aimed at shifting the public's education attitudes (Public Agenda Foundation and the Business-Higher Education Forum, 1992).

AMERICA
The Throwaway Society

ONE OUT OF EVERY FOUR AMERICANS
DOESN'T FINISH HIGH SCHOOL. BY 1999, MORE THAN
TEN MILLION ADULTS WILL NOT HAVE FINISHED SCHOOL.
IS THIS ANY WAY TO COMPETE?

SECOND-RATE SKILLS MEAN A SECOND-RATE AMERICA. WE'VE GOT A JOB TO DO.

Read about HELP WANTED in the (newspaper). Learn about HELP WANTED on (television).
Look for your HELP WANTED ballot in the (date and newspaper). Mark it and mail it in.

CRISIS IN THE
WORK FORCE
HELP
WANTED

for whether this policy goal alone will improve schools or the prospects of all students—dropouts or not—who feel alienated by the current system.

Rhetoric to the contrary, dropout rates are declining. This does not, however, lower the concern. We can expect to see the popularization of a new social identity, that of the "in-school dropout" and continuing pressure on young people to conform to the demands of the school, to compete on the basis of grades, and to continue their schooling into postsecondary institutions.

By transposing the perceived economic crisis onto the schools, concerns about global competitiveness wind up dictating educational policy—often in conflict with other aims for schooling, such as equity and good citizenship. In addition, schools get set up for attack by raising public expectations for what is not fully within the educational system's control to deliver. No one is arguing against advising children to get more and better education. But the idea that every student will be educated to become highly paid problem-solvers in the high technology economy (the "symbolic analysts" Reich speaks of) creates false hopes. In an increasingly bifurcated economy in which good jobs are globally mobile, as Reich himself argues, would there be rewarding work for everyone if we were to achieve the magic 10% dropout figure? It is a question rarely asked in the dominant policy discourse but raised often in this book.

The dominant discourse contains many other questionable assumptions. Examples: Students exercise a clear choice to leave school without graduating rather than being pushed out or fading out. Dropouts are below average in intelligence, psychologically disturbed, or otherwise deviant. "Dysfunctional" families, "burned out" teachers, or both are to blame. Making the curriculum more "relevant" (read: more vocational or therapeutic) will prevent "at-risk" students from dropping out. More special programs are the answer. A growing body of critical research challenges every one of these assumptions using a variety of methods (Fine, 1991; Gaskell, 1992; Kelly, 1993; LeCompte & Dworkin, 1991; Wehlage et al., 1989; Weis, Farrar, & Petrie, 1989; Wexler, 1992).

The following three chapters are a contribution to that challenge. Together they make a strong case for the importance of continuously scrutinizing the language we use in framing policy issues as well as attending to inequality. The authors highlight discourses associated with oppositional movements—feminism, antiracist and antipoverty organizations, and organized labor—that contest the dominant stance. These alternative discourses suggest ways of reframing the issues around dropouts, a theme revisited in Part III.

In Chapter 1, Kari Dehli lays out a useful way of analyzing policy documents and debates, focusing on their form, implicit assumptions, and the social and political contexts in which they are produced and disseminated. She examines three influential Canadian policy reports on education, reading them as "stories" which invite readers to see social problems—and hence their solutions—in particular ways and not others. Dehli argues that the increasingly common use of business–

government–labor "partnerships" in creating key policy documents can provide an illusion of consensus even as they make room for subordinate groups to contest the dominant policy discourse. She observes that policy formation practices often exclude those most directly affected by social problems, such as marginalized youth. One effect of the dominant policy discourse, Dehli points out, is that the emphasis on training and retraining subtly shifts responsibility onto individuals to adjust themselves to global economic restructuring. Dehli's chapter thus sets the stage for a more in-depth analysis of the concepts of "lifelong learning" (Chapter 2) and the supposed dependency of "at-risk" youth (Chapter 3).

Would leaving school "early" be a concern to policy makers if students found it easy to return at age 18, or 25, or 35? Should the educational system be organized for easy reentry in order to realize the ideal of lifelong learning? Rubenson discusses the evolution of the lifelong learning concept in Chapter 2. He points out that the first generation of lifelong learning occurred in the 1960s and had utopian origins; first generation proponents attended closely to the structural obstacles and preconditions for lifelong learning. In contrast, the second generation of lifelong learning, which developed during the 1980s, is characterized by a lack of commitment to equality and the "total dominance of the economic imperative." Today policy talk about lifelong learning concentrates narrowly on skill training and is presented as a panacea to the dropout problem. Rubenson analyzes the complex economic and social reasons that—given conditions of society-wide inequality—opportunities for and benefits of lifelong learning will remain unequal. He also critiques the technological determinism underlying second generation calls for lifelong learning, concluding that "the consequences of new technology on the demand for and development of competencies depend on the interplay of the nature of technology, implementation strategies, work organization, and the existent competencies of the work force."

Lesko deconstructs a number of binary oppositions that pervade the policy and research discourse on "at risk" youth. Such dualisms as dropout/stay-in, dependence/independence, at risk/successful, and special/regular usually hide power relations and often result in falsely dichotomous policy choices. She asks, for example, "In what schooling situations do youth have genuine power over decision making, over resources, over how they interact with adults and peers? Can we construct schooling contexts in which *interdependence* is the norm, moving beyond the dependence/independence divide?" Lesko places her analysis in the context of the intensifying battle over resources in the U.S. welfare state. She points out that policy talk about dropouts and at risk youth is often linked to wider fears about public dependency. "Independence," Lesko argues, "is defined solely as having waged work, and since such work is believed to be available to all, dependence is escapable." In this common framing of the issue, dependence is pathologized and dropouts are viewed as morally or psychologically blameworthy. She discusses strategies for calling into question the dependency of at risk youth and concludes that the "goodness" of the norm of independence has been selectively applied.

REFERENCES

Fine, M. (1991). *Framing dropouts: Notes on the politics of an urban public high school.* Albany: State University of New York Press.

Gaskell, J. S. (1992). *Gender matters from school to work.* Toronto: OISE Press.

Houston, S. E. (1993, March). *School attendance and its competition in 19th century "Canada."* Paper presented at the Dropping In/Dropping Out Conference, University of British Columbia, Vancouver, B.C.

Kelly, D. M. (1993). *Last chance high: How girls and boys drop in and out of alternative schools.* New Haven, CT: Yale University Press.

LeCompte, M. D., & Dworkin, G. D. (1991). *Giving up on school.* Newbury Park, CA: Corwin Press.

Public Agenda Foundation and the Business-Higher Education Forum. (1992, February). *Crisis in the work force: Help wanted.* New York: Author.

Reich, R. B. (1991). *The work of nations: Preparing ourselves for 21st century capitalism.* New York: Knopf.

Wehlage, G. G., Rutter, R. A., Smith, G. R., Lesko, N., & Fernandez, R. R. (1989). *Reducing the risk: Schools as communities.* London: Falmer Press.

Weis, L., Farrar, E., & Petrie, H. G. (Eds.). (1989). *Dropouts from school.* Albany: State University of New York Press.

Wexler, P. (1992). *Becoming somebody: Toward a social psychology of school.* Washington, D.C.: Falmer Press.

CHAPTER 1

Unfinished Business? The Dropout Goes to Work in Education Policy Reports

KARI DEHLI

One evening in October, 1991 I received a phone call from a friend. She was worried and wanted to talk. Michael, her oldest son who was 17, refused to go to school. He had been skipping classes for several weeks and she knew that he wasn't happy at school. My friend had tried to talk with him, but he would only say that he was bored and that there was no point in going. "Michael used to love school," she despaired. "What happened? Where did I go wrong?" As it turned out, Michael did leave school that fall. He got a job cutting vegetables and washing pots in a trendy restaurant. For a while he seemed to thrive in his new surroundings. But the pay was poor and soon the novelty wore off. By March of the following year, he was ready to go back to school. He decided to attend one of the smaller, public alternative schools in the city rather than the local collegiate he had dropped out of. Within the next year he managed to complete the number of high school credits required to get into university.

Since the early 1980s, numerous policy reports that declare state-funded schools to be in a condition of crisis have been issued in the United States, Britain, Australia, and New Zealand. These reports place education in the context of an increasingly competitive and harsh economic market, and schools are frequently depicted as both a source of economic problems and as the road to future individual and collective prosperity in industrialized capitalist countries. Although there are important differences between these reports, they have argued that there are serious problems at all levels of schooling because students are not being sufficiently prepared for the changing world of work, because standards are falling, and/or because school systems fail to operate efficiently, cost effectively, and accountably. They variously call for schools to return to the "basics" in the curriculum; for a new emphasis on "excellence" in performance, particularly in math, science, and technology; for a stronger vocational orientation; for standardized forms of testing; for school "restructuring," deficit reduction, and financial "efficiency"; and for increased parental involvement in the name of "consumer choice." (For critical reviews of such reports and debates, see Apple, 1993; Arnot & Barton, 1992; Bailey, 1989; Bowe, Ball, & Gold, 1992; Brown, 1987; Dale, 1992; Kenway, Bigum, & Fitzclarence, 1993; Lauglo, 1992; Marginson, 1992; Shapiro, 1989.)

Similar reports and policy statements have been issued in Canada by the federal and provincial governments, by state-funded research councils and institutes, by government commissions, and by "private" organizations, notably in business and labor. These documents have titles such as *Success in the Works: A Profile of Canada's Emerging Work Force* (Canada, Ministry of Employment and Immigration [MEI], 1989), *Focus 2000: Report of the Task Force on Harnessing Change* (Canadian Chamber of Commerce, 1988), *People and Skills in the New Global Economy* (Ontario Premier's Council, 1990), *Learning Well . . . Living Well* (Canada, Ministry of Employment and Immigration, Ministry of Industry, Science and Technology, and Ministry of International Trade, Prosperity Initiative, [MEI/MIST/MIT], 1991a), and *A Lot to Learn* (Economic Council of Canada, 1992b), all of which suggest the strong claims being made about the links between education and training on the one hand, and individual and national economic growth and performance on the other. Although their focus, scope, and particular recommendations vary, these Canadian reports share important assumptions about the purposes of education by privileging the needs of business and by foregrounding relationships between schools, economic development, and the labor market in public debates about education reform. Like their counterparts elsewhere, these reports have been widely circulated, quoted, and discussed. They have given shape to the agenda of public debate about education in Canada in the late 1980s and 1990s.

The concern with young people who leave school before completing their course of study has not been the only major focus in most of these reports, or even a major focus at all (but see Radwanski, 1987), although it is a topic often discussed. I argue in this chapter, however, that particular representations of dropouts are "at work" even in policy texts that do not take dropouts as their major focus. I want to explore how "the dropout" is represented and inserted into broader and more general educational policy texts. What kind of conceptual and political work is this category mobilized to accomplish in texts that investigate educational questions in relation to economic production and labor markets in the late 1980s and early 1990s? What are some of the intended and unintended effects of the category's deployment in policy texts themselves, in broader education and public policy debates, and in struggles over the organization and provision of state-funded and state-managed education?

I argue in this chapter that the dropout is put to work in recent Canadian (and other countries') policy reports to accomplish several (and not always consistent or intended) discursive and political effects (insofar as intentions can be "read off" from policy texts). It is one of a small number of categories deployed in these texts that paints a picture of schools in crisis and out of step with the kind of education young people today (and tomorrow) need. In view of claims that most jobs now and in the future will require higher levels of formal education, the prospect of large numbers of "dropouts" is not only a problem for those individuals themselves, it is also seen as a potential "drain" on the national (or/and provincial) economy. At the same time the dropout rate provides a measure of schools' ability to produce their expected "outcomes," thus offering a way to evaluate schools' productivity or quality. This way of framing dropouts (Fine, 1991) is especially evident in policy statements or reports that draw heavily on economic analyses and discourses.

Drawing on somewhat different sociological and psychological discourses, the dropout also serves to both "individualize" and "totalize" (Foucault, 1982) the varied experiences of contradictions endemic to modern forms of compulsory schooling. Along with a small number of related categories ("illiterate," "truant," and "at risk" students, to mention some), this term focuses on characteristics presumably shared by individuals and groups who do not react in "normal" ways either to the social relations and practices of schools, or to the changing structure of labor markets and paid and unpaid work (LeCompte & Dworkin, 1991; Watson, 1975). Furthermore, although the term *dropout* is used to individualize the effects of contradictory social relations and practices, its deployment in education policies and practices also facilitates general definitions of what will count as issues warranting organized regulation of populations of children and young people. Finally, I argue, the dropout is mobilized in policy reports and debates where social and political subjects are being repositioned in relation to school provision, employment, and public decision making (Dehli, 1993; Fraser, 1989).

Also in this chapter I trace how the dropout is put to work in three recent Canadian reports: *Learning Well . . . Living Well,* issued by the fed-

eral government's so-called Prosperity Initiative in 1991 (Canada, MEI/
MIST/MIT, 1991a); *A Lot to Learn,* the last report to be published by the
Economic Council of Canada in 1992 (before federal funding was withdrawn); and the Ontario Premier's Council's report, *People and Skills in the
New Global Economy,* issued by the Liberal government on the eve of the
Ontario provincial election in the summer of 1990. I examine how the
three reports are structured and how they tell their story. My interest here
is not to analyze whether young people's experience and behavior are
being fairly or accurately investigated and reported on in these policy
documents. That is, my aim is not to argue about the truthfulness or
integrity of the reports, but to ask about the forms that their arguments
take and the possible effects of truth claims (Alonso, 1988) made in and
through them. The different uses of the dropout have many educational
and political effects, of course, and I deal with only some of them here
(see also Chapter 3).

I am more interested in the form and structure of the reports, i.e., in
their implicit assumptions and choice of frameworks, than in their content
and veracity. I situate the three reports in the social and political contexts
in which they were produced, circulated, and discussed, and then read
them as "stories" that deploy particular kinds of rhetorical strategies and
narrative structures in which the dropout (and related categories) plays an
important part. Whether these strategies and structures work is subject to
interpretation, contestation, and struggle over specific recommendations,
but also in terms of the broader "regimes of truth," they work to define
problems and propose solutions (Foucault, 1982). In a discussion about
state commissions of inquiry, Ashforth (1990) argues that such commissions and the "truths" they engender are effective as "reckoning schemes
of legitimation" (p. 1), even when their specific proposals are not adopted.
It seems clear that the plethora of policy statements and reports in the
1980s and 1990s have contributed in major ways to altering the terms of
public debate about education in Canada and the United States. As Marginson (1992) has argued for Australia, these reports position education as
a "branch of economics," thus evaluating its successes and failures in terms
of economic rationalism (see also Clandfield, 1993; Shapiro, 1989). One
feature of these perspectives is a reconsideration of the "cost-effectiveness" of schooling, that is, what types of education (and other) services
ought to be provided by the state, what kinds of claims can reasonably be
made on state-provided or state-funded schools, and a shift in how, where,
and by whom such claims should be put forward. Thus, one important
effect of recent policy debates in Canadian education is a struggle to define who has a legitimate right to speak and act, or, in the language of
many of these reports, who is a desirable and credible "stakeholder" or
"partner" in educational decision and policy making.

READING POLICY TEXTS AS STORIES

The account that introduced this chapter would be commonly recognized as a story about particular individuals who live and act in specific times, places, and conditions. Reports such as those issued by governments, government-appointed institutes and councils, or private organizations and think tanks can also be read as stories told in order to make sense of experiences, relations, and events, and to recommend, initiate, or organize courses of action in or by governments and public institutions. Like Michael, his mother, and me, those who produce such reports also have reasons for telling their stories, and they too are particularly located social subjects. They too use narrative devices and rhetorical strategies to convince readers of the seriousness of the problems they discuss, or to garner support for the arguments they make.

But there are some differences. Michael's story is one that would usually be told by one person to another, face to face, perhaps on the telephone or in a letter, addressed to someone in particular. Stories told in policy reports appear to speak from no particular place and they are addressed to everyone, or to the general public. Policy reports are produced with the aid of paid staff, printed in hundreds or even thousands of copies, quoted in newspapers and magazines, presented at conferences, and reported as "facts" in educational and government institutions. Although they rely on a complex division of labor and the mobilization of vast resources, such stories appear as if they come out of nowhere. And although many of the reports I referred to earlier privilege the interests of employers and corporations, they present their positions as though they promote the interests of "all of us." Dorothy Smith (1990) has written about how "the conceptual practices of power," including those organized through policy formation and debates, work to organize "relations of ruling" as though they comprise a normal and inevitable state of affairs. In the passive voice that such reports often use, one might also say that the telling of stories through commissions, research councils, and policy groups also contributes to notions of who and what the public is, what can count as important issues to be publicly debated and acted upon, and how and where such debates should occur (Corrigan & Sayer, 1985).

THREE CANADIAN REPORTS

The three Canadian policy documents I analyze have all had a significant impact on policy discussion. They are all dominated by the business/government agenda for schooling. *A Lot to Learn* was published by the Economic Council of Canada in April 1992, only a few months after the

Council was abolished by the Tory federal government. A larger and more detailed follow-up and background report, *Education and Training in Canada,* was released later in the year (Economic Council of Canada, 1992a). According to its president, Judith Maxwell, the Council's objectives in any research project were threefold: "to provide relevant policy advice to decision makers, to enhance public understanding of key economic issues, and to advance the boundaries of knowledge of those issues" (Economic Council of Canada, 1987, p. ix). At the time of its closing, the Council had 25 members, about half of whom were drawn from the corporate sector. Others were recruited from the leadership of labor unions, postsecondary education, or voluntary or social service organizations (Economic Council of Canada, 1992b, pp. 63–64). It was fully funded by the federal government. The Council's research staff, consultants, and the reports they wrote gained a high reputation for their credibility and thoroughness. Some of the reports took positions that were quite critical of prevailing government policy. This was particularly true of the Economic Council's 1990 report *Good Jobs, Bad Jobs,* which warned of increasing polarization in Canada's labor market.

As the name and objectives suggest, the Economic Council of Canada focused its work on what its staff and members defined as economic issues, or as issues with important effects on economic production, trade, and markets. It is not surprising, then, that *A Lot to Learn* positions education and training in direct relation to paid work, or that education is treated as an industry. In the foreword to the report, Judith Maxwell claimed that *A Lot to Learn* "is the first comprehensive examination of the way primary and secondary schools and the training system in Canada prepare young people for employment." She explained how Council members and staff had begun to see the need for such a study in "the late 1980s and early 1990s," while they were working on reports into technological change, trade relations, and changes in employment patterns. In the course of those studies, Council members and researchers grew concerned that "high levels of participation in education obscured high rates of illiteracy and unemployment, and serious mismatching between jobs and skills" (1992b, p. vii). Moreover, the Council expressed a concern it took to be shared by "many Canadians," that the country's education system was not providing an adequate return on individual and collective investments in it. The resulting policy statement (as well as the larger research report that followed) provides an interesting version of economic rationalism, in the form of human capital theory, applied to education.

Learning Well . . . Living Well was published jointly by the federal Ministry of Industry, Science, Technology (MIST), the Ministry of International Trade (MIT), and the Ministry of Employment and Immigration

(MEI) in 1991. With a companion document, *Prosperity Through Competitiveness,* it was intended to serve as a consultation paper on key national economic issues. These two documents are known as the "Prosperity Initiative" documents. In the words of the two Ministers, "[W]ith the release of this paper and *Prosperity Through Competitiveness,* the Government of Canada intends to stimulate a national discussion on the factors that determine our future prosperity."[1] Whereas the Economic Council of Canada's study resulted in a comprehensive report and a shorter policy statement, the Prosperity Initiative documents are slim, although they too draw on some versions of economic theory to make their claims. These latter documents were not meant just to produce facts and figures for debate, however, they were intended to produce a national consensus on economic and educational goals and strategies. They are more openly political in that they are concerned with garnering support for federal government policies. To quote the Ministers again: "The goal is to develop a consensus on a national action plan for the balance of the 1990s to be implemented by governments, business, labor and individual Canadians" (1991, p. i). As faculty members of a postsecondary institution, my colleagues and I received a copy of a draft of *Learning Well . . . Living Well,* with an accompanying memorandum from the director of our institution urging us to respond to "the challenge of this document." According to the final draft, "60 business, labor, academic and social action groups, as well as provincial governments" (p. i) were consulted in the preparation of the document, which Canadians were then invited to discuss.

The Ontario Premier's Council on Technology was formed on the initiative of Liberal Premier David Peterson in April 1986. Peterson appointed members to the 36-member Council and chaired its meetings. With a membership dominated by the premier, key cabinet ministers and corporate executives, senior education managers and researchers, three leaders of trade unions, and with only four women and even fewer members of visible minorities, the Council was hardly representative of the Ontario population. Nevertheless, through its research staff and consultations with education and labor market "experts," the Council's analysis did not reproduce an unqualified corporate perspective. Moreover, some of its recommendations in *People and Skills in the New Global Economy* suggested a much greater role for governments in regulating the economy than those reports issued by the federal Canadian government in the same period. This report, issued in the summer of 1990, was the third document produced and circulated by the Premier's Council. When the New Democratic Party (NDP) won the provincial election later that year, the new government quickly decided to follow up on many recommendations made in that report. In particular, the government began to reorganize secondary schooling to "de-stream" (or "de-track") 9th grade, and to provide a more comprehensive and open curriculum. The NDP also pursued the creation of a semi-autonomous and multipartite board that would develop and implement "training and adjustment" policies and programs (Dehli, 1993).

FRAMING QUESTIONS: HOW THE POLICY STORIES BEGIN

In these three reports, and in many similar reports and policies produced and circulated in Canada, the United States, Britain, Australia, and New Zealand, readers are presented with a sense of urgency and crisis. The foreword to the Economic Council of Canada's background report to *A Lot to Learn* begins by arguing that education is pivotal to "maintaining the competitiveness of the Canadian economy in an increasingly globalized trading environment, in strengthening its ability to adapt to changes in the industrial structure and in technology, and in improving the distribution of income and employment" (1992a, p. vii). The message in *Learning Well . . . Living Well* echoes this perspective by claiming that "two great challenges face our country: national unity and future prosperity" (Canada, MEI/MIST/MIT, 1991a, p. i). For the Canadian government, mired in years of constitutional debates, these two challenges are intertwined, not in the least because Canadian provinces have jurisdiction over education. Appearing to rise above such political disputes, the Conservative government's Prosperity Initiative promoted an agenda of "excellence and . . . provincial efforts to improve the acquisition of knowledge and skills. These are essential elements of our future prosperity and economic security" (Canada, MEI/MIST/MIT, 1991a, p. i). One way of reading these opening statements suggests that the economy is positioned beyond politics, and that a national consensus can be achieved in the pursuit of knowledge and skills.

The first pages of *People and Skills in the New Global Economy* (Ontario Premier's Council, 1990) invoke a similar sense of urgency by arguing that "there are signs that [economic] growth is faltering" and that this is due to "concealed structural weaknesses in the provincial economy and the vulnerability of many Ontario industries to international competition" (p. 1). The task at hand is to facilitate the "transition to a higher value-added economy," which is, according to the authors, the only kind of economy that will ensure collective and individual prosperity and well-being. Following some of the same lines of argument as the other two documents here, the Premier's Council goes on to make connections between "the new economy" and the people and skills that will bring it into being:

> A critical determinant of whether we can make the transition to a higher value-added economy will be the education, skills, ingenuity and adaptability of our workers. They must be prepared for work which will demand the sophisticated knowledge and talents that are the trademarks of a truly developed nation. Our raw materials, our infrastructure and our capital will not be utilized to their fullest without the enhancement that a competent, innovative and adaptable work force can bring to such advantages. (p. 1)

The authors of all three reports foreground the qualification of labor as the key issue facing not just governments, but other partners or stakeholders as well. (I will return to a discussion of who comes to be positioned as having a "stake" in these matters.) References to global relations in the reports do not just pertain to firms and markets, but suggest an explicit contrasting with "we" and "us" inside the boundaries of the Canadian nation-state. In *People and Skills* this contrast is set up as between the "sophisticated" workers in "truly developed nations" and the presumably less sophisticated workers populating the not-yet or not-quite developed nations. Elsewhere in *People and Skills* it appears that "our" choice of "high value-added" and highly skilled production presumes that "other" workers will take up, or continue, production of "low value-added" goods, with low pay and highly intensive and exploitative conditions. Leaving aside for a moment whether all or most of "us" partake in decisions about what is produced and how, the authors' vision of broad distribution of prosperity in Ontario (and the rest of Canada) only appears attainable in an international division of labor where "other" workers and people continue to be subjected to extreme exploitation. Such others are positioned both as "out there," beyond "our" borders, and as "in here," in the form of individuals and groups who are rendered marginal in relation to waged work and economic production. One of the uses of the dropout is as a key explanation for why such marginalization occurs.

An effect of the frequent invocation of the term "global" in these reports is to paint a picture of threat and danger coming from outside, against which "we"—the nation, the province, the workers, the citizens, the students, the teachers, the parents, and so on—must abandon our differences and work together. Only by coming together around a consensus can "we" survive and prosper in the new world of global competition. At an individual level, "we" must adjust to change by acquiring the skills and knowledge that will ensure continual learning and be in demand, or by adopting the flexible, competitive, and innovative behaviors that will lead to individual and collective growth. Forging a linear path through schooling, with a clear eye on returns on investment of time, effort, and expense, is described as the normal trajectory that young people ought to follow. In this story line of social and economic difference, those who deviate from this path risk becoming excluded from prosperity, and indeed, by becoming "too dependent" on state welfare, detract from the prosperity that "we" might otherwise enjoy.

In this context, the need to forge a tighter "fit" between education and the labor market is taken for granted, although there is considerable debate about the means whereby schools can become more vocational and more effective in fulfilling their economic functions. There are some differences in the reports' emphases. *People and Skills* spends far more time than the other two discussing how education can be altered to achieve goals of equity and justice. Although it clearly foregrounds the need to prepare Ontario's young people for "the new global economy," the Ontario Premier's Council's report (1990) is at the same time concerned to develop "a people strategy that also aims for inclusiveness and fairness" and that is "founded on several universal entitlements" (p. 11). Thus, their report recommends a gradual end to practices of sorting secondary students into different streams or tracks, for example. This report's recommendations are also more explicit than the other two concerning a strong and directive role for government in the regulation of production and markets, including the labor market. The Economic Council of Canada, on the other hand, recommends that parents (and students) be provided with greater degree of "choice" in the schools they attend, that schools be allowed to develop more specialized and flexible programs to meet local needs and preferences, and that national standards be developed to ensure that schools operate efficiently and effectively (1992b, pp. 47–58). Although they acknowledge that conditions are not equal, the analysis and recommendations of the Economic Council are steeped in assumptions about individuals operating as rational actors in pursuit of the greatest possible return on their (or their children's) human capital investment.

ENTER THE DROPOUT

From this initial placement of education in relation to international economic competitiveness, the reports move to make comparisons of school and student outcomes. In two sections, entitled "Quality: An Essential Issue," and "Education and Training: An International Perspective," the Economic Council of Canada's report *A Lot to Learn* (Economic Council of Canada, 1992b) draws up several indicators to measure the effectiveness and quality of Canada's education system against "the international scene" (see also Economic Council of Canada, 1992a). I will not go into their discussion of how to measure "inputs" and "outputs," how to separate one from the other, and how to define what is to count as quality in education. But it is here that the term *dropout* begins to be used. The incidence of students leaving school before graduating appears measurable in numbers, capable of historical and geographic (and other) comparisons. There is, of course, a great deal of discussion among managers of school systems, policy makers, and researchers about who can be identified as a dropout (Charbonneau, 1989; LeCompte & Dworkin, 1991; Watson, 1975). Much to the chagrin of economists writing policy reports, school boards and provinces use different criteria to define and measure dropout rates, and their systems of record-keeping are not consistent. Nevertheless, the reports discussed here make use of the dropout rate as telling evidence of the problems facing Canadian schools at the end of the twentieth century. Moreover, they use it (and a small number of other categories) to identify groups who fail to adopt properly sequenced and cumulative schooling careers.

The summary of *Learning Well . . . Living Well* declares:

> Despite . . . significant achievements, too many Canadians still lack basic learning skills. Nearly four adults out of 10 cannot do math tasks or cope with written instructions, if they are unfamiliar or too complex. Three students out of 10 drop out of high school, adding to the growing pool of the unskilled unemployed. (In Japan, there was much public hand wringing when the dropout rate fluctuated by a small fraction to just 2 percent.) (Canada, MEI/MIST/MIT, 1991a, p. vi)

The Economic Council of Canada puts the matter slightly differently, but here too connections are made between early school leaving and future unemployment. In the foreword to *A Lot to Learn,* Judith Maxwell writes:

> Our findings confirm that education is a cumulative process— skills that are learned well in the early years provide the foundation for future success. And early setbacks in learning are hard to correct, often leading to dropping out, followed by a lifetime of low wages and unstable employment patterns. (Economic Council of Canada, 1992b, p. vii)

In a chapter of *People and Skills* entitled "The Pivotal Years," the Ontario Premier's Council (1990) also takes up the dropout problem. In context of an otherwise sensitive discussion of the systemic disadvantages that continue to structure many young people's schooling experiences and outcomes, the authors talk about "lost potential: dealing with the dropout problem." Although elsewhere in the report they discuss philosophies and practices of education, and particularly the negative effects of sorting students by ability, the concerns with the "one in three students in Ontario who leave secondary school before graduating" are introduced as matters of "economic competitiveness." Thus, they write: "If Ontario is to improve its economic competitiveness, there must be a substantial increase in the proportion of young people who graduate from secondary school and a consequent increase in the quality of their preparation to participate fully and effectively in the labor market" (p. 30).

The many complex reasons why many young people leave school before acquiring a diploma are taken up only indirectly in these reports. Dropouts deviate from the Economic Council's normative model of individuals who realize that they will gain future rewards from formal education, and who manage to conduct themselves rationally in pursuit of these goals. Its analysis suggests that dropping out results from a failure to develop good working habits and a motivation to learn in the early years of schooling, or even before those years. This vision of the progressive accumulation of knowledge and skills renders invisible and irrelevant the complex and often contradictory practices and relations of power that operate within schools and in the lives of teachers, students, and parents (Bailey, 1989; Marginson, 1992).

In addition, the category "dropout" is constituted in relation to other categories in the text or in discourses with which it intersects. Significantly, the dropout takes its negative meaning in relation to its opposites, the successful and competitive student, the lifelong learner who will, in turn, become the skilled and knowledgeable worker, capably and flexibly adjusting to a rapidly changing and increasingly technological future. In contrast to "normal" children, who (presumably) enjoy school and do well, the dropout comes to stand as a pathological marker for school failure, family (and especially mothers') ignorance or neglect, family poverty, and barriers to opportunity (Walkerdine, 1986). Moreover, and for the authors of these reports this seems most urgent, the dropout is joined by other pathological categories of feared "others" who will not be able to compete on the job market and contribute to national prosperity. Thus the authors of *A Lot to Learn* write:

> So it is hardly surprising that about one third of secondary school students drop out and spend haphazard periods of casual work and joblessness. The failure to provide these students with basic skills means that nearly a quarter of young Canadians are both functionally illiterate and innumerate. If present trends continue, our schools will release one million more functional illiterates into the work force by the year 2000. When they do find a job, their

employers are unlikely to offer them world-class on-the-job training. (Economic Council of Canada, 1992b, pp. 47–48)

Here is the school system that is subject to criticism. The dropout conjures up conclusions that the quality and efficiency of schools are inadequate, and that curriculum and teaching methods are too rigid and out of step with what employers, in particular, want from graduates. That employers can now expect and demand that young people are turned to the labor market with all the qualifications required to perform a job suggests that corporations are taking even less responsibility for training workers on the job than in the past. In many areas of manufacturing jobs, for example, it was not so long ago that generations of workers were recruited at age 16 and trained by coworkers on the job. Although each report discusses and recommends apprenticeships, none of them has much to say about how or why such learning practices are disappearing, nor about what it means that more and more of the work and cost of qualifying labor power will be borne by individual workers and the state. Even in the discussions of apprenticeships, it is clear that publicly funded schools are meant to take on a much greater share of their provision, linking them to better technical and vocational programs. The Ontario Premier's Council and the Economic Council of Canada both promote more "flexible" apprenticeships, linked to programs in secondary schools as well as in community colleges. Such programs, these reports argue, will not only provide more relevant schooling for disaffected youth, they will also redress the skills gap and boost the country's ability to compete in the new global economy.

The word "release" in the last block quotation conjures up images of pollutants slipping out into the environment. Aside from the Economic Council's interesting use of an environmental metaphor, it is implied that people who leave school before graduating constitute a serious current and future problem for the national economy. In the pages of policy texts we do not encounter people who agonize over decisions, who feel guilty, or who are too exhausted from a long work day to check up on children's homework. We do not see how racism pushes many Black students out of schools, or how homophobia forces others to leave as soon as they legally can. The complexity of students' lives in and out of school is flattened and for many, constituted as a pathology.

Although the reports do not critically discuss the shifts in responsibility for reproducing labor power, they do provide some historical perspective to explain why schools now and in the future must do their job differently. *Learning Well . . . Living Well* suggests that "our learning system

has served Canada well in the past. We have made significant progress
over the past quarter century" (Canada, MEI/MIST/MIT, 1991, p. v).
Although this may sound like a compliment to teachers and schools, it
becomes clear as we read on that it is meant as a comment on low expectations in the past. Whereas this might have been adequate earlier,
"Canada's learning performance is simply not good enough to prepare us
for the future" (Canada, MEI/MIST/MIT, 1991, p. vii):

> The Ontario Premier's Council (1990) likewise argues that we cannot cling
> to low-wage, low value-added activities where we have no competitive ad-
> vantages, but must move into the high value-added, high-wage goods and
> services wherein lies our best hopes for prosperity over the long term. This
> shift will require continuing improvements in the productivity of both capital
> and labor. (p. 1)

In the "new" world of high technology and global competition "we"
cannot be satisfied with what was good enough in the past, leaving aside
the question of who was served well by schools. Even as they recognize
the problems of predicting future skill requirements, the reports proceed
on the assumption that more people will need more and higher levels of
skills, and that such skills can and should be developed in public education. Schools must become more oriented to such requirements, whatever
they may be, and the entire curriculum must be rethought in terms of
a skills discourse, that is, in terms of observable behaviors, outcomes, or
performances.

BUILDING CONSENSUS

In face of a huge and complex education and training system, the division
of jurisdiction between the federal and provincial government, and a history of adversarial relations between employers and workers and among
regions in Canada, each of the reports is concerned that education become an area of consensus. At a different level, the writers worry that
young people are confronted with confusing messages and choices, and
do not receive enough support and motivation for learning.

A Lot to Learn frames this latter set of questions in the following
manner:

> Our research also shows that employers and parents—and indeed, society
> as a whole—give conflicting signals to students and teachers. This lack of
> "coherence" is most evident in the transition from school to work. Large
> numbers of young Canadians do not value education. They cannot see clear

pathways from school to work and therefore follow a process of trial and error that is in stark contrast to the clear passages laid out in other industrial countries, particularly Japan and Germany. (Economic Council of Canada, 1992b, p. vii)

The problem here is said to be "conflicting signals" and a "lack of coherence" and motivation. The Economic Council uses the strategy of comparing "us" with "them" to argue that competing nations do a better job of structuring the path of young people from school to work. *Learning Well . . . Living Well* (Canada, MEI/MIST/MIT, 1991a) puts the problem somewhat differently, suggesting both that young people face contradictory messages and that the school curriculum has moved too far from its "basic" functions:

> Canadians do expect a lot from learning institutions, but these expectations are sometimes expressed ambiguously. For example, Canadians ask both too much and too little of our learning system. On the one hand, many Canadians demand that schools function like institutional parents—babysitting our kids in the younger years, providing basic social and health services, and counselling them on drugs and sex when they become teenagers. On the other hand, while Canadians want excellence and would never accept second-class status in learning, we appear surprisingly undemanding when it comes to the real business of learning. Opinion polls confirm that Canadian parents are generally quite satisfied with the educational status quo when it comes to their own children. Our learning system produces as many drop-outs as it does university graduates, but the public has not demanded a reduction of the disturbingly high drop-out rate. It has not demanded (except through trade unions) that corporations play a much larger role in the learning system. It has not demanded that the system produce measurable results comparable to those of other countries. (p. vii)

Again, the authors suggest that what worked in the past is not good enough anymore. Moreover, the curriculum has become "crowded" with matters that detract from the real business of learning, by which these writers mean preparation for the labor market. A connection is then made between these claims and the disturbingly high dropout rate, so as to convince the public, and especially parents, that their satisfaction with schools is actually misplaced.

Beyond the workings of the dropout in this particular report, it is important to remember that the government which produced it has no direct jurisdiction over education. At the same time, however, this government's pursuit of deficit reduction, another feature of corporations' demands, has caused a massive disintegration of social and health programs, while leaving huge numbers of families without adequate incomes

(Mahon, 1990). Adding to the many negative effects of economic restructuring, including unemployment, poverty, and homelessness, the government's own policies have increased the need for all those extra programs that "crowd" the school day. In addition, it is possible to read these reports (and the effects of the government's pursuit of deficit reduction) as an attack on those who are most vulnerable in the current economic upheaval and crisis: the poor, Native people, people of color, disabled people, and women.

Consensus building is not just a matter of creating coherence in young people's movement from school to work. It is also about inviting *some* groups and individuals to take an active part in devising policies and programs. That is, it is about positioning certain groups as legitimate political subjects in relation to educational decision making. The pursuit of consensus around the urgency of educational reform is one of the overarching themes that tie these reports together. *Learning Well . . . Living Well,* for example, was intended as a consultation document that would be used to forge consensus and "stimulate a national discussion on the factors that determine our future prosperity," where Canadians would be given "the widest possible opportunity to be heard and to participate in creating a consensus on ways to generate stable income and employment and to assure our economic security and prosperity in the future" (Canada, MEI/MIST/MIT, 1991a, p. i). This opportunity to consult is not so wide-reaching as to include all Canadians equally, however.

The authors of these reports recognize that consensus has to be struggled for and won. Indeed, the repeated emphasis on consensus, both at the level of rhetoric and in the context of the formation of a plethora of councils and boards that invite "stakeholders" to become partners in decision making, is remarkable (Ontario Premier's Council, 1990; Canadian Labour Market and Productivity Centre, 1990). Most Canadians have not actually been invited or expected to share in the partnerships envisioned by corporate think tanks and government commissions, and the politics of who can be seen as a stakeholder and how such groups should be represented and heard are extremely problematic and contentious (Dehli, 1993). Nevertheless, the invitation to take part in such bodies as the Canadian Labour Force Development Board and the Ontario Training and Adjustment Board has been taken up and used quite strategically by a number of different groups and movements. In the case of the former, a broad and diverse coalition of women from across the country, many of whom work in nonprofit and community-based training and education programs, have had a significant impact on the Board's deliberations (Marcy Cohen, personal communication, 1993). At the same time, those women who are involved in these boards have struggled among themselves, with governments, and with other stakeholders both to take and transform the ways in which they are designated as a constituency with shared interests in relation to training and education (Fraser, 1989). In addition to those designated as the major partners on these boards, business and labor, both the federal and Ontario provincial governments have identified a small number of so-called equity groups that can each send one representative: women, visible minorities, Native people, disabled people, and (in Ontario) Francophones. Sorting out membership in each of these categories for purposes of political representation is extremely difficult. At the same time, the positioning of business and labor as the major players and all the others as equity groups is also very suggestive of what counts as the key questions to be discussed, and what is seen as marginal.

SOME TENTATIVE CONCLUSIONS

By looking at policy texts as stories, I have tried to show how three recent Canadian reports construct particular interpretive frameworks that orient readers' attention toward certain definitions of social problems and possible political and institutional courses of action rather than other definitions (Smith, 1990). Although these texts rarely attend to the specific troubles of individuals or groups, their ways of framing issues and proposing solutions do affect how ordinary people come to understand and make sense of their experiences (Fraser, 1989). Moreover, as Hall (1988, 1991) has argued, such texts would not achieve credibility unless they resonated in at least some way with people's own understandings. At the same time, however, their status as official knowledge (Apple, 1993) also derives from their source among experts and from the large expenditures on their production and distribution (Ashforth, 1990).

Although they are produced at a great distance from those who experience schooling, this kind of text does generate meanings that people draw on to make sense of their worlds and the problems they face. To continue with the story that started this chapter, my friend and I were trying to make sense of what her son was doing, and she was sorting out what to do and how to respond. She connected this event in their lives to what she understood about the links between education, her son's present experiences, and his future; she worried that he might not have a very good future. Our shared social positionings as White, heterosexual, well-educated, and professionally employed women who live in a large, central-Canadian city shaped our (and Michael's) access to discourses with which to make sense of his temporary withdrawal from school. These positionings also enabled Michael to benefit from resources that provided him with several school and work alternatives. Although he was "turned off" by school, the material conditions and "cultural capital" available to Michael gave him important "home advantages" (Lareau, 1988) and school advantages, to which many other young people do not have the same access (see Chapter 9). He was able to find a job through his parents, and some family friends knew of the alternative school where he later enrolled.   That school, in turn, was populated by other middle-class youths who had become disenchanted with regular schools.

At the same time, my friend was also positioned in a gendered "mothering discourse" (Smith, 1991) through which she was made to feel responsible and guilty for her son's disaffection with school. Although she is well educated, has a "good job," and, like most parents, has encouraged Michael's learning, she has also learned over the years that her status as a single mother was seen as a problem by many of his teachers. Women's work as mothers is taken for granted in the ways that schools' and teachers' work is organized (Smith, 1991). Children's educational failure is frequently attributed to women's failure to provide adequate mothering, either because they engage in waged work or because they inhabit "deviant" family forms. The policy reports that I review here suggest that many children's failure in school, including their dropping out, can be attributed to a lack of parental support and to an "inappropriate" transfer of responsibilities from families to schools. Such claims and arguments are gendered in that their assumptions and effects are quite different for women and men (David, 1992). The practical and negative consequences of transferring services out of schools and other public-sector institutions are already experienced by many women, particularly women who are poor and living in single-parent families.

My friend certainly worried that she had failed her son, that perhaps she was not a "good enough" mother or that she, as a single-parent and working mother, had not provided Michael with the environment he needed. At the same time, she could draw on other discourses to reject such arguments and come up with different explanations. She thought, for example, that the working conditions of teachers in Michael's school were getting worse, and that it was becoming more and more difficult for them to teach. She also felt, as Michael did, that the hierarchical social relations that structured the large collegiate that he attended were counterproductive to young people learning to work collectively and to accept social responsibility. In retrospect, she concluded that his absence from school had probably been a good thing for Michael. She certainly rejected the notion that he constituted a drain on the national economy, or that his withdrawal from school demonstrated a pathology on his part. There are many other examples of more organized opposition and questioning of official definitions of and explanations for educational problems (Martell, 1993), although the terrain on which the politics of education is being waged is changing.

I have argued elsewhere (Dehli, 1993) that the production and circulation of policy texts establish, affirm, or change different subject positions and their relation to each other. It is crucial to notice that the people whose lives and work have been disorganized through current upheavals in capitalist economies are not present as knowers or active agents in these reports. Rather, they or their families and communities are identified as pathological, as individuals or groups warranting particular kinds of intervention, discipline, and regulation. Those who might leave school before obtaining a diploma, for example, become subjected to various technologies of surveillance and intervention. Only a narrow group of people are named as stakeholders in education and training debates: educators, academics and researchers, civil servants, politicians, and representatives of employers, trade unions, and so-called equity groups. At the same time, however, those who read and use policy reports do not comprise a homogeneous audience, nor do all students, teachers, and parents adjust to normalized forms of conduct and behavior.

It is possible that many of the specific recommendations of these reports will not be implemented. Even so, they work to provide a framework for discussing the issues they raise. Thus, it is now very difficult to find public debates about education which do not automatically trot out "the new global economy" or "the needs of industry" as their obvious reference points. Likewise, it seems to be taken as a given that dropout rates in Canada are alarmingly high, and that our students are performing poorly compared to other countries. As a group of documents issued by governments, business organizations, or research councils, these reports have obtained legitimacy and have profoundly shaped contemporary debates about educational change in Canada. The fact that they echo similar reports and debates in the United States, Britain, Australia, and New Zealand reinforces the strength of their claims. These reports seem to form part of a new or, perhaps, a reemerging hegemonic educational discourse, in which economic rationalism is privileged as the framework for debate, and where corporate interests and property rights comprise the "new" consensus (Apple, 1993).

It is not as if the reports I have considered in this paper all say the same thing, or that they are deliberately biased. However, they do provide a consistent framework of urgency and crisis to describe contemporary issues in education and to propose solutions. They move from these beginnings to argue that schools must become more "efficient" and more "relevant" to the needs of the labor market, although they differ somewhat in specific recommendations. I am arguing neither that these accounts are false nor that Canadian schools are beyond criticism. Clearly, there are major changes taking place in the organization of production and markets, and there is much room for improvement in education. What I have tried to show is how one version of a complex and contradictory story about change has become reified as the only and most important story. A message repeated often enough in official and semi-official reports has the effect of transforming contradictory realities into simple categories—such as the dropout—which, in turn, enables the development of apparently simple mechanisms to redress problems. The reports I have discussed, then, have effects not only in relation to the specific issues and institutions they address. They are also important in a broader cultural sense, because they contribute to a narrowing of the agenda for debates in and about education, about what education is for, and about what it means to become and be an educated subject.

The deepening crisis of capitalist accumulation beginning in the 1970s constitutes a crisis in political and institutional modes of representation and regulation, as well as in production relations and the labor process. Qualification of labor power has taken on new significance in production and market relations that appear to be increasingly relying on knowledge-based labor. It is also clear, though, that a great deal of employment in Canada and elsewhere, will be performed for low pay, under precarious contract relations and hazardous conditions. Indeed, these and several similar reports provide explanations for the growing difference between the center and the margin within Canada and North America, and between the northern and southern hemispheres. Moreover, one effect of this new policy discourse is to alter individual and group expectations of employers and of the state by suggesting that individuals, rather than employers, are responsible for insuring themselves against the harsh economic competition of the labor market. On the other hand, employers are provided with considerable scope to define what state-funded public schools should or should not do, and how they should be funded, evaluated, and regulated.

My critique of the most recent crop of reports on education is not that they are dishonest attempts to lure people into accepting budget cuts or exclusion from educational programs. Instead, I argue that these reports contribute to an ideological and epistemological shift in official knowledge about education, training, and work. The reports work up a rationale for changing the content, structure, regulation, and governance of schools in Canada, and for altering relations between workers and employers and citizens and the state. In order to mount effective resistance and counter-discourses to these and similar reports, we need a better understanding about how policy documents constitute and legitimate some forms of knowledge about the social world, rather than other forms of knowledge as well as how their knowledge production is embedded in and has important effects on changing social relations of class, gender, race, and ethnicity.

NOTE

1. At the time, Bernard Valcourt was Minister of Employment and Immigration, while Michael Wilson was Minister of Industry, Science and Technology, and Minister for International Trade.

REFERENCES

Alonso, A. M. (1988). The effects of truth: Representations of the past and imagining community. *Journal of Historical Sociology, 1* (1), 58–89.

Apple, M. W. (1993). *Official knowledge: Democratic education in a conservative age.* New York: Routledge.

Arnot, M., & Barton, L. (Eds.). (1992). *Voicing concerns: Sociological perspectives on contemporary education reforms.* Walingford, Oxford: Triangle Books.

Ashforth, A. (1990). Reckoning schemes of legitimation: On commissions of inquiry as power/knowledge forms. *Journal of Historical Sociology, 3* (1), 1–22.

Bailey, C. (1989). The challenge of economic utility. In B. Cosin, M. Flude, & M. Hales (Eds.), *School, work and equality* (pp. 223–237). London: Open University.

Bowe, R., Ball, S. J., & Gold, A. (1992). *Reforming education and changing schools.* London: Routledge.

Brown, P. (1987). *Schooling ordinary kids: Inequality, unemployment and the new vocationalism.* London: Tavistock.

Canada, Ministry of Employment and Immigration [MEI]. (1989). *Success in the works. A profile of Canada's emerging work force.* Ottawa: Ministry of Employment and Immigration.

Canada, Ministry of Employment and Immigration, Ministry of Industry, Science and Technology, and Ministry of International Trade, Prosperity Initiative [MEI/MIST/MIT]. (1991a). *Learning well . . . Living well.* Ottawa: Author.

Canada, Ministry of Employment and Immigration, Ministry of Industry, Science and Technology, and Ministry of International Trade, Prosperity Initiative [MEI/MIST/MIT]. (1991b). *Prosperity through competitiveness.* Ottawa: Author.

Canadian Chamber of Commerce. (1988). *Focus 2000: Report of the task force on harnessing change.* Ottawa: Canadian Chamber of Commerce.

Canadian Labour Market and Productivity Centre. (1990). *Report of the CLMPC task forces on the Labour Force Development Strategy.* Ottawa: Canadian Labour Market and Productivity Centre.

Charbonneau, J. (1989). *School dropouts: Annotated bibliography.* Ottawa: Youth Affairs, Canada Employment and Immigration Commission.

Clandfield, D. (1993). The NDP and the corporate agenda in Ontario. *Our Schools, Our Selves, 5* (1), 8–26.

Corrigan, P. R. D., & Sayer, D. (1985). *The great arch: English state formation as cultural revolution.* Oxford, UK: Basil Blackwell.

Dale, R. (1992). Whither the state and education policy? Recent work in Australia and New Zealand. *British Journal of the Sociology of Education, 13* (3), 387–395.

David, M. (1992). *Parents, gender and education reform.* Oxford, UK: Polity Press.

Dehli, K. (1993, Summer). Subject to the new global economy: Power and positioning in Ontario labour market policy formation. *Studies in Political Economy, 41,* 83–110.

Economic Council of Canada. (1987). *Innovations and jobs in Canada.* Ottawa: Economic Council of Canada.

Economic Council of Canada. (1990). *Good jobs, bad jobs.* Ottawa: Economic Council of Canada.

Economic Council of Canada. (1992a). *Education and training in Canada.* Ottawa: Economic Council of Canada.

Economic Council of Canada. (1992b). *A lot to learn.* Ottawa: Economic Council of Canada.

Fine, M. (1991). *Framing dropouts: Notes on the politics of an urban public high school.* Albany: State University of New York Press.

Foucault, M. (1982, Summer). The subject and power. *Critical Inquiry, 8,* 777–795.

Fraser, N. (1989). *Unruly practices: Power, discourse and gender in contemporary social theory.* Minneapolis: University of Minnesota Press.

Hall, S. (1988). The toad in the garden: Thatcherism among the theorists. In G. Nelson & L. Grossberg (Eds.), *Marxism and the interpretation of culture* (pp. 35–57). London: Routledge.

Hall, S. (1991, March). Brave new world. *Socialist Review, 1,* 51–64.

Kenway, J., Bigum, C., & Fitzclarence, L. (1993). Marketing education in the postmodern age. *Journal of Education Policy, 8* (2), 105–122.

Lareau, A. (1988). *Home advantage: Social class and parental intervention in elementary education.* London: Falmer Press.

Lauglo, J. (1992). Vocational training and the bankers' faith in the private sector. *Comparative Education Review, 36* (2), 227–236.

LeCompte, M. D., & Dworkin, A. G. (1991). *Giving up on school: Student dropouts and teacher burnouts.* Newbury Park, CA: Corwin Press.

Mahon, R. (1990). Adjusting to win? The new Tory training initiative. In K. A. Graham (Ed.), *How Ottawa spends, 1990–91: Tracking the second agenda* (pp. 73–111). Ottawa: Carleton University Press.

Marginson, S. (1992). Education as a branch of economics: The universal claims of economic rationalism. *Melbourne Studies in Education 1992. (Rationalising Education), 26,* 1–14.

Martell, G. (1993). A democratic socialist response to the failure of the NDP educational reform. *Our Schools, Our Selves, 5* (1), 68–91.

Ontario Premier's Council. (1990). *People and skills in the new global economy.* Toronto: Queen's Printer.

Radwanski, G. (1987). *Ontario study of the relevance of education, and the issue of dropouts.* Toronto: Ontario Ministry of Education.

Shapiro, S. (1989, Fall). Towards a language of educational politics: The struggle for a critical public discourse of education. *Educational Foundations, 3,* 79–100.

Smith, D. E. (1990). *The conceptual practices of power: A feminist sociology of knowledge.* Toronto: University of Toronto Press.

Smith, D. E. (1991). Women's work as mothers: A new look at the relations of class, family and school achievement. In F. Forman et al. (Eds.), *Feminism and education* (pp. 219–244). Toronto: OISE Press.

Walkerdine, V. (1986). Progressive pedagogy and political struggle. *Screen, 27* (5), 54–60.

Watson, C. (1975). *Focus on dropouts: An abridged version of the Report of the Ontario Secondary School Dropout Study, 1974–75.* Toronto: Ontario Ministry of Education.

CHAPTER 2

Lifelong Learning: Between Utopia and Economic Imperatives

KJELL RUBENSON

While dropping out is the focus of this book, dropping in also reflects the ongoing changes in educational behavior among youth as well as adults. The traditional front-end model, where one moves into the labor market after an initial period of education—where there is a distinct break between education and work—no longer prevails: It is being replaced by a recurrent model. In this new model, lifelong learning has become the catchword of the day, and the panacea for the problematic relationship between education and the economy, now exacerbated by the emergent information economy. The purpose of the school is no longer only to give a good initial education but to prepare students to become lifelong learners. In this perspective the "dropout" phenomenon is seen as a major problem. Traditionally, dropping out is discussed with regard to a specific form of initial education, primarily high school but also college. With the shift to a recurrent model of education, however, it will be increasingly important for policy makers and researchers concerned with the link between education and opportunity structure to address the dropping in/out problem from the perspective of lifelong learning.

This chapter contributes to a broadening of the perspective addressed in this book by presenting a preliminary analysis of the concept of lifelong learning as it appears in public policy documents. The point of departure is the new politico-economic imperative framing discussions and policies around education.

A NEW POLITICO-ECONOMIC IMPERATIVE FOR
EDUCATIONAL POLICY

Almost every day the media in one way or another expresses concern about the dismal situation in Canadian schools, problems in postsecondary education, and low investment in education and training of the labor force. The discussions are framed within a new politico-economic imperative that places importance on highly developed human capital, science, and technology to support Canada's needs for economic restructuring and greater international competitiveness. The business section in daily papers frequently carries articles on education. Ministers of finance have started to sound like ministers of education, whereas books like *The Work of Nations* by Robert Reich (1990) have become the new bibles of educational policy makers.

Over the last 10 years, Statistics Canada has changed its measurement of participation in adult education in ways that reflect the new politico-economic imperative. Its first survey, in 1984, financed by the Department of Secretary of State, looked at adult education generally and treated employer-related education and training as just one category among others. The three subsequent surveys, financed by Employment and Immigration Canada, are called surveys of adult education and training. In these three surveys there has been a shift in purpose, giving increased importance to work-related education, and particularly employer involvement in the training and education process. Adult education for general interest has now become a residual "rest" category.

The present economic imperative is quite different from the reform period based on the human capital theories that affected educational planning in the 1960s. The focus during the 1960s was on increasing the percentage of youth continuing on to secondary and postsecondary education. Reforms were aimed at increasing the number of students admitted to the traditional higher education system, and at the creation of new institutions such as community colleges. In short, the arena was the formal system and the target group was the youth. With the exception of a few lonely voices calling for recurrent and lifelong education, no one seriously questioned the use of a front-end model for educational policy. What was in the 1960s a demand for more education for more young people, resulting in an explosion in financial support for, and enrollment in, secondary and postsecondary education, has, in the 1990s, become a debate about lifelong learning throughout the education system, training and education for adults, and a focus on the world of work as a place of learning. The Speech from the Throne on May 13, 1991, the Canadian equivalent to the State of the Union address in the U.S. (Canada, House of Commons, 1991), proclaims the following: "In the dawning knowledge age, how well we live will depend on how well we learn. Canadian men and women must have access to both the skills and lifelong learning opportunities necessary to improve their job prospects and ensure their own prosperity" (p. 16). Similarly, the report from the government task force "Prosperity Initiative" concludes: "We face the challenge of equipping all Canadians with the basic skills necessary for lifelong learning" (Canada, Ministry of Employment and Immigration, p. 8). With the projected demands for skilled labor increasing and with two thirds of those who will be in the labor force in 2005 already in the work force today, there are two major problems: (1) how to get the educationally disadvantaged who have already quit school to return, and (2) how to create a future school system that solves the dropout problem and fosters within individuals a willingness to engage in learning throughout the life cycle. It is in this context that lifelong learning has become the panacea to economic problems and the solution to the dropout problem.

Another important difference between the 1960s and the 1990s is that the pressure for an expansion of educational opportunities in the 1960s had both economic and social roots. Proponents of human capital theory maintained not only that there exists a strong link between investments in education and economic growth (Denison, 1962; Schultz, 1960) but also that a more even distribution of investment in education would equalize individual earnings (Schultz, 1960). In the 1960s, this assumption was important because it linked the economic justification for the reform of education with social demands for equality of opportunity. Greater equity in educational opportunity was seen as a major leveling force in society.

Looking at policy documents written during the 1980s in various countries, the erosion of a commitment to equality and the total dominance of the economic imperative is evident. This is an effect not only of the evolving information economy and the focus on global economic competitiveness but also of the ascendancy of a politico-economic perspective that praises the free marketplace and sees any involvement of government as something evil in itself. Within this perspective, accountability, standards, relevance to the needs of the economy, cost-effectiveness, and not equality, have become the key issues.

Although the concept of lifelong learning might now be in its second generation, the original philosophy of lifelong learning, introduced by intergovernmental organizations like UNESCO and the European Council in the late 1960s and early 1970s as a master concept for educational planning, has very little in common with what is happening today in schools and society.

FIRST GENERATION OF LIFELONG LEARNING

The 1972 UNESCO report *Learning to Be: The World of Education Today and Tomorrow* (UNESCO, 1972) recommended "that to address the problems facing education in developing as well as developed countries," existing education systems should be transformed into a system aiming at the principle of lifelong learning. Following the advice of the Faure report, UNESCO's Institute for Education concentrated its policy and research effort on the conceptualization of lifelong education. When it was first presented, the appeal of lifelong learning was its potential to respond to the new challenges caused by rapid and unprecedented change by continuing the process of renewal of knowledge, skills, and values throughout life. These changes were not specifically discussed within an economic imperative but in all spheres of political, cultural, social, and economic life. "In fact, the far-reaching socio-economic developments accompanied by a special emphasis on the principle of democratization have contributed a great deal to the present phenomenon of change" (Dave, 1976, p. 16). From within a humanistic tradition, the proponents of lifelong learning called for a better society and a new quality of life, where people adapt and control change in a way that allows the full development of their individual personalities; "making themselves" rather than "being made" were the catchwords. Through self-evaluation, self awareness, and self-directed learning, humans were expected to work toward achieving the central goals of democracy, humanism, and the total development of self.

The conceptual work within UNESCO stressed that the evolution of lifelong learning should not be seen as a purely educational venture but as a societal one. It would involve the horizontal integration of education and life, not simply as a result of finding educative experiences in everyday life but through ensuring that the experiences consist continuously of "educational situations." A precondition for lifelong learning was a changed conceptualization of education, encompassing formal (e.g., schools), nonformal (education organized by trade unions, libraries, recreation centers, churches, etc.) and informal (newspapers, TV, etc.) settings for learning. People were warned against narrowly conceptualizing lifelong learning as merely an extension of the idea of re-training without taking into account the humanizing qualities of individual and collective life. It was pointed out that a crucial weakness in the structure of society is an absence of political will, not only toward the democratization of education but also toward the democratization of society. Consequently, the existing social relations of production provide a major obstacle to the true realization of lifelong learning—indeed lifelong learning will become a new arena for social struggle because it will require a much more equal society (Vinokur, 1976, p. 362). Finally, time after time, it has been stressed that in order for lifelong learning to become a reality, people must want engagement in learning.

A comparison of the first and second generations of lifelong learning suggests that the concept has lost its utopian origin and has been reduced to a narrow definition centered on meeting the needs of the economy by equipping the work force with the necessary skills and competencies. Another major difference is that whereas the earlier debate gave a lot of attention to the obstacles and preconditions for lifelong learning, today's discussion is simply concentrated on the need for lifelong learning, paying very little notice to the prerequisites or hindrances to fostering a lifelong learning culture. The research on participation in adult education and training, and the "role" of education in selection, stratification, and reproduction is ignored. Rather than declaring "The New Jerusalem," it seems important to look at the present situation in light of the initial discussion about obstacles to lifelong learning.

OBSTACLES TO LIFELONG LEARNING

The readiness to engage in lifelong learning has to be understood in relation to the processes that govern the social construction of attitudes toward adult education and the provision of adult education in society. The vicious circle of poor childhood conditions, short formal education, repetitive jobs, reduced opportunities to participate in political life, and so on, have made "factual" opportunities to participate far from equal. Thus, the common assumption in much of the adult education literature—that the adult is a conscious, self-directed individual in possession of the instruments vital to making use of the available possibilities for adult education and lifelong learning—becomes highly problematic. The consequences of the "vicious circle" for the probability of "dropping into" education as an adult have over the years been demonstrated in adult education participation research.

The general conclusion arrived at by Johnstone and Rivera (1965) in their comprehensive study on participation in adult education in the U.S. is as true today as it was 30 years ago:

> One of the most persistent findings emerging from the inquiry is that a great disparity exists in the involvement in continuing education of segments of the population situated at different levels of the social hierarchy. (p. 231)

A close look at different forms of adult education points to the fact that the better an education pays off in terms of income, status, occupation, political efficacy, cultural competence, and similar matters, the greater the differences in socio-economic status between participants and nonparticipants (Rubenson, 1980). Thus, it is interesting to note that the rapid rise in participation in adult education accompanying the emergent information economy which occurred in Canada between 1985 and 1992 has been accompanied by increasing socio-economic differences (Rubenson & Willms, 1993). This and other findings point to the crucial links between the structure and nature of work, the preparedness of different adults to engage in education, and the nature and amount of informal learning. I will use Collins' (1988) theory of stratification to explore briefly the link between the education credential stratification on the one hand and the way in which the work role encourages or discourages participation in adult education on the other.

The allocation of work roles influences participation in at least three ways. First, certain roles provide more opportunities to take part in adult education than others. Data on participants in some form of employer-sponsored education show that regardless of country, there are major differences in access to education and training for various groups of the labor force. The participation pattern is linked to the work hierarchy, and the more qualifications required for a position, the more common it is that an employer will sponsor some form of education and/or training. An analysis of the 1992 Adult Education And Training Survey (Rubenson & Willms, 1993) shows that whereas only 13% of workers with less than a high school education received employer support for education and training, the figure for those with a university education was 50%.

The participation rate differs greatly not only by level of occupation but also by the nature of the education and training. Künzle and Büchel (1989) found that in Switzerland 70% of general managers who had participated in adult education had taken a course outside their organization, compared to 26% of unskilled workers. The latter had mainly followed some shorter form of on-the-job training.

Second, those in higher positions have the best chances to learn on the job. The differences existing among various groups entering the labor market become more and more pronounced throughout the life span. Those who are favored find themselves in a work situation which is constantly generating a need for knowledge, whereas the complete opposite applies to those who suffer de-qualification.

Third, we have to look at the way work roles have an indirect impact on a person's likelihood of participating in some form of adult education. This is something seldom discussed in the literature on participation, but it is crucial to an analysis of these issues. I will, therefore, discuss it at some length, relying primarily on research linking the world of work and the world of learning that can help inform our understanding of participation and, more broadly, lifelong learning.

What we are exploring is how the "objective world" influences the perception of reality, or, as Mannheim put it, how mental structures are inevitably formed differently in different societal and historical settings (Mannheim, 1936). This is reflected, for example, in the established relationship between job design and the individual's life outside of work. Meissner (1971) was able to demonstrate a direct connection between the shaping of work tasks and the life of the individual outside working hours. When the scope for individual initiative at work was limited by factors in the work process, the ability of workers to participate during their leisure in activities posing demands of this kind appeared to diminish. A similar tendency emerges regarding the effect of work that provides limited opportunities for social contact. When workers are allowed more control over their work, they show more interest in participating in decision making processes. Accompanying changes also occur in their leisure activities and lead to a more active leisure. Meissner's findings support Leontjev's (1983) thesis on the link between praxis of work and our structures for thinking.

From the point of view of lifelong learning, it is interesting to note that there is a close resemblance between the discussion about humanizing the workplace through the reorganization of work and the principles for effective learning and instruction based on cognitive sciences. "Action regulation theory," developed primarily by Hacker (1985) and Volpert (1989), focuses on the impact of working conditions on peoples' socially constructed cognition and learning processes, among other things. A central assumption in the theory is that by striving for autonomy in action, a person tries to satisfy a basic need for control. Action regulation theory attempts to explain how such a motivated and autonomous individual actor sets goals and reaches them. These processes are considered a psychological aspect of action referred to as "regulation." The transformation of a general goal into a sequence of operations occurs through the

FIGURE 2.1. Relationship between work organization, knowledge, and personality before democratization (from Svensson, 1985).

hierarchical-sequential organization of action. There are various levels of action units differentiated by levels of regulation that determine the scope of action. Thus autonomy, that is, the degree of freedom in the setting and reaching of goals, plays a crucial role. As long as the basic patterns are flexible, there is a broad scope for autonomous action which is an essential characteristic of personality development. According to this perspective, regulation chances (the scope to act) are very important determinants of the socialization process. They influence the way people think about themselves as well as their aspirations and willingness to act, thus having far-reaching consequences for individual competencies. The implications for the qualifications of the work force and the ways to acquire and use them are apparent. In a hierarchical, inflexible work organization, there will be restricted ability to act. When the individual is cut off from central processes of decisions and planning, he or she is incapable of learning more elaborate actions, which diminishes his or her motivation and competencies. The negative effect on people's feeling, thinking, and acting of restrictive regulation requirements (as Hacker and Volpert call it), or lack of control of working conditions, is well documented in the research literature (Lennerlöf, 1986). There is also strong evidence that increased control has positive effects on people's well-being and motivation.

An illustration of the links among structure of work, perception of reality, and adult education can be found in a Swedish study of local struggle for industrial democracy (Svensson, 1985). Figure 2.1 represents the situation before the organization of work was radically changed and shows the link between structure and agency. According to Figure 2.1, the original work organization stimulated the development of a work force characterized by individualism and uncritical acceptance of the situation (herein called uncritical knowledge).

In the process of changing the workplace, employees, who were the subjects of the research, came together in study circles to explore ways in which they could strengthen their influence over the organization of work. During this process, the workers created what Svensson (1985) calls their own critical knowledge, and their meetings acted to strengthen solidarity among the union members (all workers were unionized). As the workers' solidarity and critical awareness increased, they gradually managed to achieve a more fully realized industrial democracy. This in turn resulted in a further strengthening of solidarity and increased critical insight into the conditions of labor. According to some of the workers interviewed in Svensson's study, the most important element in this spiraling process of solidarity and insight was the learning that occurred in the study circles. The workers' point of departure was their own experience, which they related to course material on industrial democracy and which in turn led them to visualize alternatives to the system in which they were working. These alternatives, the practical result of the interplay of study circle material and everyday experience, were then presented to the employer under the auspices of the local union.

The structural changes that occurred in these employees also affected the workers' sense of agency; their values, expectations, and demands were higher, and their class awareness and sense of solidarity with the working class was greater. The changes that occurred are a good example of the dualism between human agency and structure that Giddens (1984) draws attention to.

The vast differences in participation in adult education between various social groups cannot be explained only by the economic functions of adult education. One also has to take into account adult education as a form of cultural consumption. Bourdieu's (1977) concept of habitus provides a fruitful perspective on this phenomenon. Through socialization in the family, the school, and later on in working life, a positive disposition toward adult education becomes a part of the habitus of some groups but not of others. It is this phenomenon that Bergsten (1977) refers to when he shows that noncompetency-oriented adult education is linked to a leisure style consisting of types of cultural activities usually found in the middle and upper classes. The relationship between habitus and conceptions of adult education is further elaborated on by Larsson, Alexanderson, and Fransson, 1986. They found that nonskilled workers with little formal education in occupations offering limited possibilities for growth were characterized by a very restrictive conception of adult education. According to this restricted view, participation in adult education is meaningful only when it results in better and higher-paying work.

Participation must be understood in relation to the link between supply and demand for adult education, and the processes that govern who gets what kind of adult education. Broström and Ekeroth (1977) claim that to understand why the effects of adult education on equity are so small, we have to look at the way in which demand determines what the adult education organizations offer. They also claim that the activities of these organizations have been a response to manifest social and individual demands rather than to needs stemming from inequalities in society. A policy for equity would imply a striving for equalization, which, in turn, entails a hope that certain groups will make use of what is available. This raises two problems that are very seldom solved. The first is to stimulate demand among the groups for which a measure is taken. The second is to understimulate the demands from groups that are not the direct objects for a measure. A financial formula based on market forces will make this policy impossible to achieve and reflects the "true" social functions adult education has been awarded in society.

CONCLUDING COMMENTS

Lifelong learning has been framed within two totally conflicting imperatives. The utopian imperative spurred much rhetoric but had no effect on educational planning. This is understandable, because it questioned not only the education system but also the structure of society at large and particularly the division of labor. The current imperative presents a restricted notion of lifelong learning framed within the presumed demands of the economy. Whereas the "Utopianists" gave serious attention to prerequisites for the realization of lifelong learning, this has not been done within the economic imperative. It is true that lifelong learning has become the reality for a substantial segment of the population in the industrialized world and that the notion of a learning society is more true today than 20 years ago. The closing of the gender gap in the industrialized world is also worth noting: Recent statistics on participation in various forms of education show that although there are still marked gender differences in choice of program/courses, women participate to the same or greater extent than men. However, the major problem within the second generation of lifelong learning is that it neglects to examine critically some of the underlying assumptions about work, the link between education and work, and the combined effects of family and school on the unequal development across class and ethnicity of the disposition to engage in lifelong learning.

The future of lifelong learning will be closely related to what happens in the world of work. Despite all that is said and written about the need for a highly skilled labor force, there is substantial evidence to show that there is not a general development toward higher-skilled jobs but rather toward a bifurcated labor market with the middle level disappearing, particularly in North America (Krahn, 1992; Kunin & Knauf, 1992;

Myles, 1988). Esping-Andersen (cited in Myles, 1988) notes that the rapid expansion of low-service jobs in the U.S. is not occurring in Germany and Sweden. Labor politics and public policy in these countries create an inhospitable environment for low-wage, unskilled service industries.

It is important to note that despite the general cry for a better qualified work force and worries about skill shortages, new technologies do not themselves result in demands for higher qualifications or in better possibilities for employees to develop and broaden their skills. On the contrary, the research literature is full of findings with claims of deskilling, up-skilling, polarization, and reskilling (not more but different qualifications needed). There are good reasons to be skeptical of the more optimistic as well as the more pessimistic positions. Both are expressions of technological determinism, which states that technology will more or less automatically result in positive or negative effects on skill demands and opportunities for the development of competencies (Ellström, 1992). A more plausible position, and one that has support in recent research (Löwstedt, 1989; Zuboff, 1988), is that the consequences of new technology on the demand for and development of worker competencies depend on the interplay of the nature of technology, implementation strategies, work organization, and the existent competencies of the work force. It is the strategic use of technology, not the technology itself, that determines what kind of skills are needed and hence governs employees' opportunities for developing their competencies. Thus, the question of skills cannot be discussed from only a narrow economic perspective on efficiency, but also must be understood in terms of labor's struggle for the humanization of work and workplace democracy. Studies like *Made in America* (Dertouzos, Lester, & Solow, 1989) show that although some industries have adopted the new modes of production, there is very little diffusion of their practices to the majority of firms.

In short, the literature on structural changes in the labor market and studies of links between new production technologies and skill requirements suggest very unequal opportunities for lifelong learning. Even the most superficial reading in the sociology of education makes it apparent that the pedagogic actions of families from different ethnic groups and social classes, as well as those of the schools, do not work together harmoniously to promote lifelong learning in a fair and equitable way.

The issue of how preparing to engage in lifelong learning and the opportunities for education and training are socially constructed is, of course, as relevant from a utopian point of view as it is from the new politico-economic imperative. The latter, however, seems to assume that market forces have, in some mysterious way, created a general demand for lifelong learning.

The concept of lifelong learning can be used to integrate various areas of research that address the link between different forms of education and the distribution of life chances through a person's life cycle. Collins' notion that every micro situation is surrounded by other micro situations and that the micro–macro link is really a micro–micro link—"macro is the medium through which micro situations are connected to each other" (Collins, 1988, p. 397)—could be used as a starting point to see how the world of work structures opportunities for lifelong learning both directly and indirectly through its effects on family life and schooling. It also calls for longitudinal research, through which one could follow the cumulative effects of family life, schooling, and work on the readiness to engage in lifelong learning.

The dream of a learning society is rapidly becoming a reality for the well-educated few, and a major policy concern surrounding lifelong learning remains beyond the expectations of large segments of the Canadian and U.S. populations. Given the bifurcation of future skill demands in the economy, it is obvious that the information economy in and of itself will not solve the problem of dropping out in today's high schools. What is needed is a comprehensive framework for promoting lifelong learning that integrates various policy sectors: the economy and the labor market, education, and social services.

REFERENCES

Bergsten, U. (1977). *Adult education in relation to work and leisure*. Stockholm: Almquist & Wiksell International.

Broström, A., & Ekeroth, G. (1977). *Vuxenutbildning och fördelningspolitik* [Adult education and distributive politics]. Uppsala: Sociologiska Institutionen, Uppsala Universitet.

Bourdieu, P. (1977). Cultural reproduction and social reproduction. In J. Karabel & A. H. Halsey (Eds.), *Power and ideology in education*. New York: Oxford University Press, 487–510.

Canada, House of Commons. (1991, May 13). Speech from the Throne. Ottawa: Author.

Canada, Ministry of Employment and Immigration, Ministry of Industry, Science and Technology and Ministry of International Trade. Prosperity Initiative. 1991. *Learning Well . . . Living Well*. Ottawa: Author.

Collins, R. (1988). *Theoretical sociology*. San Diego, CA: Harcourt Brace Jovanovich.

Dave, R. H. (Ed.) (1976). *Foundations of lifelong education*. Oxford: Pergamon Press.

Denison, E. F. (1962). *The source of economic growth and alternatives before us*. New York: Committee for Economic Development.

Dertouzos, M., Lester, R., & Solow, R. (1989). *Made in America: Regaining the competitive edge.* Cambridge: MIT Press.

Ellström, P.-E. (1992). *Kvalifikation, utbildning och lörande i arbetslivett* [Qualification, education, and learning at work]. Linköping: University o Linköping.

Giddens, A. (1984). *The constitution of society.* Berkeley: University of California Press.

Hacker, W. (1985). Activity: A fruitful concept in industrial psychology. In M. Frese & J. Sabini (Eds.), *Goal-directed behavior* (pp. 96–121). Hillsdale, N.J.: Erlbaum.

Johnstone, J., & Rivera, R. (1965). *Volunteers for learning.* Hawthorne, N.Y.: Aldine.

Krahn, H. (1992). *Quality of work in the service sector.* Ottawa: Statistics Canada, General Social Survey Series 6.

Kunin, R., & Knauf, J. (1992). *Structural changes in our labor market: The 80's and 90's or of doughnuts and layer cakes.* Unpublished manuscript, Employment and Immigration Canada. Regional Economic Services Branch, British Columbia/Yukon Territory.

Künzle, D., & Büchel, D. (1989). *Weiterbildung als Strategie für Region und Betrieb* [Continuing education as strategy for regional and workplace development]. Zürich: Verlag der Fachvereine.

Larsson, S., Alexanderson, C., & Fransson, A. (1986). *Arbetsupplevelse och utbildningssyn hos icke facklärda* [Work experience and attitudes to education among low-skilled workers]. Göteborg, Sweden: Göteborg Studies in Educational Sciences.

Lennerlöf, L. (1986). *Kompetens eller hjälplöshet? Om lärande i arbete. En forskningsöverskrift* [Competence or alienation: learning at work. A review of the literature]. Stockholm: Arbetarskyddsstyrelsen.

Leontjev, A. (1983). *Virksomhed, bevidsthed, personlighed* [Activity, knowledge, and personality]. Köpenhamn, Denmark: Progres.

Löwstedt, J. (Ed.). (1989). *Organisation och teknikförändring* [Organization and changing technology]. Lund, Sweden: Studentlitteratur.

Mannheim, K. (1936). *Ideology and utopia: An introduction to the sociology of knowledge.* London: Routledge & Kegan Paul.

Meissner, M. (1971). The long arm of the job: A study of work and leisure. *Industrial Relations, 10,* 239–260.

Myles, J. (1988). The expanding middle: Some Canadian evidence of the deskilling debate. *The Canadian Review of Sociology and Anthropology, 25* (3), 335–364.

Reich, R. B. (1990). *The work of nations.* New York: Random House.

Rubenson, K. (1980). Background and theoretical context. In R. Hoeghielm & K. Rubenson (Eds.), *Adult education for social change* (pp. 1–54). Lund, Sweden: Liber.

Rubenson, K., & Willms, D. (1993). *Human resources development in British Columbia.* Victoria: Ministry of Skills Training and Labor.

Schultz, T. (1960). Capital formation by education. *Journal of Political Economy, 64,* 1026–1039.

Svensson, L. (1985). *Arbetarkollektivet och facket* [Workers and the union]. Lund, Sweden: Lund University.

UNESCO. (1972). *Learning to be: The world of education today and tomorrow.* Paris: UNESCO.

Vinokur, A. (1976). Economic analysis of lifelong education. In R. H. Dave, (Ed.), *Foundations of lifelong education* (pp. 286–337). Oxford: Pergamon Press.

Volpert, W. (1989). Work and personality development from the viewpoint of the action regulation theory. In H. Leymann & H. Kornbluh (Eds.), *Socialization and learning at work* (pp. 215–234). Aldershot: Avebury.

Zuboff, S. (1988). *In the age of the smart machine: The future of work and power.* New York: Basic Books.

CHAPTER 3

The Dependency of Independence: At Risk Youth, Economic Self-Sufficiency, and Curricular Change

NANCY LESKO

Youth stand on the cusp between dependence and autonomy. Teen-agers—"at the threshold" or in "transition to adulthood"—are referred to in terms that speak of "becoming." The contemporary American sense of a teenager is located in temporariness and movement toward something else. Among other things youth are expected to become independent in a number of ways: emotionally, socially, legally, and, most importantly, economically. Nevertheless, independence has become more difficult and complex in that the supports for becoming independent are eroding (Gaines, 1994; Lipsitz, 1994).

The expectation for youths' movement toward economic independence is presently heightened in the U.S. In a time of economic decline, job insecurity, and massive youth unemployment, especially among young males of color, the social profile of youth is elevated in gang activity, sexuality, and violence. Half of the U.S. population designated as poor consists of children under the age of 18 (Barringer, 1989). Young people have once again become significant social problems (Gilbert, 1986; Gus-field, 1986; Lesko, 1990) at a time in which as a group, youth have fewer and fewer resources (Fine & Mechling, 1993; Gaines, 1994).

Much of the research and policy making surrounding increasingly needy youth tend to focus upon their personal characteristics and how they will not accomplish the "transition to independence" (e.g., Carnegie Council on Adolescent Development, 1989; Dryfoos, 1990; Hamburg,

1993). Social structural inequalities are turned into personal deficiencies (Fine, 1993). When we speak of "at risk" youth, we are discussing young people whose future independent status is jeopardized.

In this chapter I argue that *dependence* is highly significant for thinking about youth at risk of dropping out and about school policy and curricular responses to dropouts—a fact which has been missed by researchers and policy makers. My starting point for examining dependence highlights the paradoxical relationship of independence and dependence for youth. In a very real way, dependency is necessary for future independence, but the long view is not generally adopted by policy makers.

This chapter examines the conception of at risk students in relation to the unacceptability of dependence in the contemporary U.S. and in relation to the peculiar "independence" promoted in secondary schools. I see fear of *dependence* as a significant contributor to the narrowing of thinking about school responses to youth at risk of dropout. The definition of adolescence, as a time of becoming, assures an indefiniteness and thereby provides a prime arena for cultural politics (Gusfield, 1986). But its indefiniteness also means an ongoing contested, contradictory arena, with slippage across categories of youth such as dependent and independent, or at risk and successful.

BACKGROUND

The roots of this chapter extend back to the fall of 1980, when I collaborated on a study of six Wisconsin programs for at risk youth. During a visit to LEAP (Lincoln Educational Alternative Program), an alternative high school program in Wisconsin Rapids, WI, I observed a "regular" social studies class and introduced myself to the teacher and students as a visitor studying LEAP. The class discussion came to be centered on the rightness of alternative programs like LEAP. The White male teacher and several White students said that "students shouldn't be coddled." Having programs like LEAP was coddling or babying them, and they should be expected to make it or not in the same classes with everyone else.

These discussions remain vivid for me, perhaps because of their emotional intensity, perhaps because I never knew how to respond adequately. I will explore how persistent these ideas regarding student autonomy and self-sufficiency are, and how they influence efforts to make schools more humane and equitable places. I trace the constellation of ideas encoded in the refrain, "special programs 'coddle' students," and how those ideas affect policy and programs for dropouts.[1]

DEPENDENCY

The broad discourse on dependency in the United States forms an important context for school programs for at risk youth. *Dependency* is a keyword of the U.S. welfare state (Fraser & Gordon, 1994), and is denounced from economic, political, legal, and moral perspectives (Gilder, 1981). In other historical periods particular kinds of dependence were accepted, although postindustrial America sees dependence as avoidable and blameworthy. Independence is defined solely as having waged work, and since such work is believed to be available to all, dependence is escapable. Individuals are blamed for dependence, and the problem is seen as moral and psychological, not stemming from legal, economic, or political structures (Fraser & Gordon, 1994). The awareness of how dependence has been pathologized and how it is only discussed as moral and/or psychological properties of individuals provides important ground for responses to at risk youth.[2]

Fraser and Gordon's work on the contemporary demonizing of dependence is supported by literature in education. For example, Robert Dreeben's (1967) influential article "The Contribution of Schooling to the Learning of Norms" links school practices with the production of individual independence. Schools inculcate norms that have "particular relevance to economic and political participation in industrial societies" and independence tops the list: "Independence has a widely acknowledged though not equivocal meaning . . . doing things on one's own, being self-reliant, accepting personal responsibility for one's behavior, acting self-sufficiently" (Dreeben, 1967, p. 221).

Dreeben ties the reasonableness of this norm to his view that full adult status requires occupational employment "at least for men" (p. 216). In line with Fraser and Gordon's thesis, Dreeben links independence and waged work. Dependence is reasonable for children within their families and, implicitly, for women as wives.[3]

More recently, Joy Dryfoos (1990) states a common view[4] of at risk youth, which also has the specter of dependence at its center:

> Many children are growing up in the United States today without a hope of enjoying the benefits that come with adulthood. *They are not learning the skills necessary to participate in the educational system or to make the transition into the labor force. They cannot become responsible parents because they have limited experience in family life and lack the resources to raise their own children.* The gap between achievers and nonachievers is expanding. . . . *There is growing concern in this nation about the future status and work potential of these high-risk youth* [emphasis added]. (p. 5)

On the following page, Dryfoos writes, "One goal of this study is to identify and quantify a broadly defined segment of the population: young people who are at risk of not maturing into responsible adults" (p. 6). To that end, "it is necessary to understand what problems create barriers to maturing into responsible adulthood" (p. 4). "Adulthood" has been defined by Dryfoos as being in the labor force and being a responsible parent.

The Carnegie Corporation's *Turning Points* report deals with the problem of dependence more broadly:

> Unfortunately, by age 15, *substantial numbers of American youth are at risk of reaching adulthood unable to meet adequately the requirements of the workplace, the commitments of relationships in families and with friends, and the responsibilities of participation in a democratic society*. These youth are among the estimated 7 million young people—one in four adolescents—who are extremely vulnerable to multiple high-risk behaviors and school failure. Another 7 million may be at moderate risk. . . . In these changed times, when young people face unprecedented choices and pressures, all too often the guidance they needed as children and need no less as adolescents is withdrawn. *Freed from the dependency of childhood, but not yet able to find their own path to adulthood, many young people feel a desperate sense of isolation.* Surrounded only by their equally confused peers, too many make poor decisions with harmful or lethal consequences [emphasis added]. (p. 8)

Adulthood for the framers of this report included waged work, ongoing relationships with family and friends, and participation in democratic institutions, all of which are at risk for millions of contemporary young adolescents. The *Turning Points* report suggests a pathological isolation, or suspension, between dependency and independence that portends evil things for young adolescents.

In an introduction to another recent report on young adolescents, Deborah Meier (1990), principal of the Central Park East secondary school in New York City, negotiates this lack of middle ground—the suspended state—by saying that young adolescents are both dependent and independent and need opportunities in school to be both. Although her tone is different, Meier uses the same terms to locate young adolescents' position.

In examining just a few documents, a conflicted, shifting view of dependence and independence in relation to youth arises: fears of failure to become independent, suspension between dependence and independence, and the need for opportunities for both independence and dependence. Each of these accounts problematizes teenagers' position regarding dependence/independence and asserts that schools, rightly organized, can remedy the situation. In school, states Dreeben (1967), "pupils learn to acknowledge that there are tasks to be done by them alone" and "that others have a legitimate right to expect such independent behavior" (p. 221). Dreeben discusses how the ratio of students to a teacher, rules about cheating, and formal testing all "teach" the expectation for independence that employers and colleges demand, since both these groups "want to know how well each person can do" (p. 225). The *Turning Points* report recommends different avenues to achieve independence, which include smaller school communities, a core of common knowledge, and close teacher–student relationships.

Despite Dreeben's argument that schools rightly teach independence (or in Meier's view, both dependence and independence), there is competing evidence that schools in fact enforce prolonged *dependence*. Fraser and Gordon (1994) argue that the dependence of industrialized waged work is invisible and glossed as economic *in*dependence. Schools appear to mirror this ideological inversion. Aaron Pallas (1993) writes persuasively on the dependence demanded of students:

> The current organization of schooling in the U.S. and many other countries makes students very dependent on adults in school . . . the impact of the dominant public image of teaching and learning as the process of filling passive student receptacles with predetermined knowledge . . . is to make students dependent in ways that nonstudents are not. Students typically have little control over what they study, how time is spent in school, or with which students and teachers they will interact. (p. 413)

Pallas acknowledges that most social roles involve dependence; for example, workers are dependent on other workers, but he asserts that most of these examples actually involve *interdependence*, in which independent action is still valued. "In schools, students typically depend on the actions of their teachers, but the converse is not as obvious, and students' own independent actions are quite constrained" (Pallas, 1993, p. 443, note 2). The ethnography of two junior high schools by Mary Metz (1978), for example, demonstrates how teachers depend upon students' compliance with school authority; however, interdependence is not labeled as such by the teachers. Rather, when students act independently, it is generally seen as a discipline or management problem.

Scholars of youth have designated modern adolescence as a state of dependency (Keniston, 1970).[5] More recently, historian Michael Grossberg (1993) termed youth "doubly dependent"—dependent both on their families and on the state. How to educate "doubly dependent" youth for economic independence (which Pallas and Fraser and Gordon claim is masked dependence) is especially thorny. Educational policies and programs to foster independence can appear Byzantine at best, and are often self-serving for adults.[6] For schools to declare that youth are independent, although they are unable to sign leases, be paid a full minimum wage, or receive social services as individuals, is to detach independence from any power to act by/for oneself. If youth are "doubly dependent," they may thereby be "doubly neglected" by families and the state.[7]

To label youth "at risk" marks them as needing more adult supervision and fewer independent actions and opportunities.[8] A bigger question remains: Should teenage students be independent or dependent?[9] The slippery ground of defining (in)dependence for youth is illustrated in the case of single mothers, one particular at risk group. In Rickie Solinger's (1992) history of Black and White single pregnancy in the U.S., single mothers are pathologized as too dependent and too independent. For example, one policy recommendation to the director of the U.S. Children's Bureau (which oversaw federal efforts in 1949) from a psychiatrist discussed dependency as a psychological problem:

> Unmarried, pregnant girls are dependent people and that's the reason they got pregnant—to stay in a dependency situation. . . . So an agency working with unmarried mothers shouldn't offer a maternity home or other assistance too quickly. If the unwed mother is relieved of her anxiety in these matters too quickly, she continues her feeling of dependency, which complicates treatment. (cited in Solinger, 1992, p. 96)

Simultaneously, mental health workers diagnosed unwed mothers as "too independent, aggressive, and masculine" (Solinger, 1992, p. 96) and a substantial dimension of the overt curriculum of maternity homes in the 1945–1965 era was to help single mothers become more feminine. The language of Dreeben, Dryfoos, and the *Turning Points* report is more acceptable to contemporary audiences than the language Solinger reports, but the ideas stem from similar sociocultural constructions of what independence and dependence are.

Clearly, the legitimacy of being dependent varies with particular gender, race, social class, and age positions (Abramovitz, 1988a). Feminist sociologists find that women who followed norms for dependency as middle-class wives were pathologized for the same behavior—for example, looking to other people to provide an income—when they became homeless (Golden, 1986). The media praises high-powered professional women who return home to care for children, but denigrates welfare mothers who want to care for their own young children (Abramovitz, 1988b). Programs for school-age mothers may preach independence, but teach a curriculum that omits extensive career education, implicitly assuming that their students will be dependent upon a male wage (Lesko, 1990).

PROBLEMATIZING YOUTH DEPENDENCE/INDEPENDENCE

Independence has been severed from a consideration of power relations— to declare a youth independent but without power to act renders independence meaningless. Fraser and Gordon's (1994) analysis is directed toward changing women's position in the welfare wars over resources by seeing the dependence of mothers in a different light. I have drawn on their historical analysis of dependence to call attention to the bind of secondary schools in the preparation of youth for independence. Fraser and Gordon's analysis helps clarify the "doublespeak" around teenagers' independence in a school system that expects and demands their dependence, and suggests that we replace or supplement those considerations with analyses of power relations. In what schooling situations do youth have genuine power over decision making, over resources, over how they interact with adults and peers? Can we construct schooling contexts in which *interdependence* is the norm, moving beyond the dependence/independence divide? Part of such a move is to emphasize the *present* power relations, rather than some future position in work or family (Fabian, 1983). An emphasis on present relations, however, is undermined by the way youth signifies "becoming" or "in transition." To emphasize the present in working with youth, without blotting out the future, is to work strongly against the grain.

Clearly, the postindustrial economic decline and realignment will continue to vilify individuals and lower-status groups for succumbing to structural problems. When discussing dropouts and *dependence* in the U.S., the close ideological relationship between schools and capitalism becomes clear, since both "return individuals to self-reliance while maintaining structural barriers related to economic, racial, and sexual class that limit and curtail the individual" (Eisenstein, 1982, p. 587).

To call simple notions of dependence into question, we can also examine the production of independence. In the way that Michelle Fine (1991) demonstrates how youth are dependent on the whims of teachers, administrators, and counselors, other research could document the dependencies of successful students, and how autonomy and independence require enormous supplies of dependency (economic, psychological, emotional). Part of this strategy to deconstruct dependence/independence rhetoric in relation to at risk youth could show how some forms of dependence are invisible, even necessary, for independence and how some aspects of dependence are acceptable because they meet adults' demands for control over youth. Such a strategy would make visible what is presently overlooked: the resources provided for some youths' successes, that is, the dependency of independence.

I believe that policy questions regarding dropouts are firmly embedded in this broader social pathologizing of dependence, which is selectively and variously defined and applied. We need to have a critical approach toward the dependence/independence oppositional pairing as it operates in research, policy, and programs for at risk youth. The next section examines curricular issues with issues of independence and dependence in mind.

PREPARING FOR DEPENDENCY: SOCIAL SERVICES IN SCHOOLS

In this section, I inquire into the curricular implications of the keyword *dependence,* that is, its relationship to school programs for at risk and regular students. What kinds of dependence are presumed and facilitated in school programs? What kinds of independence are presumed and facilitated? What are the relationships among the play of dependence and independence in "special" programs and "regular" programs?

I draw in broad strokes some ways that well-established programs for at risk students define themselves and their students and how those definitions look in relation to the conferred identities of students in "regular" school programs. In this analysis I rely heavily, although not exclusively, on the case studies of 13 programs that colleagues and I conducted at the Center for Effective Secondary Schools during 1986–1988 (Wehlage, Rutter, Smith, Lesko, & Fernandez, 1989). In reexamining these programs, I ask how the identities of at risk students are created. A simple formulation would be that programs for at risk youth form an additional lower track in schools, and that these students are treated as having lower capabilities and given fewer opportunities (Oakes, 1985). Other studies of lower-track classrooms and different forms of curriculum differentiation, however, find more ambiguity in the meanings of differentiated curricula (Page, 1991) and uncertain effects, some nearly identical to those in regular classrooms and others showing positive attributes (Page & Valli, 1990). Page and Valli (1990) conclude that curricular differentiation is "paradoxical, complex, and contextualized" (p. 240), cautions I try to keep in mind here.

Research and policy studies of at risk students generally begin by listing the students' characteristics, the factors that make them at risk. Dryfoos (1990), in this normative vein, lists "antecedents to at-risk," which are demographic, personal, family, and community factors (p. 8). Dryfoos describes "a problem behavior syndrome" which may involve delinquency, dropout, pregnancy, and drug use. Although analyses now try regularly to portray the range and variety of students at risk (Wehlage at al., 1989), the very process of specification of "antecedents" marks these young people as different, since attention to the contexts in which youth live are considered "nuisance" variables in many studies of adolescents and, thus, are not attended to by many researchers (Lipsitz, 1991). In contrast to such reports as *A Nation at Risk,* in which students are generic and undifferentiated, the noting of personal and social characteristics is synonymous with problems. Dryfoos (1990) speaks of "the significant differentiation between children who are 'making it' and those who are not" (p. 26). What are the consequences of accepting a characterization of dropouts as "significantly different" from stay-in-school youth?

A common element of programs for at risk youth is their attention to youth's social–emotional situations. Such programs accomplish this through counselors, discussion groups, weekly family meetings, and cognizance of individuals' particular living problems or personal dilemmas. One common effect can be the diminution of the cognitive or intellectual aspects of schools, often referred to as lowering standards (Wehlage et al., 1989). This is a crucial difference between lower-track classrooms and other alternative programs; Page (1991) reports that students in lower-track classes get "bits and pieces" of knowledge, easier texts, and are passive recipients of knowledge. Although students in the programs studied by Wehlage et al. (1989) did get a similarly "banal" academic curriculum that did not add up to anything, they also got attention from staff and extra chances to start again and be a version of a successful student.

In general, the tagging of youth as having social and emotional problems cancels out their academic needs and their need to be intellectually stimulated and challenged (Wehlage et al., 1989). This apparent forced choice between a program that emphasizes academic content or one that recognizes social and emotional issues is, however, a trap. Dryfoos's (1990) conclusions regarding themes across programs for at risk youth provide a good portrait. She synthesized 11 components of successful prevention programs for at risk youth:

(1) intensive attention for individuals;
(2) community wide and multiagency approval;
(3) program location in schools;
(4) early identification;
(5) administration of school programs located outside of schools;
(6) community-based programs outside of schools;

(7) additional staff training;
(8) social skills training for youth;
(9) peers involved in intervention;
(10) parent involvement;
(11) links with the world of work. (pp. 228–233)

Nowhere in this list is attention to intellectual development, or to the touted "higher-order thinking skills" that are present in general secondary school reform reports (Resnick, 1987) and in calls for general access to postsecondary schooling (Cole, 1992).

Dryfoos (1990) synthesizes six "theoretical concepts" supported by the research on successful programs for at risk youth:

(1) no one solution;
(2) risky behaviors are interrelated;
(3) grouping services is required;
(4) aim to change institutions, not individuals;
(5) timing of the intervention is critical; and
(6) continuity of effort is necessary. (pp. 233–234)

Important for this analysis is the fact that these are administrative concepts. When they are read alongside the 11 characteristics of effective programs, one sees the outline of a social service agency, not an educational organization. At risk students' needs are defined as administrative and therapeutic, not in terms of their right to a first-class education (Fraser, 1989). Such a definition of needs skews the discussion of school responses further toward social services and further away from school knowledge and curriculum-centered discussions. Given an administrative and therapeutic framework, it is commonsense that at risk youth need social skills training and links to the world of work. Other needs such as for strong mathematics foundations, which are necessary for college entrance examinations (Jetter, 1993), are never discussed. Given binary thinking (invoked in "at risk" and "successful" students) and limited economic resources for youth, highly individualized and personalized programs have difficulty not slighting the academics.[10]

Reporting on Australian curricular efforts to develop girls and boys' equality, Yates (1993) finds that the real problems for any special population of students arise at the level of substantive curricular decisions. Even though state policy reports appear progressive, the differentiation then moves to the level of concrete choices in curriculum strategy, that is, "the degree of emphasis given to a common knowledge and expectation of students, as compared with that given to the 'needs' of students" (p. 181).

In the U.S. context, common formal curriculum and common expectations of students usually capitulate to the special needs of at risk students (Dryfoos, 1990; Wehlage et al., 1989). The practice of defining students with particular characteristics and their needs leads to "special" programs for them that usually remain inferior to the college-bound track. Attempts to maintain the common formal curriculum for non-college-bound students often produce a caricature (Page, 1991), however.

These examples demonstrate the stalemate of current curricular strategies for at risk youth. Two choices appear consistent. One choice is to remake the curriculum toward the needs of students, which involves strong attention to social and emotional needs and little attention to traditional academic needs, such as math knowledge, reading and comprehension, and writing abilities. The second substantive curricular choice is to keep the common formal curriculum and common expectations (e.g., for attendance), and many at risk youth will drop out. This either–or choice means second-class or truncated schooling for many at risk youth.

Researchers, policy makers, and educators must give greater attention to specifying which aspects of schooling for at risk youth need to be different and which can be similar to those of schooling for "regular" students. Are social bonding, personalized instruction, educational basics, and preparation for work necessary and appropriate for at risk youth? As advocates for youth at risk of dropping out, we need to be aware of the specific kinds of differences and the politics of specific differences articulated in any district or school. We also need to distinguish which aspects of curriculum differentiation are necessary and which are detrimental. What possibilities for enhanced learning exist with special programs? What risks for second-class education accompany special curricula? Some differences in programs and policies will need to be rejected and others advocated. This will have to be done within particular historical, geographic, and political contexts. These are hard questions, but they must be answered in ways that are both critical of commonsense language and assumptions about students and capable of making substantive curricular differentiations and comparisons.

SUMMARY AND IMPLICATIONS

We need to develop a way to see separate or special programs and curricula in relation to regular curricular strategies (Young, 1990). If "regular" school programs demand greater measured competence in math and science, for example, to define the needs of at risk youth as primarily social, emotional, and linked to waged work is likely to give these youth a second-class education. This means that educators must begin to specify which differences are salient for schooling and which are not; which differences are aspects of commonalities for all students and to be written into school reform; and which differences can reasonably provide a groundwork for programmatic alternatives.

In this chapter, I have emphasized the relation in the present time period between a pathologizing of dependence and a mystifying of waged work as independence, a pattern that appears to characterize much of U.S. secondary school practices. First, I drew connections between the terms dependence and independence, calling into question their presumed opposition and the contradictory ways they are invoked in relation to school aims and practices for different groups of teenagers.

Similarly, I have sketched how curricular practices for at risk youth must also be seen in relation to regular curricula. To avoid the worst problems of curriculum differentiation and to improve curricula for all groups of students, we need to consider how programs relate to one another, in terms of formal knowledge taught, pedagogical practices, staffing issues, and program aims. I also presented an approach to examining formal curricular knowledges and their connections to independence and dependence, but did not examine pedagogies or staffing. We must scrutinize which differences make a difference for curricula adjustments and alternatives, and which differences can be acknowledged while keeping curricula common.

Finally, curricula for both at risk and successful students must be revamped, and considered together as parts of a whole picture. All curricular reforms must address persistent student complaints, such as that school is boring, school knowledge is meaningless, and teachers are uncaring (Donmoyer & Kos, 1993; LeCompte & Dworkin, 1991). Such system-wide changes will affect curricula and programs for different groups of students, each of which can become more viable when seen in relation to other programs and practices.

NOTES

1. Joan W. Scott's (1990) deconstruction of equality and difference in policy toward female workers is important for this analysis. Although I emphasize dependence and independence, those concepts are intertwined with the principles of treating all secondary school students as equal and/or different.

2. See Lesko (1990) for a description of this pathologizing/redemptive approach in a program for school-age mothers.

3. Dreeben (1967) articulates and elevates independence to an important functional characteristic of persons in industrial and democratic societies. This

functionalist, ahistorical perspective is called into question by such scholars as Fraser and Gordon (1994), who show conceptions of independence as changeable, and by historian Mary Ryan (1987), who traces the production of the "self-made man" among middle-class, nativist households during industrialization in the mid–1800s in New York state.

4. Dryfoos's (1990) research was funded by the Carnegie Corporation of New York.

5. For an overview of adolescents in relation to pre-industrialized and industrialized economies, see Modell and Goodman (1990).

6. Patricia Meyer Spacks (1981) has incisively captured the catch–22 of youth in society with her phrase "our psychology confirms our sociology" (p. 290). That is, our conception of youth as deficient confirms their powerless position in our social order. Thus, I see much of what passes as knowledge and policy on youth as confirming our sociology.

7. Melinda Henneberger reported in the February 15, 1993 *New York Times* that youths of all social classes are running away from abusive families and asking for public assistance. Heretofore, caseworkers have sent teenagers back to their families, believing the parents' stories, which typically deny abuse. Teenagers are too young to sign leases or qualify for public housing, and getting public assistance drags on, as long as 6 months. Middle-class teenagers generally have an even harder time convincing caseworkers that their parents cannot provide a safe and stable home. This upswing in homeless teenagers points to the dilemma of the "doubly dependent" teenager who is denied help in both the domestic and the state spheres.

8. An interpretation of the Carnegie Corporation's *Turning Points* report on reforming middle schools is that it mandates closer controls over young adolescents as well as the teaching of critical thinking, for instance. See Lesko (1994), for such an analysis.

9. Elsewhere (Lesko, 1995), I inquire into whether school-age mothers—who are simultaneously mothers, youth, and students—are *properly* independent or dependent.

10. There are exceptions to the pattern of lowered academic emphasis. The Media Academy in Oakland, California is an alternative program with a substantive academic curriculum focused upon broadcast and print journalism (Wehlage et al., 1989).

REFERENCES

Abramovitz, M. (1988a). *Regulating the lives of women: Social welfare policy from colonial times to the present.* Boston: South End Press.

Abramovitz, M. (1988b). Welfare, work, and women: How "welfare reform" is turning back the clock. *Christianity and Crisis, 48* (12), 292–297.

Bailey, T. (1993). Youth apprenticeship in the context of broad education reform. *Educational Researcher, 22* (3), 16–17.

Barringer, F. (1989, October 18). 32 million lived in poverty in '88, a figure unchanged. *New York Times*, p. 1.

Carnegie Council on Adolescent Development. (1989). *Turning points: Preparing American youth for the 21st century.* New York: Carnegie Corporation.

Cole, J. (1992). Higher education. In B. Clinton (Ed.), *President Clinton's new beginning* (pp. 185–188). New York: Donald I. Fine.

Donmoyer, R., & Kos, R. (Eds.). (1993). *At-risk students: Portraits, policies, programs, and practices.* Albany: State University of New York Press.

Dreeben, R. (1967). The contribution of schooling to the learning of norms. *Harvard Educational Review, 37,* 211–237.

Dryfoos, J. G. (1990). *Adolescents at risk: Prevalence and prevention.* New York: Oxford University Press.

Eisenstein, Z. (1982). The sexual politics of the new right: Understanding the "crisis of liberalism" for the 1980's. *Signs, 7,* 567–588.

Fabian, J. (1983). *Time and the other: How anthropology makes its object.* New York: Columbia University Press.

Fine, G. A., & Mechling, J. (1993). Child saving and children's cultures at century's end. In S. B. Heath & M. W. McLaughlin (Eds.), *Identity and inner-city youth* (pp. 120–146). New York: Teachers College Press.

Fine, M. (1991). *Framing dropouts: Notes on the politics of an urban public high school.* Albany: State University of New York Press.

Fine, M. (1993). Making controversy: Who's 'at risk'? In R. Wollons (Ed.), *Children at risk in America: History, concepts, and public policy* (pp. 91–110). Albany: State University of New York Press.

Fraser, N. (1989). *Unruly practices: Power, discourse and gender in contemporary social theory.* Minneapolis: University of Minnesota Press.

Fraser, N., & Gordon, L. (1994). A genealogy of *dependency:* A keyword of the U.S. welfare state. *Signs, 19,* 309–336.

Gaines, D. (1994). Border crossing in the U.S.A. In A. Ross & T. Rose (Eds.), *Microphone fiends: Youth music and youth culture* (pp. 227–234). New York: Routledge.

Gilbert, J. (1986). *A cycle of outrage: America's reaction to the juvenile delinquent in the 1950s.* New York: Oxford University Press.

Gilder, G. (1981). *Wealth and poverty.* New York: Basic Books.

Golden, S. (1986). Daddy's good girls: Homeless women and "mental illness." In R. Lefkowitz & A. Withorn (Eds.), *For crying out loud: Women and poverty in the U.S.* (pp. 28–42). New York: Pilgrim Press.

Grossberg, M. (1993). Children's legal rights? A historical look at a legal paradox. In R. Wollons (Ed.), *Children at risk in America: History, concepts, and public policy* (pp. 111–140). Albany: State University of New York Press.

Gusfield, J. R. (1986). *Symbolic crusade: Status politics and the American temperance movement* (2nd ed.). Urbana: University of Illinois Press.

Hamburg, D. A. (1993). The opportunities of early adolescence. *Teachers College Record, 94,* 466–471.

Hamilton, S. F. (1984). *Raising standards and reducing dropout rates.* Washington, D. C.: American Educational Research Association.

Hamilton, S. F. (1993). Prospects for an American-style youth apprenticeship system. *Educational Researcher, 22* (3), 11–15.

Henneberger, M. (1993, February 15). Increases in homeless youth burden shelters. *New York Times,* p. 12.

Jetter, A. (1993, February 21). Mississippi learning. *New York Times Magazine,* pp. 12–15.

Keniston, K. (1970). Youth as a stage of life. *American Scholar, 39,* 631–854.

Kliebard, H. (1986). *The struggle for the American curriculum, 1893–1958.* New York: Routledge.

LeCompte, M. D., & Dworkin, A. G. (1991). *Giving up on school: Student dropouts and teacher burnout.* Newbury Park, Ca.: Corwin Press.

Lesko, N. (1990). Curriculum differentiation as social redemption: The case of school-aged mothers. In R. Page & L. Valli (Eds.), *Curriculum differentiation: Interpretive studies in U.S. secondary schools* (pp. 113–136). Albany: State University of New York Press.

Lesko, N. (1994). Back to the future: Middle schools and the *Turning Points* report. *Theory Into Practice, 33* (3), 143–148.

Lesko, N. (1995). The "leaky needs" of school-aged mothers: An examination of U.S. programs and policies. *Curriculum Inquiry, 25* (2), 25–38.

Lewis, A. C. (1990). *Making it in the middle.* New York: Edna McConnell Clark Foundation.

Lipsitz, J. (1991). Public policy and young adolescents. *Journal of Early Adolescence, 11* (1), 20–37.

Lipsitz, G. (1994). We know what time it is: Race, class and youth culture in the nineties. In A. Ross & T. Rose (Eds.), *Microphone fiends: Youth music and youth culture* (pp. 17–28). New York: Routledge.

Meier, D. (1990). Foreword. In A. C. Lewis (Ed.), *Making it in the middle* (pp. 5–9). New York: Edna McConnell Clark Foundation.

Metz, M. H. (1978). *Classrooms and corridors: The crisis of authority in desegregated secondary schools.* Berkeley: University of California Press.

Modell, J., & Goodman, M. (1990). Historical perspectives. In S. S. Feldman & G. R. Elliott (Eds.), *At the threshold: The developing adolescent* (pp. 93–122). Cambridge: Harvard University Press.

Oakes, J. (1985). *Keeping track.* New Haven: Yale University Press.

Page, R. N. (1991). *Lower track classrooms.* New York: Teachers College Press.

Page, R. N., & Valli, L. (Eds.). (1990). *Curriculum differentiation: Interpretive studies in U.S. secondary schools.* Albany: State University of New York Press.

Pallas, A. M. (1993). Schooling in the course of human lives: The social context of education and the transition to adulthood in industrial society. *Review of Educational Research, 63,* 409–448.

Resnick, L. (1987). Learning in school and out. *Educational Researcher, 16,* 13–20.

Ryan, M. P. (1987). Privacy and the making of the self-made man: Family strategies of the middle class at midcentury. In H. G. Graffe (Ed.), *Growing up in America* (pp. 238–267). Detroit: Wayne State University Press.

Scott, J. W. (1990). Deconstructing equality-versus-difference: Or, the uses of poststructuralist theory for feminism. In M. Hirsch & E. F. Keller (Eds.), *Conflicts in feminism* (pp. 134–148). New York: Routledge.

Solinger, R. (1992). *Wake up little Susie: Single pregnancy and race before Roe v. Wade.* New York: Routledge.

Spacks, P. M. (1981). *The adolescent idea: Myths of youth and the adult imagination.* New York: Basic Books.

Wehlage, G., Rutter, R., Smith, G., Lesko, N., & Fernandez, R. (1989). *Reducing the risk: Schools as communities of support.* London: Falmer Press.

Yates, L. (1993). Feminism and Australian state policy: Some questions for the 1990s. In M. Arnot & K. Weiler (Eds.), *Feminism and social justice in education* (pp. 167–185). London: Falmer Press.

Young, I. M. (1990). The ideal of community and the politics of difference. In L. Nicholson (Ed.), *Feminism/postmodernism* (pp. 300–323). New York: Routledge.

PART II

FRAMING RESEARCH ON DROPPING OUT OF AND RETURNING TO SCHOOL

This part provides examples of the ways in which the dominant policy discourse shapes research on the process of leaving school. By providing resources for particular kinds of research and posing the questions in particular ways, governments, academics, and interest groups shape what we discover as "facts." By both accepting the dominant frame and by trying to contest it, researchers become part of the politics of discourse around school leaving.

Much academic research takes a problem that is posed by policy makers and examines the accuracy of its assumptions or the adequacy of proposed solutions. What is the best estimate of the rate of school leaving? What is the effect of programs designed to reduce school leaving? In the past few years these questions have been researched and argued increasingly in both the United States and Canada. The 30% dropout rate that was first estimated by the Canadian government in 1991, when the panic about dropouts was at its height, was revised in 1993 to 18%, when the figures were more carefully examined (Barlow & Robertson, 1994). In the United States during the 1970s, concern existed that schools were holding tanks for too many young people who should be somewhere else; in the early 1990s, it turned to concern about high dropout rates, and then to a debate about which formula and which interpretation of the numbers was best (Ligon, 1994). The volatility and political importance of the research was perhaps best illustrated in the debate about the fate of the Sandia Report, a national study of education that was suppressed by the Bush administration because of its optimistic view of how the schools were reducing the dropout rate and increasing the achievements of students (Tanner, 1993). Releasing the 1995 report on the conditions of education (National Center for Education Statistics, 1995), Secretary Riley "pointed to the steady progress being made by American education in the years since *A Nation at Risk* (1983). Significantly more students are taking difficult courses, math and science test scores are up, and the dropout rate is declining" (p. 1). These statements are part of a fight to retain the Office of Education by pointing to the effectiveness of federal interventions.

Researchers become political actors by contributing a certain expertise and authority to positions in the public discussion of education, whether they wish to remain outside politics or not. This makes the way they frame their research, and whose questions they ask, a matter of political as well as academic import—and one of responsibility.

Researchers do not just take up the dominant policy discourses to see if they are correct on their own terms. They try to shape the public conversation by defining and redefining the issues, and often provide new concepts. Researchers who work inside schools frame the problems from the point of view of young people themselves and try to get these points of view on the policy table. They bring in issues like social class, race, ethnicity, and language, which are important in the way lives are lived in school although ignored in the larger debate. Researchers doing this kind of work use their privilege to speak for those whose voices are not often heard in public spaces, although ways of doing this responsibly are very controversial (Alcoff, 1991). Can anyone speak for others without appropriating and changing what is said? Without inserting their own interests into the conversation?

These observations challenge the notion that researchers can be above or beyond politics. Their words and findings are used politically, and they must carry out the research with a clear awareness of political consequences. Research paradigms reflect values and assumptions that are value laden. Every researcher must simplify the real world in order to carry out research, and these simplifications reflect the concerns of some, and ignore the concerns of others. They are always partial.

The papers in this section all start in one way or another from the dominant policy frame outlined in Part I. They illustrate the various ways in which researchers work from and within these frames to become public intellectuals, making public policy points.

In Chapter 4 Harvey Krahn and Julian Tanner, citing the labor market statistics that have heightened concern about early school leavers, provide information about the work experiences of a group of young people in Edmonton, Alberta who have left school without a high school diploma. The researchers are interested in how young people understand their work, how satisfied they are, and what they aspire to. Although these young people have unstable employment histories and work in lower level service jobs, surprisingly, "Only a handful clearly disliked their job." This research confirms the general view that dropping out is a problem because it leads to marginal employment. It also raises questions about the meaning of this marginal employment, by paying close attention to how young people themselves understand it. The research thus works within dominant concerns about employment, while allowing young people a voice in redefining the problem.

Paul Anisef and Lesley Andres (Chapter 5) describe a data set collected by Statistics Canada under the auspices of the federal Stay-in-School Initiative, begun in Canada in 1990. Partly because of the structure of the Canadian state, where education is a provincial responsibility, and partly because there has been no national educational research agency, little data was available to monitor or substantiate the concern about school-leaving. "According to the Project discussion paper, six out of ten provinces reported that they did not collect data on high school graduates and/or dropouts." The school-leavers survey was designed to "explore the environmental, social, attitudinal, personal, and economic factors that may contribute to the early departure of students from school." Anisef and Andres discuss both what was discovered and what was not. This is a case study of policy research framed by the dominant discourse.

Program evaluation is another major form of policy research. One of the most important policy initiatives designed to cope with youth who are in danger of dropping out of school is the creation of alternative programs crafted to meet their needs. Exploring the meaning and structure of such alternative programs in California, Deirdre Kelly (Chapter 6) argues that they represent examples of a long running and unresolved competition of missions: that of providing a safety net for students, and of providing a safety valve for the mainstream schools. She sketches the historical antecedents of these schools and examines the concept of "choosing" an alternative program. The chapter illustrates the dilemma of well-intentioned school reform "on the ground" as teachers, students, and administrators contest its meaning and structure. School reform engenders contradictions and always poses new dilemmas, which research can clarify. The best efforts of researchers are, however, unlikely to have the questions posed in the school supplant the questions posed by the dominant discourse.

In Chapter 7, Margaret LeCompte also starts with a look at reform efforts, but this time with an attempt to develop a "learning community" and create a culturally compatible curriculum in a school on a Navaho reservation. As both a consultant and a researcher in the district, she was identified with the reform in various roles, teaching courses to teachers and giving speeches, developing ideas for restructuring and stimulating resistance, and documenting and writing up the conflicting findings. She concludes that such reform efforts do not change practice in the classroom. Teachers and administrators do not trust each other enough to work together. Anglo teachers do not understand their own cultural specificity or the culture of the Navaho. Time, resources, and understanding are scarce. Underlying patterns of power come together to prevent change, and the researcher tries to understand why.

REFERENCES

Alcoff, L. (1991). The Problem of speaking for others. *Cultural Critique, 23*, 5–32.
Barlow, M., & Robertson, H. (1994). *Class warfare: The assault on Canada's schools.* Toronto: Key Porter Books.
Ligon, G. (1994, April). *Getting to the point and counterpoint of dropout reporting issues.* Pre-

sented at the Annual Meeting of the American Educational Research Association, New Orleans, LA.

National Center for Education Statistics (NCES). (1995). *Condition of education 1995* (Stock No. 065–000–00791–6). Washington, DC: U.S. Government Printing Office.

Tanner, D. (1993, December). A nation truly at risk. *Phi Delta Kappan,* pp. 289–310.

U.S. Department of Education. (1983). *A nation at risk.* Washington, DC: Author.

CHAPTER 4

Coming to Terms with Marginal Work: Dropouts in a Polarized Labor Market

HARVEY KRAHN AND JULIAN TANNER

Educators have long viewed high dropout rates as a serious problem; now concern is being expressed in other sectors as well. In 1990, the Canadian government launched the 5-year, $300 million "Stay-In-School Initiative" to "respond to the serious threat that the secondary school dropout rate poses to the future productivity of the Canadian economy" (Employment and Immigration Canada, 1990, p. 14). Several years earlier, in 1987, the Ontario government commissioned a major study of high school dropouts and of the relevance of education in the emerging service economy (Radwanski, 1987). A number of national research and lobbying organizations (Conference Board of Canada, 1992; Economic Council of Canada, 1992) have portrayed high dropout rates as one indicator of an education and training system that needs to be restructured.

Although it is not apparent that lower dropout rates will quickly lead to higher national productivity, it is very clear that in a more polarized labor market (Economic Council of Canada, 1990; Krahn, 1992), high school dropouts will be increasingly disadvantaged. Compared to the situation several decades ago when full-time, semiskilled or skilled occupational positions were reasonably available to those with limited formal education, today's labor market is much less welcoming. The increasingly difficult employment prospects faced by today's young dropouts constitute an immediate and serious social problem of growing inequality.

Dropouts are more likely to be unemployed and, when employed, to earn much less than graduates (Ekstrom, Goertz, Pollack, & Rock, 1986;

Gilbert, Barr, Clark, Blue, & Sunter, 1993; Lawton, Leithwood, Batcher, Donaldson, & Stewart, 1988; Rumberger, 1987). Recessions and economic restructuring over the past decade have simply amplified this pattern. While lower tier service sector jobs have expanded (Krahn, 1992), we have seen a sharp decline in the number of desirable entry-level positions offered by employers in the goods-producing sector and the upper tier services. Consequently, many high school graduates and even some university graduates are being forced to accept part-time, temporary, and lower-status jobs (Krahn & Lowe, 1990; Myles, Picot, & Wannell, 1988). In turn, finding a good job has become much more difficult for high school dropouts, a group always near the end of the job-seekers' queue.

In this chapter, we examine in detail the labor market experiences of a large sample of high school dropouts in a western Canadian city during the mid-1980s.[1] Although the research literature clearly documents dropouts' more frequent unemployment and lower incomes, their actual work experiences have seldom been studied. Our interview results provide a much more detailed picture of the work histories and employment prospects of early school-leavers. In addition, we ask how dropouts react to their marginal employment status in a polarized labor market. Although the original study was completed a decade ago, the results remain relevant today. The work histories of these young people highlight the generally precarious and disadvantaged labor market position of early school-leavers, a position that has not improved and may have even deteriorated further.

RESEARCH DESIGN

This study was completed over a 4-month period in 1984–1985 in Edmonton, Alberta, a large western Canadian city with a population of around 600,000. During the 1970s and early 1980s, the local economy had expanded rapidly, largely due to increases in international oil prices. But heavy dependence on oil also meant that the recession of the early 1980s had a devastating effect on the local labor market. Edmonton unemployment rates (annual averages) jumped from around 4% in the 1970s to 14.1% in 1984. The 1984 provincial unemployment rate for teenagers (15 to 19 years old) was 18.2% compared to 15.4% for young adults (age 20 to 24). While estimates of unemployment among young dropouts in Edmonton during this period are not available, they were no doubt considerably higher, probably well above 20%.

A quota sampling technique was used to contact 168 individuals who had left high school in the previous few years. An attempt was made to balance the number of female and male and employed and unemployed respondents, and to include in the sample dropouts who had been in contact with social service agencies, along with others who were coping on their own or with family assistance. About two dozen had returned to school by the time they were interviewed. A few of the subjects were living in youth shelters, and several interviews were completed with dropouts serving time in a local corrections center.

Semistructured interviews were conducted in public places by a team of trained interviewers. The interviews were taped and subjects were also asked to complete a short questionnaire containing additional questions. Taped interviews and completed questionnaires were obtained from 162 of the dropouts originally contacted. Despite the inclusion of possibly sensitive questions about school and work problems, relationships with parents, and deviant behavior, respondents appeared comfortable answering the questions or skipping those they did not wish to answer. To ensure anonymity, all identifying information about respondents was destroyed after the interviews were completed.

Just over half of the respondents were male and most (85%) were between the ages of 17 and 23. On average, both females and males were 20 years old when interviewed and had been out of school for about 3 years. Nine out of 10 sample members had completed 9th grade, 69% had managed to finish 10th grade, but only 36% had stayed in school till the end of 11th grade. Apparently half of the subjects were employed when interviewed. More than half were living with their parents.

DROPOUTS' EMPLOYMENT HISTORIES

The labor market behavior of the majority of the sample appeared to be rather unstable, with frequent movement between jobs and in and out of employment. Over one-third (37%) of the 76 employed sample members were working part-time when interviewed. More than half (55%) of the employed dropouts had held their job for less than 6 months. Both employed and unemployed sample members reported an average of about four jobs in their employment history.

Unemployment figured prominently in the work histories of both the currently employed and the jobless. The 86 unemployed dropouts had been without a job for an average of 9.2 months. About three-quarters also reported earlier periods of unemployment. On average, the unemployed sample members had experienced a total of just over 12 months in this state. A large majority (82%) of the employed dropouts had also been unemployed at some time in the past. This subgroup reported an average of 9.4 months of unemployment.

The distribution of jobs currently held by the employed sample members (Table 4.1) highlights the limited range of work opportunities available to most young high school dropouts. Only a handful had found work outside the service industries and, with a few exceptions, the jobs were of low status. Food service positions were most common, especially waiting tables and fast-food jobs, followed by sales clerk positions. Young dropouts were also employed in warehouse jobs, janitorial work, and a number of other low-skilled positions. In addition, Table 4.1 demonstrates that gender-based occupational segregation exists even at the bottom of the service industries. Food service and sales positions were particularly common among the female dropouts, none of whom were employed outside of the service industries.

A small number of these dropouts had managed to find somewhat better jobs. One woman was managing a restaurant and two other respondents were employed as chefs. Several waitresses in better restaurants reported reasonable incomes, with tips supplementing low hourly pay. In addition, seven female respondents were in what could be described as "mid-status" service jobs (clerical positions or working as assistants in the helping professions). By working many hours of overtime, the young man employed in a steel mill was earning considerably more than most respondents. And the machine shop employee had begun an apprenticeship which might turn into a secure and well-paying job in the future.

Table 4.1 profiles the marginal labor market within which young dropouts obtain their work experience and in which many remain trapped, a labor market within which periods of unemployment are common and job mobility is primarily horizontal. Although respondents reported frequent job changes, upward mobility was very limited, as indicated by the work history of a 22-year-old female currently driving a catering truck:

> I worked in a butcher shop right after I quit for a year, and then . . . I worked for the Bay in . . . a self-serve restaurant and then I went to work for Grandma Lee's as a baker . . . for a year and a half. It's early, early hours but it's all right. The pay was no good—at Grandma Lee's you don't get paid anything. And after that I went to work for a delicatessen again. I worked there for seven months and then I went to the Renford Inn and I worked there for six months. . . . I cooked [there]. I learned how to fast-food cook and then I went back to Grandma Lee's again as a baker and I baked there for six months and then I got promoted to an assistant manager—and it's seven days a week any time they want you for a measly $1100 a month . . . . But then my boss told me not to bother his girls because he had them trained the way he wanted them. So I quit there and now I've got this job.

TABLE 4.1. Present job by industry and gender.

Present Job	Female	Male
Restaurant manager	1	-
Chef	1	1
Hostess	2	-
Waitress	6	-
Bartender	1	-
Catering truck driver	1	-
Kitchen assistant	1	1
Busperson	-	2
Fast food (McDonald's/etc.)	4	1
Total Food Services	17 (40%)	5 (20%)
Sales manager	2	-
Sales clerk	11	3
Stock clerk	-	2
Telephone salesperson	-	1
Total Sales	13 (30%)	6 (24%)
Warehouse worker	3	2
Security guard	-	2
Janitor	-	3
Car rental assistant	1	-
Other personal services worker	2	1
Total Other Low-Status Services	6 (14%)	8 (32%)
Secretary	2	-
Data entry clerk	1	-
Telephone operator	1	-
Bank teller	1	-
Physiotherapy aide	1	-
Daycare assistant	1	-
Youth training project assistant	-	1
Total Other Mid-Status Services	7 (16%)	1 (4%)
Auto repairer	-	1
Steel works/machine shop worker	-	2
Textile processor	-	1
Laborer (construction)	-	1
Total Blue-Collar Industries	-	5 (20%)
TOTAL	43 (100%)	25 (100%)

JOB LIKES AND DISLIKES

Most studies of job satisfaction ask questions like "All in all, how satisfied are you with your work?" These general measures typically reveal a large majority of satisfied employees despite the evidence that many jobs pay little, require few skills, offer few intrinsic satisfactions, and may be very insecure. This apparent contradiction is easier to understand when we recognize that many workers have little chance of obtaining a better job. Given few reasonable alternatives, most workers will report that they are relatively satisfied with their job (Kalleberg & Griffin, 1978; Rinehart, 1978). As Stewart and Blackburn (1975) put it: "Satisfaction is expressed within a framework of what is possible, liking is expressed within a framework of what is desirable" (p. 503).

This is an important theoretical distinction, particularly for a study of young dropouts in a restricted labor market. If, in fact, these young people see few alternatives to their present employment, most might be inclined to report satisfaction with their current job. The point is not to question such reports, but to get beyond them to any particular likes and dislikes an individual would have of her or his job. Consequently, in this study interviewers were instructed to ask dropouts what they liked and disliked about their current job, rather than if they were satisfied or dissatisfied. A detailed content analysis of answers enabled us to categorize employed respondents as generally liking their job (58%), appearing ambivalent (35%), or generally disliking their job (7%).

It is apparent that job dissatisfaction was not particularly widespread even though most of these dropouts held rather low-level service jobs. However, some of the older respondents described their jobs less positively. To examine this pattern more systematically, we combined the "ambivalent" and "generally dislike" categories and separated the sample of employed dropouts into two groups, those under 20 and those 20 years of age and older. Two-thirds (66%) of the younger dropouts appeared generally to like their jobs, compared to only 46% of their somewhat older peers. This simple test suggests that job satisfaction was more common among younger dropouts, reversing the consistently observed pattern of greater satisfaction among older workers (Krahn & Lowe, 1993). In the following discussion of specific job assessments, we speculate about the reasons for this unusual age difference.

Positive Job Evaluations

Job characteristics that respondents said they liked are categorized in Table 4.2. The social aspects of the job—meeting interesting people and/or

TABLE 4.2. What respondents liked about their job.

	(n)
Meet/talk to nice/interesting people	18
Nice/fun/interesting co-workers	14
Pay	12
Promotion/advancement possibilities	5
Hours (set your own/flexible)	4
Benefits	2
Office environment	1
Interesting work/interested in the area	12
Responsibility	7
Variety in tasks	5
Challenging	3
In area of training	1
Chance to get some training	1
No supervisor/work at your own pace	6
Good management/expectations clearly defined	2
Keeps me busy/time goes quickly	7
Easy work	2
Gets me out of the house	1
Job is fine/I like everything/general answers	5
Total (number of answers)	108
Total (number of respondents)	(61)

enjoying the company of co-workers—were identified most often as positive features. A 17-year-old waitress expressed it this way: "There isn't really anything I dislike about it. It's fun to work there, people are great to get along with."

Extrinsic or material work rewards were mentioned less often. Although 12 respondents said something positive about their wages, not all of these individuals were so well paid. One was a 17-year-old female impressed with the $5.00 an hour she was receiving. Another three mentioned pay in the "at least I get paid" sense. Only two listed fringe benefits as an attraction, one of whom was pleased about being given paid holidays. Five of these dropouts spoke positively about the possibility of promotion, although it was by no means certain that they themselves would be so fortunate.

Intrinsic work rewards were evaluated positively about as often as material rewards. A dozen respondents said they found their work interesting, including a physiotherapy aide, a secretary, several sales clerks, a young man employed as a cook in a fast-food restaurant, and a young woman working in a warehouse. About half a dozen mentioned responsibility and variety in tasks, and three considered their work to be challenging. A 23-year-old male chef said, "I like the responsibility, calling your own shots. . . . There's a lot of pressure . . . a lot of times when it gets really hairy, but you get used to it. It's always different, you can't blueprint your job."

A handful of respondents mentioned management practices as things they liked in their job. Some of these dropouts were noting that they were being trusted to work unsupervised. The positive answers provided by seven of these employed dropouts suggested that they had held previous jobs where time dragged. A 19-year-old female employed as a cook/restaurant hostess said, "I think what I like the most is that the work is fast-paced and the time just flies by."

Jobs in the secondary labor market are typically described as offering few intrinsic and extrinsic rewards. Most of these recent dropouts were employed in this marginal work world, although a few of the older sample members had managed to find somewhat better jobs. This probably accounts for why the older group provided four of the five positive comments about career advancement possibilities. Thus, in general, these results reinforce the negative characterization of the labor market in which most young dropouts find employment.

More interesting, perhaps, is the degree to which workplace social relationships were evaluated positively. Younger employed dropouts were more likely to mention nice/interesting customers and clients (13 times) than were older respondents (only 5 mentions). Younger subjects also said positive things about their co-workers more often (9 mentions versus 5 from the older subgroup). Greater emphasis on workplace social relationships among younger dropouts might reflect a different set of work orientations, more of a preoccupation with fun and friends, and less concern about careers and personal self-fulfillment at work.

This interpretation suggests that young dropouts would not be aware, or take little notice of, the largely absent intrinsic and extrinsic rewards in their job. For example, a 17-year-old male warehouse worker stated enthusiastically, "Oh yeah, everything, everybody's just perfect" and then later reported matter-of-factly that the job was temporary and would be ending in a week. For others, somewhat more aware of what they were missing, the emphasis on positive aspects of social interactions at work might have been a form of coping with, or compensating for, absent extrinsic and intrinsic work rewards.

A similar argument has been used to explain why, in the labor force as a whole, instrumental work orientations focusing on material job rewards are relatively common. Individuals working in jobs with few intrinsic rewards will stress the importance of good pay (Rinehart, 1978, p. 7). Since the labor market inhabited by young dropouts is also rather short on well-paying jobs, positions where co-workers and customers are interesting and fun may come to be seen as "better" jobs, particularly by the youngest dropouts.

Negative Job Evaluations

Table 4.3 lists the fewer negative characteristics of jobs reported by employed dropouts. Absent extrinsic rewards were reported somewhat more often than other job dislikes. Low pay was mentioned most often: "I only bring home about $600 a month so that covers like all of our living expenses, our food and everything, but it doesn't cover the rent or nothing like that," said a 22-year-old female driving a catering truck and living with her boyfriend.

Several respondents disliked the long hours they were working, while a few were working part-time and wanted more hours. But complaints about irregular hours, shift-work or night-work were more common. Only a few of these dropouts commented on the absence of other extrinsic work rewards such as promotion opportunities or fringe benefits. However, 8 respondents mentioned hard-to-please customers as a dislike. This is not surprising, given the number employed in retail sales and food service positions where contact with the public is extensive. Another 5 were irritated by lazy co-workers, and 6 commented negatively on their supervisor or manager. A 20-year-old waitress described her manager's expectations of her and other waitresses in the hotel dining room:

> I don't like working in the hotel that I'm working in now 'cause the management is just too much, but we all hope that that's going to change pretty soon . . . they're just really, really bad. . . . He treats us really bad, but he expects a lot from us. He really gives us a hard

TABLE 4.3. What respondents disliked about their job.

	(n)
Low pay	9
Hours: too long	3
too few	3
irregular/nights/poor shifts	7
No promotion/advancement possibilities	3
Unpleasant/unhealthy working conditions	2
No benefits	1
Problems with customers/clients	8
Unpleasant/lazy co-workers	5
Unpredictable/unpleasant management	6
Having to supervise and be responsible	2
Boring/tedious work	6
Lack of challenge/no variety	3
Stressful work	1
Having to look busy	2
Transportation (to work) problems	1
Total (number of answers)	62
Total (number of respondents)	(49)

time, he wants us all to come in with as little [clothing on] as possible, and work in as little [clothing] as possible, and take a lot of abuse that I won't take.

Job dislikes focusing on intrinsic work rewards were also noted by some of the respondents. One of the chefs found his supervisory position to be stressful, but his case was unusual. Respondents were more likely to complain about limited task demands. Half a dozen respondents, in a range of different jobs, said they disliked the boring or tedious nature of their work. Two of these dropouts disliked having to look busy (in sales positions), and a handful found little challenge in their job. A 24-year-old secretary characterized her job succinctly: "It's boring, it's menial, it's got no challenge."

Summing up, we find these dropouts identifying in their list of job dislikes some of the negative aspects of work often attributed to jobs in the secondary labor market (low pay, irregular hours, boring work, problematic management, and so on). But with respect to job dislikes, we observed no obvious age differences in the pattern of answers. Younger and somewhat older respondents were equally likely to criticize these and a handful of other aspects of their jobs.

COMING TO TERMS WITH MARGINAL WORK

The interview data clearly show that a large majority of these young dropouts were employed in very marginal jobs. It is particularly noteworthy, then, that so few spoke negatively about low pay, few benefits, absent promotion chances, and boring, menial work. This lack of criticism does not mean that most dropouts were enjoying extensive work rewards. If they had been, presumably they would have said so when asked what they liked about their work (Table 4.2); instead, many appeared to like their work despite the absence of intrinsic and extrinsic rewards. We have already suggested that workplace social relationships may fill some of this gap, particularly for the youngest dropouts. But there are additional factors, some of them age-related, which help account for these relatively positive job evaluations.

Limited Occupational Goals

When asked about their occupational goals, over half of the employed sample members had vague or no work-related ambitions. It is impossible to tell whether the absence of occupational goals was a precipitating factor in dropping out of school or whether the failure to finish high school meant that occupational goals did not develop. Whatever the causal direction, these interviews reveal substantial numbers of young dropouts with vague or unformed career goals. Those under 20 were less likely to report specific occupational goals (61% compared to 48% of those aged 20 and older).

The absence of such goals was associated with positive job evaluations, probably because negative comparisons between a low-level job and personal ambitions would be less likely to emerge. Alternatively, the presence of occupational goals increased the probability of a current job being disliked. A 17-year-old female generally liking her job at Burger King said, "As long as I'm working, I'm happy." When asked, "So you have no definite career goals?" she replied, "No."

INTERVIEWEE (a 20-year-old woman managing a video shop and ambiva-
    lent about her job): Sure would like to become a nurse, but I don't
    think I ever will.
INTERVIEWER: So you don't think you will be doing a job like that in five
    or ten years?
INTERVIEWEE: No, I don't. . . . I feel like I'm going to be stuck at that
    [video store] for the rest of my life sometimes.

Among the female respondents, reports of no clear occupational goals were frequently accompanied by comments about wanting to get married, have children, or both. Alternative central life interests would obviously reduce the possibility of dissatisfaction with a low-level job. Eight of the women in the employed sample (20%), including some of the older re-spondents, mentioned such traditional female goals when asked about jobs they would like to hold in the future.

INTERVIEWEE (22-year-old female driving a catering truck; about to get
    married): What are my major goals in life? I really don't have any
    right now.
INTERVIEWER: What kind of job would you like to have in five or ten
    years?
INTERVIEWEE: I don't want to be working in five or ten years. I want to
    be at home having kids.

Some sample members reported what must be considered unrealistic occupational goals. Several mentioned careers in popular music, even though none appeared to have the aptitudes and skills needed for success in this area. One wanted to be a psychologist, another a scientist, and one a lawyer. It is difficult to tell whether these were real occupational goals or just expressions of youthful bravado. Whatever they were, it is clear that such "goals" were so far removed from current labor market realities that they were unlikely to breed dissatisfaction with the jobs currently held. A 15-year-old female "helping Dad with his books" part-time and generally liking her job said:

Well, I just want to finish high school and then I'll think about that
later. I want to sing. I want to become a singer . . . I'm going to

take guitar lessons. I've never taken singing lessons, but . . . I sing pretty good.

Job Hierarchies and Opportunities for Advancement

One way of coping with a menial job was to point to others that were even less desirable. There seemed to be some agreement among sample members about the hierarchy of jobs within the lower level service industries. White-collar jobs were more highly valued than restaurant jobs, according to several sales clerks who spoke disparagingly about their previous jobs in the food services. But it was unskilled jobs like dish washing and in fast-food restaurants that received the most criticism from those who had done better. A 20-year-old stock clerk in a music store called them "piddly jobs." A 19-year-old woman, ambivalent about her present temporary job as a data entry clerk, added telephone soliciting to the list of worst jobs:

> I'm looking right now but there's not much out there except telephone soliciting. . . . I did it once before and I don't want to do it again. . . . If I get another dishwashing job, I better start thinking about the direction of my life.

Reminding oneself (and the interviewer) that there were even worse jobs was one way of maintaining face in this secondary labor market. Another was to point out the possibilities for advancement from the present position. A number of the sample members had obtained their present job through participation in a "job-finding club." Government job-training funds subsidized their salaries, but only for a limited time. Almost all of these respondents were confident that the subsidized "training" position would turn into a real job when the program ended, a hope that was bound to be unrealized for some. Sales clerks were frequently told that they were starting low in the job hierarchy, but that there were opportunities to move into management or to become a "buyer," if you stuck with the job. And employees in fast-food restaurants were generally provided with a description of how they could move up the ladder to better jobs. A 17-year-old female who clearly likes her job at A&W said:

> I'm a car host. I go out and take people's orders, and tell them to have a nice day and enjoy their food, and I have been training in the kitchen as well. I would like to train for supervisor, that's what I would like to do. They have been putting me in the kitchen and I have been cooking, and doing fries and things like that.

In a sense, these young dropouts were quite normal in how they rationalized their low labor market position. Like older and better educated workers, they looked down the job hierarchy for reassurance and up the promotion ladder for hope. But, unlike more advantaged workers in the primary labor market, they were much closer to the bottom of the occupational hierarchy and were also looking up a much shorter ladder.

Experiences of Unemployment

Most sample members had been unemployed at some point, often for long periods of time. For a few of the younger respondents, unemployment had not been very stressful. Living at home reduced money problems, although it also meant putting up with concerned parents. But most had found unemployment to be a relatively unpleasant experience. Depression and boredom were mentioned most often, along with problems of getting by on very little money. For some of those living independently, the latter meant constant worries about paying bills. For those still living at home, the problem was more often one of being embarrassed when friends with jobs had more money for leisure-time activities. A 19-year-old female who likes her job as a "hiker" in a car-rental firm said:

> Times were really tough. . . . you really had to save. . . . [I felt] really insecure . . . 'cause at the time all my friends had jobs and they were always going out. . . . And you couldn't go out with them 'cause you didn't have any money.

Working in a marginal job might not seem so bad when compared to unemployment. Furthermore, since these dropouts tended to socialize with others like themselves, their friends were also often unemployed or working in similar types of jobs. And because, on average, these dropouts tended to come from lower socio-economic backgrounds, other family members might also be employed in the same labor market. Thus, comparisons with the jobs and work histories of friends and family members would not, in many cases, lead to negative assessments of an individual's own job. Here is a 17-year-old female who generally likes her job as a hostess in a restaurant:

INTERVIEWER: How far did your mom go in school?
INTERVIEWEE: I think she got halfway through grade twelve.
INTERVIEWER: And what does she do?
INTERVIEWEE: Right now, nothing, she was a waitress. She's unemployed, last night she quit.

Here is a 19-year-old female ambivalent about her temporary job as a data-entry clerk:

INTERVIEWER: What kinds of things does your boyfriend do?
INTERVIEWEE: He was a stockboy at K-Mart, he was a gas attendant, a cab driver, door-to-door salesman.
INTERVIEWER: Is he working now?
INTERVIEWEE: No, it's always, "If we need you, we'll call you."

In general, then, many of these dropouts had only a limited understanding of employment alternatives. Most had never worked outside of the secondary labor market and only a minority had friends or family members employed in primary labor market positions. Many could not even imagine alternatives, since they had vague or unformed career goals. As Blackburn (1988) notes in a discussion of the relationship between stratification structures and ideologies of work, "Those at the bottom of the stratification hierarchy not only have the least attractive jobs but also the most constrained experience" (p. 232).

Education Values and Plans

Most of these young workers probably did not consider the labor market implications when they first dropped out of school. Despite limited experience with employment alternatives, however, most were beginning to recognize that they were handicapped by not having a high school diploma:

> I haven't had any problems with finding jobs, like I've been working steady ever since. One thing about it is without the schooling, waitressing is about the only good job you can make money at. Every now and then I think that I would like to get a regular daytime job and I can't think of anything I can do without having more education than I do.

One of the surprising findings to emerge was that only a minority of these dropouts appeared to have totally rejected the education system. Most still placed considerable value on education, despite having chosen to quit high school. In fact, when asked, 70% of the total sample stated that they would like to get more education at some future time. Within this subsample of currently employed dropouts, 60% answered the question positively, 33% thought that they might get some more education in the future, and 7% were certain that they would not.

Some of these dropouts would, no doubt, follow through on these promises. Several sample members had already returned to alternative schools to complete their high school education. But for others such plans would probably not translate into future action. Nevertheless, such plans do reveal a value system shared with the rest of society, and equally important is that such public statements might serve an important function for young people beginning to recognize that they might be trapped in a marginal labor market. Like university students telling themselves that menial jobs are "just for the summer," dropouts could promise themselves, and others, that their current labor market situation was temporary. Once they obtained their high school diploma, new opportunities would open up. Thus, expressions of future education plans could be a means of coping with marginal work.

SUMMARY AND IMPLICATIONS

Portraying high dropout rates as an economic problem diverts our attention from a much more immediate and serious social problem. In an increasingly polarized labor market characterized by high rates of unemployment and a growing number of part-time, temporary, and frequently low-skill jobs, dropouts are severely disadvantaged. At a time when many better educated young people are having difficulty finding satisfactory employment, most dropouts have little hope of moving out of the marginal jobs found in the secondary labor market. They are at risk of becoming a class of educational "have-nots," unable to compete for better jobs requiring secondary and postsecondary credentials. Hence, the dropout problem is a problem of social inequality, particularly since young people from lower socio-economic backgrounds are more likely to leave school prior to graduation. Reducing dropout rates should be a national priority, not just in the hope that this will improve Canada's competitive position, but because fewer dropouts mean fewer labor force participants with limited opportunities.

Our account of dropouts' marginal jobs and limited career opportunities profiles part of the emerging structure of labor market inequality in the service economy. In addition, our interview data put a human face on the dropout problem by revealing the reactions of young, uncredentialed labor force participants to peripheral jobs. Dropouts are not merely passive participants in a difficult labor market. Instead, they cope and come to terms with their marginal labor market status in a variety of ways. In this respect, our observations about dropouts' job satisfaction come as somewhat of a surprise. We found reasonably high levels of job satisfaction. Furthermore, the youngest members of the sample tended to evaluate their jobs more positively, frequently emphasizing their satisfaction with workplace social relationships.

We have addressed this pattern of unusual findings in several ways. First, we argue that an emphasis on social relationships as significant job rewards is not particularly unusual when the jobs in question offer few material or intrinsic rewards. Second, the fact that younger dropouts particularly liked the social aspects of their job fits with our understanding of the "pre-career" life interests of teenagers, which frequently tend to focus on friends and fun. Third, the lower level of job satisfaction among older dropouts reflects a greater awareness of their limited labor market options. Working part-time in a low-skill, low-paying job may not be problematic when one is 16 or 17, particularly if one has friends at work and parents who cover basic living costs. But for older dropouts attempting to live independently, marginal jobs are no longer good enough; whereas within the labor force as a whole, higher incomes and better jobs tend to come with age, followed by increased job satisfaction (Hamilton & Wright, 1986, p. 288). The same kind of upward mobility is not possible in the secondary labor market inhabited by dropouts.

Our interview data suggested that young dropouts may emphasize positive workplace social relationships as a way of coping with marginal work. Vague or no career goals might also reduce the possibility of dissatisfaction with relatively dead-end jobs, as might comparisons to prior periods of unemployment. Nevertheless, our interview results showed that many dropouts still maintained some hope of moving up the occupational hierarchy, and most were aware that additional education was necessary for any real improvement in their labor market position. They recognized that the decision to quit high school had severely restricted their opportunities. Hence, many continued to promise that they might, someday, return to school.

This last research finding points to an important policy implication. Most current initiatives directed at reducing dropout rates are of the stay-in-school variety. The fact that a majority of dropouts recognize their educational handicap, are not completely alienated from the education system (Tanner, 1990) and say they would like to return, and the recent evidence that a significant minority actually do return at least for a time (Gilbert, Barr, Clark, Blue, & Sunter, 1993), suggest that return to school initiatives are equally important. Concerted efforts to develop programs that would entice dropouts back into the education system, perhaps into institutions that provided high school training in an "adult" environment

(Krahn & Tanner, 1989), are clearly a policy priority. Fewer dropouts and more "drop-back-ins" would both lead to greater equality of employment opportunity in Canada.

NOTE

1. Funding for this study was provided by Alberta Manpower (now Alberta Advanced Education and Career Development).

REFERENCES

Blackburn, R. M. (1988). Ideologies of work. In D. Rose (Ed.), *Social stratification and economic change.* London: Hutchinson.

Conference Board of Canada. (1992). *Dropping out: The cost to Canada* (synopsis). Ottawa: The Conference Board of Canada.

Economic Council of Canada. (1990). *Good jobs, bad jobs: Employment in the service economy.* Ottawa: Supply and Services Canada.

Economic Council of Canada. (1992). *A lot to learn: Education and training in Canada.* Ottawa: Supply and Services Canada.

Ekstrom, R. B., Goertz, M. E., Pollack, J. M., & Rock, D. A. (1986). Who drops out of high school and why? Findings from a national study. *Teachers College Record, 87,* 356–373.

Employment and Immigration Canada. (1990). *A national stay-in-school initiative.* Ottawa: Supply and Services Canada.

Gilbert, S., Barr, L., Clark, W., Blue, M., & Sunter, D. (1993). *Leaving school: Results from a national survey comparing school leavers and high school graduates 18 to 20 years of age.* Ottawa: Supply and Services Canada.

Hamilton, R. F., & Wright, J. D. (1986). *The state of the masses.* New York: Aldine.

Kalleberg, A., & Griffin, L. J. (1978). Positional sources of inequality in job satisfaction. *Sociology of Work and Occupations, 5,* 371–401.

Krahn, H. (1992). *Quality of work in the service sector.* Ottawa: Statistics Canada, General Social Survey Series 6.

Krahn, H., & Lowe, G. S. (1990). *Young workers in the service economy* (Working Paper No. 14). Ottawa: Economic Council of Canada.

Krahn, H., & Lowe, G. S. (1993). *Work, industry and Canadian society* (2nd ed.). Scarborough: Nelson Canada.

Krahn, H., & Tanner, J. (1989). Bringing them back to school. *Policy Options, 10* (2), 23–24.

Lawton, S. B., Leithwood, K. A., Batcher, E., Donaldson, E. L., & Stewart, R. (1988). *Student reiteration and transition in Ontario high schools.* Toronto: Ontario Ministry of Education.

Myles, J., Picot, G., & Wannell, T. (1988, October). The changing wage distribution of jobs, 1981–86. *The Labour Force,* 85–138.

Radwanski, G. (1987). *Ontario study of the relevance of education and the issue of drop-outs.* Toronto: Ontario Ministry of Education.

Rinehart, J. (1978). Contradictions of work-related attitudes and behavior: An interpretation. *Canadian Review of Sociology and Anthropology, 15* (1), 1–15.

Rumberger, R. (1987). High school dropouts: A review of issues and evidence. *Review of Educational Research, 57* (2), 101–121.

Stewart, A., & Blackburn, R. M. (1975). The stability of structured inequality. *Sociological Review, 23,* 481–508.

Tanner, J. (1990). Reluctant rebels: A case study of Edmonton high school drop-outs. *Canadian Review of Sociology and Anthropology, 27* (1), 74–94.

CHAPTER 5

Dropping Out in Canada: The Construction of a Crisis?

PAUL ANISEF AND LESLEY ANDRES

As described in previous chapters, the federal government of Canada considered the "dropout problem" a serious enough issue to launch several reports in the early 1990s warning of its dire social consequences, as well as the Stay-in-School Initiative. A cursory examination suggests that this national effort to reduce dropping out arose due to public concern about a rapidly escalating social problem. This is consistent with a model advanced by Mauss (1975, 1984, 1989) in which he describes social problems as originating at the grassroots level and, based on democratic processes, extending to influence representatives of government. Once the existence of a problem is recognized by government, its management takes the form of a society-wide approach to confront the problem, including lobbying and publicity through mass media.

Jensen, Gerber, and Babcock (1991) offer an alternative interpretation. Following their analysis of the "War on Drugs" in the United States, they contend that some social problems are created by powerful "claims makers" to serve their political self-interests. Jensen and Gerber (1993) assert that "although public concern may precede the state creation of social problems, the primary claims making activities are conducted by politicians who have a professional stake in the social construction process" (p. 454). Jensen et al. (1991) suggest that social problems can emerge from state claim-making efforts of powerful interest groups and "without prior existence of a social movement" (p. 652). They present a modified model of Mauss' (1975, 1984, 1989) original conceptualization, where

they posit four stages: incipiency, coalescence, creation and policy formation, and legitimation.

In the first or incipiency stage, some members of the public may
express concern with the emerging issue, though no informal or formal
organizations exist to further the condition as a problem. The second or
coalescence stage may or may not be present; if it occurs, informal or
formal organizations are created to act as collective claims makers. Central
to the model is the third stage, that of creation and policy formation. In
this stage, the existence of an undesirable condition is put forward by such
powerful interests as politicians and governmental agency personnel who
argue for the legitimacy of their claims and develop a solution for the
politically constructed problem in an attempt to further their own interests. In the final or legitimation stage, politicians or other state officials
attempt to create or strengthen public support for their position and legitimize their claims and remedies in order to support their political or organizational interests.

In this chapter, we endeavor to determine whether the emergence of
school dropouts as a national crisis in the 1990s emerged out of public
concern based on escalating numbers of youth departing from school, or
a crisis constructed by the state. We begin by reviewing conceptions of
dropping out in earlier decades before analyzing the Stay-in-School Initiative. We then examine the Stay-in-School Initiative in relation to
school leaving patterns over time. This Initiative and findings of the related School Leavers Survey (SLS) commissioned by Employment and Immigration Canada and carried out by Statistics Canada in 1991 (Statistics
Canada, Education, Culture and Tourism Division [ECTD], 1991) are used
to assess the degree to which the dropout problem is an artifact of limited
definitions and reified perceptions rather than a problem that warrants
national intervention. Employing a state claims-making model, we examine the extent to which the national dropout crisis in Canada was socially
constructed by a body of the federal government, namely Employment
and Immigration Canada, as a strategy to deflect public attention away
from issues of unemployment and the labor market.

HISTORICAL CONCEPTIONS OF EARLY SCHOOL LEAVING

Only in recent decades has the high school diploma become a required
credential for securing many forms of employment. Prior to the 1950s,
most Canadians left school after Grade 8 or 9 (Lawr & Gidney, 1973).
Indeed, the senior grades were marked by massive dropout insofar as those

children with no intention of pursuing a postsecondary education left school and joined the work force.

Undoubtedly, dropping out of school is as old as formal school itself. However, with the advent of compulsory education legislation, normative expectations dictated that children would stay in school until the age of 15 or 16 (Martin & MacDonnell, 1982). Until the 1950s, high schools functioned primarily to prepare a relatively small group of students for advanced studies and senior level curricula were determined by the demands of universities. Thus, in 1951 only 46% of Canada's 14- to 17-year-olds were enrolled full-time beyond 8th grade (Lennards, 1980).

In the late 1950s and early 1960s, "dropping out" altered in meaning and was no longer thought of as a natural phenomenon. Rather, dropping out became defined as a problem or threat to the well-being of the nation (Lawr & Gidney, 1973). The 1960s was a period of unparalleled public education expansion, and the majority of Canadians believed fully that schools could play a major and positive role in a new age characterized by rapid change, a highly developed technology, and a commitment to democracy and social justice. The government set a course of stable economic growth and sustained economic development based on "human capital" theories in vogue in the United States. Such theories posited that knowledge or brain power was the principal factor facilitating great increases in productivity, on which economic prosperity depended. Advanced industrial societies were "knowledge" societies and the Canadian labor force was grossly undereducated compared to that of the United States. The striking gap in educational completion led to the obvious conclusion that if Canada were to catch up to its American neighbor, dramatic expansion and reform of the education system was required. Between 1951 and 1971, the total student population in Canada more than doubled. And though part of this increase is attributable to the postwar baby boom, the largest portion of the growth resulted from increased participation levels and a rapid expansion in the number of students continuing to matriculation. Expansion of education in the 1960s served to push the school-leaving age close to the postsecondary level. As more teenagers graduated from high school, graduation eventually became an expectation and exerted a strong influence on families and students; dropping out was perceived as a departure from a newly defined age-specific norm (Dorn, 1993).

Whereas "expansion" and "individuality" were the familiar buzzwords in the 1960s, educational reformers and other critics made "efficiency" and "productivity" the watchwords of the 1970s. Concern regarding dropping out reflected the difficulties experienced by youth in making the transition to employment and the role school could play in making the transition more efficient, rather than an emphasis on individual failure to complete. There was a heightened awareness of shortages in skilled labor among those in the federal government and Canadian industry, and the latter had become increasingly dissatisfied with federal labor market policy. This concern carried into the 1980s.

THE ECONOMY, UNEMPLOYMENT, AND STAYING IN SCHOOL

Gaskell (1993) indicates that by 1981, unemployment had increased, economic growth remained low, and Canada was faced with an aging and no longer expanding labor force. The federal government became even more concerned with the fit between the education system and the labor market (Employment and Immigration Canada, 1981a, 1981b). In the 1980s, key social policy issues for most Canadians were the economy and unemployment. Livingstone and Hart (1991) report that in national time-series data, educational issues attracted minimal attention and were often included in the "other" category when reporting results. In polls commissioned by the British Columbia and Ontario governments in 1985, 5% of British Columbians and 10% of Ontarians identified current educational issues as most important; however, unemployment was identified by 66% of British Columbians and 83% of Ontarians as the most important issue facing their province.

The Task Force on Labor Market Development or Dodge Report (Employment and Immigration Canada, 1981b) signalled a conceptual shift from human capital theory to the notion of human resource development. With this shift came a new emphasis on skills rather than occupation (Smith & Smith, 1990). This resulted in the treatment of the labor force as "a resource to be managed in relation to the needs of the industrial sector competing on a highly competitive international market" (p. 186). Smith and Smith claim that this shift away from human capital theory toward that of human resource development was a "device for translating new production and labor processes into properties of the labor force" (p. 192).

High school completion in itself was being lauded as a panacea for the country's economic woes. Those with high school graduation credentials would create a "skilled and competent work force," individuals prepared to "compete in the global market of tomorrow" (Price Waterhouse, 1992, p. i). Hence, individuals who were potentially unemployable in a global economy were labeled "at risk." By the 1980s, being at risk of dropping out of high school was defined as a major threat to the economic prosperity of a society.

The economic recession and restructuring of the labor market in the late 1980s clearly affected unemployment rates, and those with the lowest levels of educational attainment were the most affected. Overall, however, the number of Canadians without a high school education was quite low. According to Labor Force Annual Averages for 1992, only 20% of all Canadians between the ages of 25 and 44 had not graduated from high school (Statistics Canada, 1992). It is also important to note that although students who failed to complete high school were less employable than high school graduates, high school and postsecondary graduates were not immune to downturns in the economy. This suggests a misplaced emphasis on the relationship among early school leaving, labor force participation, and economic prosperity of the country.

It was in an era of human resource management, high youth unemployment, and recession that the federal government created the Ministry of State for Youth in 1984 (Canada House of Commons, 1987). In 1986, this ministry was transferred to the department of Employment and Immigration and had specific responsibilities, such as coordinating the student summer employment program and reviewing various occupational training programs. Also, in April 1984 the Senate Special Committee on Youth was established to examine the problems and issues facing Canadian youth (Canada Senate Special Committee on Youth, 1986). The Committee focused attention on four major problem areas including the changing lifestyle and values of youth, Native youth, the transition from school to work, and employment and unemployment. Although mention is made of the positive relationship between formal schooling and employment, no detailed consideration of the "dropout problem" encountered by Canadian youth can be located in this report. Statements such as "We again stress that education and training programs must be flexible enough to allow young people to take up the challenge offered by new advances, and to adapt as yet newer advances occur" (p. 82) emphasized the severity and consequences of youth unemployment rather than early school leaving.

Yet, despite government and public concern about the economy and unemployment, attention at the federal level was focused on the retention of youth in school. High school students at risk of dropping out were targeted as "wastage" in human resource terms. Powerful interest groups including the Conference Board of Canada and the Corporate Higher Education Forum advanced such claims as "Canadian society will lose more than $4 billion over the working lifetimes of the nearly 137,000 youth who dropped out rather than graduating with the class of 1989" (Lafleur, 1992, p. 1). Fueled by such attacks on the education system and abetted by reports commissioned by the federal government, the "dropout problem" became common knowledge and rhetoric. The Ministry of State for Youth acted on the claim that dropping out was a national problem solvable by enacting policy to ensure that youth stay in school. In 1990, the Stay-in-School Initiative was launched as the unquestioned solution to the unquestioned problem.

THE STAY-IN-SCHOOL INITIATIVE

The central purpose of the Stay-in-School Initiative was to "respond to the serious threat that the secondary school dropout rate poses to the future productivity of the Canadian economy" (Employment and Immigration Canada, 1990, p. 14). In the introduction of the Stay-in-School Initiative document, *A National Stay-in-School Initiative* (Employment and Immigration Canada, 1990), the then-current Minister of Employment and Immigration, Barbara McDougall, asserted that "no nation that cares for its youth and its future can be indifferent to thousands of teenagers dropping out of high school in times like these" (p. 1).

The Stay-in-School Initiative was based on three assumptions. First, it assumed that in order to foster a learning culture, Canadian youth must be encouraged to stay in school. Second, in the main, Canadians are ignorant about the relationship between school and work. Hence, "all Canadians need to be informed about the dropout problem and its consequences—for themselves, their children, and the economy as a whole" (Canada Minister of State for Youth, 1992, p. 2). This assumption of ignorance is stated more blatantly in a report by Price Waterhouse (1992). According to this document, youth are expected to adapt to changing economic demands, although "public opinion surveys indicate that most Canadian parents do not understand that the changing world economy demands a new approach to learning" (p. 3). Given parents' influence on their children and their lack of awareness of the new economic reality, parents may be less likely to encourage their children to stay in school. Third, the secondary school dropout rate was deemed responsible for jeopardizing the future productivity of the Canadian economy (Employment and Immigration Canada, 1990).

In order to combat an "unacceptable" dropout rate, the Stay-in-School Initiative launched a three-pronged attack, including the following: the design and delivery of assessment, counseling, and labor market preparation programs and services; mobilization of government, business, labor, parents, teachers, social agencies, and youth as partners; and an information campaign aimed at enlightening youth, parents, and the public about "the realities of the labor market and the need for students to complete their high school education" (Employment and Immigration Canada, 1990, p. 9). Pilot assessment, counseling, and program delivery projects, national and local consultations, and demonstration projects involving various stakeholder groups would be included. The fourth component of the Initiative was the School Leavers Survey.

Despite the belief that "the national average early school leavers rate in Canada now is estimated at above 30 per cent" (Employment and Immigration Canada, 1990, p. 12) and compelling a perceived need to launch a campaign designed to encourage young Canadians to stay in school, it was acknowledged that very little information about the dropout situation existed. Unlike the United States, Sweden, and Britain, Canada does not have a strong tradition of collecting national longitudinal educational data. A report produced for the Social Trends Directorate of the Department of the Secretary of State for Canada indicated that research on retention, dropout, and success in school consisted of "scattered studies and unsystematic surveys" (Dallaire, 1985). According to the *Project Discussion Paper for School Leavers* (Statistics Canada, ECTD, 1989) 6 out of 10 provinces reported that they did not collect data on high school graduates, dropouts, or both. Also, it was acknowledged that the variation in dropout statistics across jurisdictions was attributed, in part, to the lack of a Canadian national database which was capable of tracking students through their school years. Existing available data were fraught with inconsistent definitions and measures of dropout.

Given the conviction with which the Stay-In-School Initiative was implemented and considering that the other three components of the program were intended to ameliorate a clearly delineated problem, it is ironic that a national survey of school leavers—the School Leavers Survey—was undertaken as a fourth component of the Stay-in-School Initiative. The intention of the School Leavers Survey was to determine the magnitude of the dropout problem in Canada (Employment and Immigration Canada, 1990). The purpose of the survey was to generate profiles of dropouts, high school graduates, and students who were continuing their education by "explor[ing] the environmental, social, attitudinal, personal and economic factors that may contribute to the early departure of students from school" (Statistics Canada, ECTD, 1991, p. 1). In particular, the survey sought to determine the reasons for early school leaving and the subsequent labor market experiences and quality of life of both early school leavers and high school graduates.

The School Leavers Survey was conducted by Statistics Canada under a contract from Employment and Immigration Canada. Cooperative data-sharing agreements between Statistics Canada and the provinces were sought. A stratified random sample of individuals between the ages of 18 and 20 was drawn from the Family Allowance File. A telephone survey was conducted between April and June 1991. In total, 9,460 individuals were contacted. The current educational status of respondents was self-reported. A detailed description of the sample is provided in the *School Leavers Survey Microdata User's Guide* (Statistics Canada, ECTD, 1991).

The purpose of the survey, as previously stated, would lead one to believe that the intention of this particular research endeavor was to have a conceptual function (Weiss, 1977). We seek to determine how dropping out was constructed as a problem, and the degree to which there is an observable basis for concern, by examining the way in which the dependent variable was framed, which independent variables were included and which omitted, and the overall conceptual framework in which the dropout problem was cast.

THE DROPOUT CRISIS IN CANADA: CONSTRUCTED OR REAL?

Construction of the dependent variable in the School Leavers Survey is problematic. Although the School Leavers Survey employs a variety of definitions that "reflect the stages of the early leaving process" (Gilbert, Barr, Clark, Blue, & Sunter, 1993, p. 16), analyses to date (Gilbert et al., 1993; Gilbert & Orok, 1993) dwell on only one definition—leaving high school before graduation.

Even when this limited definition of early school leaving is employed as the dependent variable, however, results of the School Leavers Survey of Canadian youth do not support the claim that the dropout rate in Canada is 30%. In total, 21% of the respondents to the School Leavers Survey (25% of males and 17% of females) indicated that, at one time or another, they had ever dropped out of high school. When analyses are confined to the 20-year-olds in the sample, the dropout rate is 18% (22% for males and 14% for females) (Gilbert et al., 1993).

Despite attempts by the federal government to cast the issue of dropouts as a national one, further analyses by province and sex illustrate that "having ever left school early" is clearly a provincial—and a gender—issue. Males in Newfoundland report the highest rate of ever leaving school (32%), compared with only 18% of British Columbia males. In all provinces except British Columbia, young women in the sample reported considerably lower rates of ever dropping out, ranging from a low of 14% in Alberta to a high of 19.4% in Nova Scotia. Only in British Columbia was the incidence of ever dropping out equal for males and females.

Although the frequency of early school leaving may be an indicator of the health of the education system of each province and the country as a whole, it provides a limited view of educational participation. Not all students who have ever left school at one point in their educational careers remain uneducated, unemployed, or both. If the question "Dropped out of school, then what?" is asked, early school leaving can be portrayed as a point of transition rather than one of exit. This alternate construction of the dependent variable reflects more accurately the movement of individuals through the education system and into the work force, and more clearly delineates those truly "at risk" of remaining uneducated and unemployable.

When students who left school before graduating were recast into three categories (noncompleters—no further education; noncompleters —further education; noncompleters—returned to elementary or high school), we find that 3% of females and 4% of males have received some form of further education and training without ever completing high school, and 2% of females and 3% of males who have dropped out in the past are currently back in high school. Also, 7% of female and 6% of male dropouts have since completed high school. Only 9% of female and 15% of male respondents had neither completed high school nor participated in any type of further study.

In all provinces except New Brunswick and British Columbia, noncompletion of high school with no further education or training is considerably higher for males than females. Almost 25% of male respondents from Newfoundland and Prince Edward Island belong to this group. New Brunswick (13%), Quebec (16%), Ontario (14%), and British Columbia (13%) boast the lowest number of male noncompleters who have not pursued further study. Females are less likely to continue after graduation to other education or training in Newfoundland (15%) and Prince Edward Island (14%). Quebec (9%), Ontario (7%), and Alberta (10%) have the lowest numbers of females belonging to this category.

Although the number is low in each province, more respondents from Newfoundland, Nova Scotia, New Brunswick, and Quebec than the other provinces report not completing high school but participating in some type of further education and training. Males in Manitoba (5%) and females in Nova Scotia (3%) report the highest incidence of returning to elementary or secondary school after having dropped out.

Our re-analyses of School Leavers Survey data in a manner consistent with the structure of the education system in Canada indicate that the number of students who "ever drop out" of school is much lower than previously estimated. Furthermore, very few students who drop out of school do so as a terminal educational act. Nevertheless, 9% of females and 15% of males drop out of school and do not continue to some other educational or training institution. It would seem important that a detailed understanding of the process of early school leaving would be part of any stay-in-school initiative. In the next section, we assess the extent to which the School Leavers Survey provides a more complete understanding of dropout as a social problem.

THE SCHOOL LEAVERS SURVEY AND DROPPING OUT AS A PROCESS

In the 1980s, a large body of literature on the topic of youth at risk of dropping out of school was generated (Fine, 1986, 1991; Kelly, 1993; Rumberger, 1987; Wehlage & Rutter, 1986) and variables at the individual, familial, school, community, and societal levels most predictive of early school withdrawal were clearly and consistently delineated. From a research perspective, identification of the myriad of variables highlights the complexity of early school leaving and indicates the necessity of dropout research to consider variables at all levels.

The major factors associated with dropping out distinguish among structures and characteristics associated with individual students, their families, the schools they attend, and the communities in which they live (Andres Bellamy, Ross, & Anisef, 1994; Natriello, McDill, & Pallas, 1986; Rumberger, Ghatak, Poulos, Ritter, & Dornbusch, 1990). These variables can be organized into the following categories: demographic, family-related, school-related, and individual.

The limitations of this survey become apparent by comparing the variables relevant to an analysis of early school leaving as identified in the scholarly literature with those variables contained in the School Leavers Survey. Because the research design was limited to one-time-only structured telephone interviews with 18- to 20-year-olds, the survey was unable to capture the complexity of the dropping out process. The resulting data set only provides information at the individual level. Unlike large American data sets such as the National Educational Longitudinal Study (National Center for Educational Statistics, 1988), information provided by the family, school, and community was not sought.

In addition to the lack of a complex, multimethod research design, several key variables that could have been obtained from respondents were omitted from the study. The most serious omission is a measure of curricular differentiation. Academic tracking or streaming has been clearly linked to student retention (Natriello, Pallas, & Alexander, 1989; Oakes, 1985; Page & Valli, 1990). Studies have demonstrated that general and basic level programs appear to be less challenging and rewarding for both students and teachers than are academic programs (Castallo & Young,

1988; McMullan, Leiderman, & Wolf, 1988). Radwanski (1988) suggests that such courses are unchallenging, boring, and appear pointless. Lawton, Leithwood, Batcher, Donaldson, and Stewart (1988) found that many teachers prefer to teach advanced courses and feel they are being penalized when they are forced to teach at the general and basic levels. Students taking classes at the general and basic levels are more likely to emerge with negative attitudes toward schooling. Moreover, tracking contributes to socio-economic status maintenance (Vanfossen, Jones, & Spade, 1987).

Since respondents to the School Leavers Survey were not asked to indicate whether they were enrolled in either an academic or general program, there is no way of determining the impact of curricular stream on attitudes toward school or on educational status. The interactive effects among socio-economic status, curricular differentiation, gender, and dropping out that have been demonstrated in other studies (e.g., Earle & Roach, 1989) cannot be supported or refuted by this data set.

Another serious omission in this study are variables on race and ethnicity. In several American studies, race and ethnicity have been shown to be strongly related to dropping out (Eckstrom, Goertz, Pollack, & Rock, 1986; Poulos, 1986; Rumberger, 1983; Willis, 1989). The Stay-in-School Initiative literature itself (Employment and Immigration Canada, 1990) reports that dropout rates are particularly high among Native youth (as high as 70% in some areas), and among members of some visible minorities. Since the public use file of the School Leavers Survey does not include an ethnicity or race variable, this data set cannot be used to enlighten us about the impact of race or ethnicity on educational attainment. Nor were analyses by race included in the official report by government entitled *Leaving School* (Gilbert et al., 1993). Since respondents to this survey were asked to identify the ethnic or cultural groups to which their ancestors belonged (Statistics Canada, 1992), omission of a race/ethnicity variable in the public user data set is most likely due to reasons of confidentiality. This suggests that its importance as a variable was not considered when devising the sampling strategy for the study.

CONCLUSION

The sobering 1970s and even tougher 1980s both challenged and reinforced the education–work nexus. However, before the late 1980s, dropping out was not yet visualized as a problem of national importance. The stage was set with the formation of the Ministry of State for Youth. Prior to the formation of this ministry, various stakeholders in different provinces of Canada had demonstrated varying degrees of concern and a spate of dropout research studies appeared (Anisef, 1994).

At first glance, the national effort to stifle dropping out appears to have resulted from a growing public concern with objective factors pertaining to young people leaving school early. A careful historical examination, however, revealed that dropping out in Canada has been defined as more or less problematic in Canada for more than 40 years. Furthermore, as Coulter (1991) points out, a persistent theme underlying discussions of dropouts has been the relationship between schooling and work.

Unlike the model advanced by Mauss (1975, 1984, 1989), where the author describes social problems as originating at the grassroots level and, based on democratic processes, influencing representatives of government and public policy formulation, Jensen, Gerber, and Babcock (1991) suggest that social problems can emerge from state claim-making efforts of powerful interest groups without previous intensification of public concern. They present a modification of Mauss's (1975, 1984, 1989) original conceptualization in which they posit the four stages mentioned earlier in this chapter: incipiency, coalescence, creation and policy formation, and legitimation. We argue that although public concern was expressed around the social problem of dropouts in the 1980s, it did not trigger institutionalization of the issue by government in the form of policy formation in the way that Mauss suggests. In fact, public sentiment, as measured by public opinion polls, did not reflect a disenchantment with Canada's education system. When asked to indicate how much confidence they had in several social institutions, 62% of respondents to a 1989 Gallop poll reported a "great deal" or "quite a lot" of confidence in public schools. This figure was higher than the level of confidence expressed for all other social institutions in the poll, including the Supreme Court, the church, organized labor, newspapers, the House of Commons, and political parties. Other public opinion polls conducted in the 1980s (e.g., Canadian Education Association [CEA], 1984) corroborated the findings of the 1989 Gallop poll. In contrast, in 1979, only 54% of respondents to a similar Gallop poll indicated the same level of confidence with public schools (Livingstone & Hart, 1991). Results of public opinion polls in the late 1980s are noteworthy in that the lack of decline in confidence in public schooling runs counter to critical stances on various facets of student outcomes by state claims makers. In other words, opinion poll data do not suggest that a grassroots movement was responsible for the shift from incipiency to coalescence, leading to subsequent policy creation and formulation by government.

As already indicated, no adequate "report card" on dropouts existed at the national level in Canada. A consistent statistical account surfaced only with the Stay-in-School Initiative and, more specifically, with the decision to conduct a national school leavers survey. It would appear that concern about dropouts as a national problem or crisis was constructed by the Ministry of State for Youth around 1986, when this ministry was transferred to the department of Employment and Immigration Canada. At this stage of creation and policy formation, the federal government was confronted by very large numbers of unemployed young Canadians. Given that education is a provincial responsibility, the federal government's ability to maneuver in recessionary times was limited, and any significant diminution of growing unemployment rates through job-creation programs appeared unfeasible. Instead, in an era of neo-conservatism which emphasized market forces, global economics, and carried with it an "unabashed disdain for egalitarian values" (Erwin & Mac-Lennan, 1994, p. 16), the federal government launched an all-out attack on what they conceived to be a "national embarrassment of 32%" ("A Measure of Hope," 1993).

Built into the Stay-in-School Initiative were two strategies of legitimation. First, the School Leavers Survey served the dual purpose of defining the nature and scope of the dropout problem and reifying conceptions of dropping out in Canada and its provinces. Ironically, findings of this survey ultimately contradicted state claims and demonstrated that the 32% figure was closer to 18%. When a more accurate dependent variable is employed, the numbers of students dropping out and staying out of school is much lower, at 9% for females and 15% for males.

The second strategy employed by the federal government was a campaign of national socialization. In 1990, the Minister of Employment and Immigration announced a 5-year, $300-million effort aimed at convincing students to remain in school. Included in this campaign was a national television advertising program in which students were invited to call a toll-free number for information on the advantages of completing secondary school. Following the TV drive, the government commissioned a series of advertisements that were shown in Cineplex Odeon movie theaters across Canada ("A Measure of Hope," 1993).

The way in which educational outcomes such as dropping out are perceived and framed has direct consequences for educational and public policy. The television and movie theater advertising campaign component of the Stay-in-School Initiative clearly reinforced the notion that individual students alone were responsible for their deviant actions, and also for the amelioration of their deviance. Furthermore, the Initiative promoted the warehousing of students in schools for a specified period of time without addressing the relationship between education and work. Neither the School Leavers Survey nor the information campaign mentioned the relationship between the individual and the relevant social structure. Research endeavors such as the School Leavers Survey create a one-sided view of dropouts by focusing on the characteristics of the students. This study does not question school policies, practices of schools, the role of the community, or the current economic and labor market climate. The survey was not adequately informed by the body of research literature replete with evidence that the problem of early school withdrawal must be placed within a framework that includes the individual, family, school, and society.

One stated purpose of the School Leavers Survey was to aid in the design of programs and services, yet Stay-in-School Initiative programs and services preceded the release of study results. Rather than launching a campaign directed at all school-aged youth, a more logical approach to a perceived national dropout problem would have been to conduct policy research to assess the magnitude of the problem, then design relevant and specific intervention strategies for target populations. Results of the School Leavers Survey demonstrate that early school leaving is a gender and a regional issue. The survey was used to create the indelible impression that early school leaving was a national crisis, whereas intervention strategies and resources would have been better directed at certain students within the context of their families, schools, and communities.

REFERENCES

Andres Bellamy, L. A., Ross, J. L., & Anisef, P. (1994). *Breaking the fingers of blame and recasting the problem of dropout.* Paper presented at the Southwest Social Science Meetings, San Antonio, TX.

Anisef, P. (Ed.) (1994). *Learning and sociological profiles of Canadian high school students: An overview of 15 to 18 year olds and educational policy implications for dropouts, exceptional students, employed students, immigrant students and Native youth.* New York: Edwin Mellen Press.

Canada, Minister of State for Youth. (1992). *Reflections on the national stay-in-school initiative.* Ottawa: Minister of Supply and Services.

Canada House of Commons. (1987, May 7). *Debates,* p. 586.

Canada Senate Special Committee on Youth. (1986). *Youth: A plan of action* (Report of the Senate Special Committee on Youth). Ottawa: Special Committee on Youth.

Canadian Education Association (CEA), Task Force on Public Involvement in Educational Decisions. (1984). *Results of a Gallop poll of public opinion in Canada about public involvement in educational decisions* (Report No. 1). Toronto: Canadian Education Association.

Castallo, R., & Young, D. (1988). *Early identification of potential dropouts: Toward a definition.* (ERIC Document Reproduction Service No. ED 316 359)

Coulter, R. P. (1991). Persistent themes: Some reflections of the history of schooling and work. In D. Allison & J. Paquette (Eds.), *Reform and relevance in schooling: Dropouts, destreaming, and the common curriculum* (pp. 28–38). Toronto: OISE Press.

Dallaire, L. (1985). *Youth and education: A study of 15–24-year-olds in the Canadian education system.* Ottawa: Department of the Secretary of State.

Dorn, S. (1993). Origins of the dropout problem. *History of Education Quarterly, 33,* 353–373.

Earle, J., & Roach, V. (1989). *Female dropouts: A new perspective.* Alexandria, VA: National Association of State Boards of Education. (ERIC Document Reproduction Service No. ED 320 970)

Eckstrom, R., Goertz, M. E., Pollack, J. M., & Rock, D. A. (1986). Who drops out of high school and why? Findings of a national study. *Teachers College Record, 87,* 356–373.

Employment and Immigration Canada. (1981a). *Labor market development in the 1980s.* Ottawa: Minister of Supply and Services.

Employment and Immigration Canada. (1981b). *Task Force on Labor Market Development.* Ottawa: Minister of Supply and Services.

Employment and Immigration Canada. (1990). *A national stay-in-school initiative.* Ottawa: Supply and Services Canada.

Erwin, L., & MacLennan, D. (1994). Introduction: Historical background and critical perspective. In L. Erwina & D. MacLennan (Eds.), *Sociology of education in Canada: Critical perspectives on theory, research and practice* (pp. 1–25). Toronto: Copp, Clark, Longman Ltd.

Fine, M. (1986). Why urban adolescents drop into and out of public school. *Teachers College Record, 87,* 393–409.

Fine, M. (1991). *Framing dropouts: Notes on the politics of an urban public high school.* Albany: State University of New York Press.

Gaskell, J. (1993). Introduction. In P. Anisef & P. Axelrod (Eds.), *Transitions: Schooling and employment in Canada* (pp. xi–xvii). Toronto: Thompson Educational Publishing.

Gilbert, S. N., Barr, L., Clark, W., Blue, M., & Sunter, D. (1993). *Leaving school: Results from a national survey comparing school leavers and high school graduates 18 to 20 years of age.* Ottawa: Minister of Supply and Services.

Gilbert, S. N., & Orok, B. (1993). School leavers. *Canadian Social Trends, 30,* 2–7.

Jensen, E. L., & Gerber, J. (1993). State efforts to construct a social problem: The 1986 war on drugs in Canada. *Canadian Journal of Sociology, 18* (4), 453–462.

Jensen, E. L., Gerber, J., & Babcock, G. M. (1991). The new war on drugs: Grass roots movement or political construction? *Journal of Drug Issues, 21,* 651–667.

Kelly, D. (1993). *Last chance high.* New Haven: Yale University Press.

Lafleur, B. (1992). *Dropping out: The cost to Canada.* Ottawa: Conference Board of Canada.

Lawr, D. A., & Gidney, R. D. (1973). *Educating Canadians: A documentary history of public education.* Toronto: Van Nostrand Reinhold.

Lawton, S. B., Leithwood, K. A., Batcher, E., Donaldson, E. L., & Stewart, R.

(1988). *Student retention and transition in Ontario high schools.* Toronto: Ministry of Education.

Lennards, J. (1980). Education. In J. Hagedorn (Ed.), *Sociology* (p. 30). Toronto: Holt, Rhinehart, and Winston of Canada.

Livingstone, D., & Hart, D. (1991). The people speak: Public attitudes toward schooling in Canada. In R. Ghosh & D. Ray (Eds.), *Social change and education in Canada* (pp. 3–27). Toronto: Harcourt Brace Jovanovich.

Martin, W. B. W., & MacDonnell, A. (1982). *Canadian education: A sociological analysis.* Scarborough: Prentice-Hall.

Mauss, A. L. (1975). *Social problems as social movements.* Philadelphia: J. B. Lippincott Company.

Mauss, A. L. (1984). The myth of social problems theory. *SSSP Theory Division Newsletter, 15* (3), 12–13.

Mauss, A. L. (1989). Beyond the illusion of social problems theory. *Perspectives on Social Problems, 1,* 19–39.

McMullan, B. J., Leiderman, S., & Wolf, W. C. (1988). *Reclaiming the future: A framework for improving student success and reducing dropout rates in Philadelphia.* Philadelphia, PA: Wolf Associates, Inc. (ERIC Document Reproduction Services No. ED 314 510)

A measure of hope. (1993, July 14). *Maclean's.*

National Center for Educational Statistics. (1988). *National educational longitudinal study of 1988.* Washington, DC: U.S. Dept. of Education.

Natriello, G., McDill, E. L., & Pallas, A. M. (1986). *Schooling disadvantaged children: Racing against catastrophe.* New York: Teachers College Press.

Natriello, G., Pallas, A. M., & Alexander, K. (1989). On the right track? Curriculum and achievement. *Sociology of Education, 62* (2), 109–118.

Oakes, J. (1985). *Keeping track: How schools structure inequality.* New Haven: Yale University Press.

Page, R., & Valli, L. (Eds.) (1990). *Curriculum differentiation: Interpretive studies in U.S. secondary schools.* Albany: State University of New York Press.

Poulos, N. (1986). *The Detroit early school leavers' project: A profile of dropouts.* Detroit: Office of Instructional Improvement.

Price Waterhouse. (1992). *Qualitative research on school leavers* (Summary final report). Ottawa: Minister of Supply and Services.

Radwanski, G. (1988). *Ontario study of the relevance of education, and the issue of dropouts.* Toronto: Ministry of Education.

Rumberger, R. W. (1983). Dropping out of high school: The influence of race, sex, and family background. *American Educational Research Journal, 20,* 199–220.

Rumberger, R. W. (1987). High school dropouts: A review of issues and evidence. *Review of Educational Research, 57* (2), 101–121.

Rumberger, R. W., Ghatak, R., Poulos, G., Ritter, P. L., & Dornbusch, S. M. (1990). Family influences on dropout behavior in one California high school. *Sociology of Education, 63,* 283–299.

Smith, D., & Smith, G. (1990). Re-organizing the job skills training relation:

From "human capital" to "human resources." In J. Muller (Ed.), *Education for work, education as work: Canada's changing community colleges* (pp. 171–196). Toronto: Garamond Press.

Statistics Canada, Education, Culture, and Tourism Division (ECTD). (1991). *School Leavers Survey microdata user's guide.* Ottawa: Minister of Supply and Services.

Statistics Canada. (1992). *Labor force annual averages.* Ottawa: Minister of Supply and Services. (Catalogue No. 71–529)

Statistics Canada, Education, Culture, and Tourism Division (ECTD). (1989). *Project discussion paper for school leavers.* Ottawa: Minister of Supply and Services.

Statistics Canada, Education, Culture, and Tourism Division. (1991). *School leavers survey.* Ottawa: Minister of Supply and Services.

Vanfossen, B. E., Jones, J. D., & Spade, J. Z. (1987). Curriculum tracking and status maintenance. *Sociology of Education, 60,* 104–122.

Wehlage, G. G. & Rutter, R. A. (1986). Dropping out: How much do schools contribute to the problem? *Teachers College Record, 87,* 374–392.

Weiss, C. H. (Ed.). (1977). *Using social research in public policy making.* Lexington, MA: Lexington Books.

Willis, H. D. (1989). *Students at risk: A review of conditions, circumstances, indicators, and educational implications.* Elmhurst, IL: North Central Regional Educational Lab.

CHAPTER 6

"Choosing" the Alternative: Conflicting Missions and Constrained Choice in a Dropout Prevention Program

DEIRDRE M. KELLY

Schools throughout North America have been shaped by an enduring tension between two ideals: democracy and competitive meritocracy. As Carnoy and Levin (1985) have argued, educational reform can be seen as a response to conflicts among constituencies with different priorities for schools, some interested in greater equality (democratization), others in greater efficiency (reproduction). Proponents of democratization often count the lowering of the dropout rate and the extension of education to more students through an array of alternative programs tailored to meet the needs of "at risk" students as a measure of success. Offering an element of choice to those students and their families is considered a sign of school administrators' good faith.

Continuation (or second-chance) schools collectively constitute the largest and oldest dropout prevention program in the United States. The idea that continuation high schools offer a choice (a broadening of educational opportunity) has become an important means of justifying the schools to students and the wider public. This invocation of the public policy discourse of choice, however, begs two questions: Under what circumstances are students choosing to attend continuation schools, and with what consequences?

My research in three second-chance, continuation high schools calls into question what counts as "choice." In one continuation program that defined itself purely as a "school of choice," students' process of choosing was so guided by the mainstream institution that students were often constrained to a single option, that of attending the continuation school. As a student at this continuation school put it, "This is a place for people between school and the street, or between school and no school." At the two continuation schools that enrolled at least some "troublemakers" involuntarily, I found that a fair number of students had deliberately manipulated the conventional schooling system in the hopes of attending an alternative school that seemed to expect less of them educationally, socially, and behaviorally, while still awarding them a credential.

In this chapter,[1] I draw on the findings of my ethnographic study to give a more complete picture of how choice played out in these three settings. I argue that these schools represent examples of a long-running and unresolved competition of two missions, providing a safety net for students versus providing a safety valve for the mainstream schooling system. Before discussing the ethnography, I highlight this structural tension by briefly analyzing how and why continuation schools became institutionalized.

THE SAFETY NET–SAFETY VALVE TENSION IN HISTORICAL PERSPECTIVE

Continuation schools assumed a prominent place on the agenda of vocational education reformers in the first two decades of the twentieth century. In its original form, continuation education took place largely in compulsory part-time schools designed to provide young workers with 4 to 8 hours of vocational tutoring per week. These part-time schools evolved into "adjustment education" for juvenile delinquents in the 1950s, and most recently they have been described as dropout prevention programs. Despite the shifting labels, continuation schools have always provided an alternative educational setting to conventional schools' misfits.

For school administrators in the 1920s, particularly those in the largest cities, continuation schools proved to be a solution to changes being brought about by industrial capitalism and calls to "Americanize" working-class immigrants. Reformers evinced genuine concern to provide an education to an increasingly diverse student body: newcomers, students with handicaps and health problems, school-age mothers, married students, those who needed to work, truants, students on probation, and students with discipline problems. Yet school administrators and school board members seemed most responsive to middle-class worries about juvenile delinquency and perceived threats to the social order as well as about what to do with students who did not or would not conform to the standard curriculum, both formal and hidden (Kelly, 1993).

The 1917 legislation that supplied federal money to this part-time bridge between schooling and work came about through the intense lobbying efforts of vocational education advocates. At the turn of the twentieth century, a coalition of professional educators allied with business people, labor leaders, politicians, and social reformers grew increasingly concerned about the number of students dropping out after elementary school and began to push for vocational education. This was an early call for choice within the curriculum.

The changing forces of production fueled concern over dropouts. New technologies—high-speed machinery, telephones, cash registers, pneumatic tubes, and other devices—were eliminating many of the unskilled jobs held by young people (Tyack, 1978). Child labor and compulsory school attendance laws, backed by trade unions and social reformers, began to limit the participation of children in the labor market.

Vocational reformers believed that "hand-minded" children and those who had to leave full-time schooling out of economic necessity needed occupational and moral guidance. They disagreed about what form this guidance should take, however. Many employers favored opening continuation schools inside factories, where young workers would alternate learning the general principles behind specific occupations with attending school (Kett, 1982). John Dewey and other humanitarian progressives argued, on the other hand, that vocational education should focus on general industrial knowledge and should not be administered separately from general public education (Cremin, 1964, p. 53). A dual school system would deny young people, particularly those from working-class backgrounds, an equal opportunity by forcing them to specialize in a trade too early. Trade unionists, too, argued against separate continuation schools outside of the public schooling system, interpreting them as an attempt to sanction child labor, whose cheaper rates undercut the unions (Katznelson & Weir, 1985). Ultimately, the Smith-Hughes Vocational Education Act sanctioned two forms of continuation education—separate classes or schools— but within a unitary public school system. This federal legislation represented a substantial victory for the "administrative progressives"—members of business and professional elites, including school administrators, who, as characterized by Tyack (1974), "urged that schooling be adapted to social stratification" (p. 126)—and they set about busily implementing its provisions.

Some professional educators tended to gloss over the class interests inherent in the debate about continuation schooling, arguing that the boundaries of public education had widened. The principal of Boston

Continuation School, for example, argued: "The continuation school is an institution typifying the real democracy of education. She has no aristocratic standards for admission" (McDonough, 1921, p. 255). This claim of nonelite admission standards was seriously misleading because continuation schools were originally designed for young workers, not children from more privileged backgrounds who would hardly choose to attend them.

Allied to this attempt to construct a practice of schooling that appeared classless were progressive educators' plans for citizenship training, which found their way into federal and state legislation on continuation schools. Citizenship training would "assimilate foreigners" and introduce them to "our customs and to the ideals peculiar to America," according to a U.S. Bureau of Education bulletin (Jones, 1907, pp. 140–141). This assimilationist vision ignored existing ethnic and racial divisions deeply embedded in U.S. society and implied that an uncontested set of customs and ideals existed.

Although most states received federal aid for part-time general continuation classes during the 1920s and 1930s, much of the enrollment was concentrated in large industrial centers in a handful of states: New York, Pennsylvania, Massachusetts, California, Illinois, Wisconsin, and New Jersey. This fact is not surprising, considering that part-time schooling had been designed primarily for city school personnel and their perceived problems: poverty, large influxes of non-English-speaking immigrants, and juvenile delinquency.

State departments of education, working with local universities to train teachers in continuation education, advised school districts to provide students affected by the part-time law with an opportunity to study trade, industrial, or commercial subjects. In the absence of a vocational focus, the professionals warned, these pupils "will constitute a problem which will be very difficult to handle" (California State Department of Education, 1919, p. 4). Reformers believed that part-timers, especially boys, were vulnerable to recruitment into crime (California State Board of Education, 1923). The continuation school was well placed to prevent delinquency, explained a New York principal, "for the continuation school alone deals with the young person in a man-to-man fashion at the most critical period of his life" (Mayman, 1933, p. 198).

Although educators and others left it unsaid, they had boys in mind when concerns about delinquency were expressed. Continuation girls were more apt to have violated middle-class norms of sexual behavior; they included pregnant girls, mothering or married teens, and runaways often assumed to be prostitutes. Continuation classes were seen as an ideal place to teach middle-class moral values and household skills to immigrant and working-class girls. For example, California's Department of Education showcased a "citizen-homemakers" course offered mainly to Mexican immigrant girls in Bakersfield. The principal purpose of instruction was the transmission of middle-class norms of self-presentation, morality, and housekeeping (California State Department of Education, 1920). Half of the girls were working as maids in local homes, and their middle-class women employers telephoned the teachers to report on their work daily. During the sewing hours at school, "all kinds of weighty problems are discussed, salaries, good taste, husbands, preference of country, U.S. or Mexico, homelife, whether it is right to break an engagement of marriage, and the right age for marriage" (p. 19).

Continuation schools continued to grow in number throughout the U.S. until the Great Depression. Thereafter, they continued to exist only in the largest cities, less as schools for part-time workers and more as sites of what became known as "adjustment education" (e.g., see Shaffer, 1955). Other "options" had emerged within the comprehensive high schools, like tracking, ability grouping, special education, and such vocational programs as school–work cooperation, work experience, and apprenticeship training. These programs superseded the original purpose of continuation education, and the latter was no longer funded after Congress passed the Vocational Education Act in 1963.

Despite the many programs that had sprung up to meet the "special needs" of youth, many young people continued to drop out. Civil rights activists focused legislators' attention on the disproportionate number of African American and Latino students who were being expelled in certain districts without recourse. Together with other youth advocates, the California Continuation Education Association (CCEA) and a part-time consultant within the state's Department of Education lobbied for recognition and increased funding of their program as the solution to the "pushout" problem.

Meanwhile, a California Assembly Legislative Reference Service study showed that "the long-term suspension mechanism has, at least in part, been substituted for the traditional and more formal [expulsion] process" (California Legislature, Assembly Committee on Education, 1965, p. 10). Validating the claims of the CCEA that continuation education was a solution to the pushout problem, the researchers found that 80% of long-term suspensions occurred in districts that did not operate continuation classes or schools (p. 8). This study persuaded the Legislature to pass a law in 1965 that required all school systems to provide continuation education (or transfer to a similar county-run school) for youths suspended ten days or more.

School districts that did not comply with the 1965 law faced having 10% of all state apportionments withheld annually. These were the teeth

that continuation leaders had been fighting to put into the compulsory attendance laws. The *Education Code* of 1967 identified a new purpose to be
served by continuation schools: to meet the "special needs of pupils with
behavior or severe attendance problems."

California, followed by New York and Washington states, has had the
largest number of public alternative schools in North America since the
movement flowered in the early 1970s, due in part to the statewide law
mandating and supporting continuation schools (Barr, 1975, p. 4; Raywid, 1982, p. 6). In the U.S., California has been credited with having
"pioneered" continuation education (Bill, 1972, p. 27). Although a number of different types of alternative schools exist, continuation programs
remain the most prevalent. In the first extensive survey of K–12 alternative programs, continuation schools comprised the single largest category (20% of the total); they provided "for students whose education
in the conventional schools has been (or might be) interrupted" (Barr,
1975, p. 8). This definition included dropout centers, reentry programs,
pregnancy-maternity centers, evening and adult high schools, and street
academies. The most recent survey of the U.S. and three Canadian provinces (Alberta, British Columbia, Ontario), focused at the secondary level,
found that about two-thirds of public alternative schools are intended for
potential and actual dropouts (Raywid, 1982; see also Young, 1990).

Despite the evolution in the continuation high school's stated purpose, the composition of its student body has remained relatively stable.
Continuation students continue to be defined as misfits within the conventional schooling system and have either dropped out or been pushed
out. These misfits include disproportionate numbers of certain ethnic
minority, working-class, or low-income students, and girls who have
violated middle-class norms of sexual behavior.

Institutional convenience, framed by a larger conflict between advocates of equality (safety net) versus efficiency (safety valve), best explains the
origins and transformation of the continuation program. In response to a
changing, hierarchically structured economy and an influx of immigrants,
professional educators were experimenting with ways to deal with students
who could not or would not conform to the dominant culture and class
standards. Social reformers argued that juvenile courts, detention homes,
reformatories, jails, penitentiaries, sanitariums, and asylums already strained
community coffers. They hailed continuation education as a humane, pre-
ventive response to these individuals' neglected needs. Yet by segregating
rebels and failures from the mainstream high school, educators stigmatized
them and the continuation program while easing their own disciplinary
load and scaring other students into relative conformity.

In the 1960s, policy makers and school administrators looked for solutions to the problems of pushouts and teen pregnancy, and the chameleon-like continuation program changed its colors to accommodate. Its expansion was boosted by the demands of protest groups for more social justice in education, and continuation schools—recolored as alternative programs—were a ready solution. Victories for greater equality in schooling were being won, such as the recognition of the right to an education for girls regardless of pregnancy and the funding of small schools for them and other continuation students. As Carnoy and Levin (1985, pp. 232–233) argue, such victories were made possible partly by favorable economic conditions in the 1960s: high employment levels and economic growth. At the same time, comprehensive high schools did not have to adapt to students; rather, those who did not fit could transfer to separate institutions, almost always devalued ones.

HOW CHOICE IS CONSTRUCTED IN THREE CONTINUATION HIGH SCHOOLS

Today, 1 out of every 10 high school students in California attends continuation classes, and 85% of continuation students are said to transfer into the program voluntarily (Hill, 1988). State officials point to this statistic as proof that continuation schools no longer function as a safety valve. The situation appears to be much more complex, however. Some students use ostensible safety-valve schools as a safety net, while some administrators use ostensible safety-net schools as a safety valve.

I base this observation on an ethnographic study I carried out in three districts located in a high-technology center in California. (To protect the anonymity of people who participated in the study, all names have been changed; I refer to the three districts and their respective continuation high schools as Beacon, La Fuente, and Willows.) At Beacon, all students officially attended voluntarily, whereas half of La Fuente and Willows students did so. These statistics tend to reflect a bureaucratic notion of choice: Before the actual transfer and after some counseling, did the student consent to attend the continuation school or not? To get a sense of the degree to which the choice was constrained, one would need to know more about the counseling, the actual range of options offered, whether the program delivered on the claims made for it, and the degree of stigma perceived to be attached to the program.

With these aims in mind, I observed the screening, transfer, and subsequent progress of students at all three schools and conducted in-depth interviews with 39 Beacon students (23 girls, 16 boys), 43 La Fuente students (24 girls, 19 boys), and 18 Willows students (11 girls, 7 boys). I

conducted a pilot study at the three sites in the spring of 1988, intensive
fieldwork at Beacon and La Fuente during the 1988–1989 school year,
and occasional follow-up visits during the 1989–1990 school year. I found
that the distinction between involuntary and voluntary transfers was not
as clear as administrative records would lead one to expect. Exploring
how choice gets constructed is important because the construction of
choice tends to mediate how students react to the continuation school
environment, which in turn builds that school's particular reputation as a
safety net or safety valve. In this section, I describe three things that contributed to the ambiguity in the choice concept: (1) the role played by
the continuation school in achieving comprehensive school discipline; (2)
the construction and perception of choice by involuntary transfer students; and (3) the perception of coercion by voluntary transfer students,
particularly pregnant girls.

The Continuation School as Disciplinary Threat

Any alternative program—in the context of a competitive struggle for,
and hierarchical distribution of, status and resources—tends to get stigmatized almost by definition because it exists in opposition to the traditional
program. Insofar as the continuation school acts as a dumping ground for
students who pose a problem to mainstream schools, it reinforces the idea
that the problem rests with a minority who can and should be segregated.

Principals at Beacon, La Fuente, and Willows were all clear that their
districts used the continuation school as "the ultimate scare tactic," as one
put it, to maintain discipline at the comprehensive schools. They were
equally forthright in saying, particularly in the two districts allowing involuntary transfers, that the continuation school serves to keep the mainstream high schools "pure"; the principal at Willows said:

> [In this district], the philosophy is send everybody here, just get rid
> of them, dump 'em; it cleans out those kinds of kids from the regular
> school and makes the regular school a better school. And it does that.
> It makes the regular school less impacted by resistant kids, truant kids,
> tardy kids, behavior problem kids.

As La Fuente's principal argued, however, there then emerges a trade-off
between offering a safety net and serving as district safety valve:

> I always felt that the biggest loophole in dropouts was in La Fuente.
> . . . But as soon as we plug that hole [by trying to reduce the high
> turnover rate in the continuation school], it creates other problems

for the district's comprehensive high schools because it becomes a bottle neck [of at-risk students].

Given these arguments of institutional convenience, continuation teachers had little or no say over which students ended up at their school. Indeed, they joked freely about the "dumping" cycle. The first dumping occurs at the beginning of November: The comprehensive schools routinely hold on to disengaging students until enrollment levels have been established for staffing purposes, and these are reported to the state at the end of October. The second dumping occurs late in the spring, when comprehensive school principals rid themselves of disciplinary cases they do not want to deal with the following year.

Beacon, unlike La Fuente or Willows, held a "screening" every other week where all teachers and the principal would meet with comprehensive school vice principals, counselors, and a district psychologist to be briefed on incoming students. Theoretically, if Beacon's principal and teachers felt that a particular student, recommended for transfer to their school by one of the comprehensive high schools, would not benefit from the continuation program, they could veto the transfer. I attended every screening except one during 1988–1989, however, and not a single student was screened out (refused), despite several instances in which Beacon's teachers and principal expressed strong concern or doubt about the wisdom of a particular transfer. Further, I recorded four separate instances in which a comprehensive high school vice principal explicitly stated that a particular student would not be allowed to return to their school, thus suggesting that the transfer to Beacon was coerced by comprehensive school staff, despite an official policy to the contrary.

In summary, all three districts used their continuation schools—even Beacon, which billed itself as a "school of choice"—as safety valves, and this fact often overshadowed these schools' role as safety nets and contributed significantly to their stigma. But students reacted differently to the program depending on their particular circumstances and the degree to which the program met their individual needs.

Much mainstream social science theory, as March and Olsen (1984, p. 737) argue, assumes that people's preferences are stable, unambiguous, and consistent, and precede a particular choice or decision in time. My data, however, call into question all three of these assumptions. Student preferences changed partly in response to what they were told and asked to consider by adults in positions of authority (and by family and friends), and partly in response to their experience of the continuation program after transfer. For many students, the mode of recruitment might best be described as semi-voluntary. Like military conscripts, they are "required to serve but are given much opportunity to feel that this service is a justifiable one required in their own ultimate interests" (Goffman, 1961, p. 118).

Students at Beacon, La Fuente, and Willows were asked several questions about the transfer process and whether they considered the transfer to have been their choice. I categorized their views by the number of options they said were available to them at the time of transfer and the value of the credential attached to each option. If students indicated that obtaining a traditional diploma was still open to them in a regular high school, they were classified as perceiving more choice. By this measure, 38% of boys and 66% of girls were voluntary transfers. Significantly more girls than boys—across ethnic groups and at all three schools—felt that they chose to come to the continuation school, reflecting in large measure the fact that boys more often were disciplinary placements, whereas girls came as counseling and pregnancy referrals.

Perception of Choice by Involuntary Transfers

The line between voluntary and involuntary can blur for new arrivals at the continuation school, depending on how administrators, parents, and particularly students construe the event. All continuation students—both voluntary and involuntary transfers—tend to be behind on credits. The major incentive that counselors and administrators at both the comprehensive and continuation schools stress is the chance to make up credits faster. Thus, students can perceive the continuation school either as an alternative route to a high school diploma or as a bridge back to the comprehensive school.

A number of involuntary transfers interpreted their presence in the continuation school as their choice once they discovered that they liked the new environment. For example, Rodney was "kicked out 'cause of fighting," but said: "It was my choice. [The principal] said I could go back, but I don't want to go back. I like La Fuente. I want to graduate early, and I can from this school." Rosa was also transferred out of a comprehensive high school for fighting: "I got kicked out because I got into a fight with a White girl 'cause she was saying that Mexicans are stupid." Rosa said she was happier at Willows—where about half the students are of Mexican descent—and perceived it as her choice.

To the extent that continuation programs offer students a better chance to succeed academically, they are more likely to be seen as true schools of choice—safety nets—by both voluntary and involuntary students. To varying degrees, all three schools in this study offered small school and class size, teachers who saw themselves less as subject-matter experts and more as concerned with educating "the whole child," more counseling (including the brokerage of much-needed social services), increased access to extracurricular activities, more opportunities for students to work at their own pace and make up high school credit, and a greater sense of community through the reduction of competition and an elimination or opening up of traditional sources of status (i.e., athletics, academic tracking, and student government). The continuation schools I studied were less successful, however, in protecting students from the ills of poverty, notably high youth unemployment, the temptations of drug use and dealing, and violence. Over one half of those enrolled at La Fuente some time during 1988–1989 dropped out or were pushed out, while about one-third at Beacon left without graduating.

Some students exercise another form of choice, one that is unofficial. They know how to behave in comprehensive high school so that they will be "involuntarily" transferred (Willows, La Fuente) or given priority for transfer (Beacon); this is necessary in schools that have waiting lists for voluntary transfers. According to one comprehensive school teacher I interviewed, "In some groups it's almost a status symbol to go to Beacon, and students will misbehave here, in a traditional high school, hoping to get kicked out so they can go to the continuation school." In formal interviews, a boy and a girl said they purposely "messed up" to get into Beacon; others boasted of it informally. Like the high school students that Page (1987) studied, who deliberately dropped down into the lower track to get an easier schedule, continuation students sometimes feel they have outwitted the credential system: They can attend a "kickback" or "easy" school and still potentially obtain a diploma.

Others, predominantly boys who had been involuntarily transferred or placed in the school by a probation officer, were clear that attending the continuation school was not their choice. Sometimes these students claimed that they had been pushed into leaving their comprehensive school, and Beacon's principal acknowledged to me that as a vice principal, he had been aware that a number of teachers "baited" students they perceived as problems until such students committed an act that warranted their removal, a practice even he had engaged in on occasion.

Perception of Coercion by Voluntary Transfers

Of the voluntary transfers I spoke with, some (e.g., pregnant or mothering girls) felt they were given little real choice. This finding is underscored by an Equality Center survey of twelve geographically and demographically diverse schools which revealed that nine of the schools may have been violating the rights of pregnant girls by channeling pregnant and mothering girls into specific courses of study (cited in Snider, 1989). Title IX requires schools to allow pregnant students to stay in regular classes if they so desire.

Both La Fuente and Willows had on-site School-Age Mothers (SAM) programs. I interviewed 12 girls at La Fuente and 5 girls at Willows who had participated in the SAM program. A few girls reported feeling coerced. According to Beverly, "My counselors were the people who were sort of pushing me over here [to La Fuente]. . . . They should talk to you and they should tell you your alternatives." Cindy said, "I would have liked to stay at [my old school] when I was pregnant . . . but as soon as it came out of my mouth that I was pregnant, they said I had to leave [that] school."

More typically, SAM girls felt "strongly counseled" into the continuation school, as Willows' vice principal described the transfer process. In other words, most SAM participants felt that counselors and other school administrators had not presented options in an even-handed way, although the girls quickly conceded that the SAM program supported them materially and emotionally in their choice to have a baby in an environment away from peers and teachers who might have ridiculed their pregnancy. Anna, a La Fuente student, explained that when she told administrators at her high school that she was one month pregnant, "They said, 'We don't want to take responsibility for you. We'll just withdraw you out of here and stick you at La Fuente.' . . . They didn't tell me I had a choice [but] . . . I probably would have said I want to try [the] SAM [program at La Fuente] first." According to Anita, the principal at her previous school "said it would be better if I came to Willows because I was pregnant. And I was having trouble with the other kids because of that." Unfortunately, this "strong counseling" can occur without the prior consent of parents, as I observed at Willows one day when a mother who spoke only Spanish called to complain.

At La Fuente, the young mothers' program staff noted in a self-evaluation: "Curriculum and class scheduling at La Fuente provides problems for special ed or college prep students (often they cannot get the classes they need); many students feel stigma attending a continuation school only because they are pregnant." This problem was echoed by students like Molly, a college preparatory student, who felt she had no choice but to attend La Fuente because she had no money for day care:

> We know that the education that we receive here is at least 50% less than what we would get at a regular school. . . . I don't think it's fair just because we have children that we should have any less of a chance than what we had before we got pregnant. Because what are we going to do?

Other voluntary transfers also described their "choice" as heavily influenced by comprehensive school personnel. Given that most students who ended up at Beacon, La Fuente, and Willows were from working-class families and significant proportions at all three schools were of an ethnic minority background (45%, 80%, and 57%, respectively), one must ask whether students and parents with less access to information and few independent resources can exercise meaningful or informed choices. For example, 4% of students interviewed at Beacon and La Fuente said that their parents had been completely unaware of the continuation transfer or of its significance; in all cases, these were non-English-speaking, first-generation immigrant parents. At Willows and La Fuente, where court-mandated school desegregation was in effect, some students spoke of not understanding their options beforehand, of being bused long distances to predominantly White schools in wealthy neighborhoods, and of subsequently seeking refuge from the ethnic conflict and academic competition in the continuation program.

Indeed, educational life histories done with a subset of Beacon and La Fuente interviewees revealed that a number of so-called voluntary transfers had already been preconditioned to exclusion from comprehensive schools by virtue of their ethnic and class background and previous schooling experiences, including suspension, detention, and placement in remedial, opportunity, and special education classes. A number of students discovered they were more comfortable in the continuation environment, interacting with peers more like themselves. Mandy, a White working-class student at La Fuente, described feeling out of place at the comprehensive school, where

> they're not rich but they're well off, whether they're Black, Mexican, or White. And here . . . we all don't have that much money and stuff. And I guess it's weird because it's so true, that if you don't have as much money, you're more laid-back.

Some voluntary transfers tended to perceive coercion after participating in the continuation school for a while and then concluding that the promises made for it—namely accelerated credit earning and the ability to return to the regular program—had been largely unfulfilled. All three schools operated under a variable credit system which did allow highly motivated, self-initiating students to succeed. The problem was that few students had been adequately prepared to work on their own. Ingrid, a Beacon student, complained, "A lot of the kids could be getting credit, they could be reading and writing something, but instead they just yak, yak, yak." A number of students described learning to put forth less effort than they were actually capable of making. David, another Beacon student, reported:

> Like the first time you come to this school, you work hard 'cause that's how you were doing at a normal high school, and then you look at other students: they're always kicking back, and you get irritated with that 'cause they're not working. . . . Then the next year, you'll be slowly kind of slacking off. Then later on, you'll be talking the whole period, and you won't even recognize it.

Too late, these students realized they were not making up the credits they thought they would.

In some instances, trying to return to the comprehensive high school from the continuation school can be like trying to back up a car over the curved spikes designed to prevent drivers from reentering a parking lot. Many students said they were told they could return to their neighborhood school and quite a few said they still planned to do so, but in reality, few ever do (less than 5% at both Beacon and La Fuente during 1988–1989). Continuation personnel often explained this by saying that students liked the alternative program and chose to stay. But this begs the question of how choice gets constructed within the schooling system.

First, the few who did return tended to be the most successful of continuation students. Teachers and administrators sometimes discouraged this group from leaving the continuation school, partly because they demonstrated to others through their attendance and academic performance that the continuation school was a place for serious students. "Our students definitely feel the stigma. They'll say, 'I need to get back to [the neighborhood school] to get the diploma,'" said one Beacon teacher, who confided: "That presses some of my buttons, obviously, because I think this is the neatest place in the whole world to go. I would love to go here; I see all its value." In addition, the return of students to their neighborhood schools undercut teachers' efforts to lessen the stigma for those who liked the continuation school and planned to remain.

Second, the rules regulating return were left vague. A few La Fuente students, whose petitions to return were signed by continuation personnel, were denied reentry by their neighborhood school principal. Others were persuaded that they would not be able to graduate if they left the continuation school. Still others saw so few of their classmates returning that they forgot or never realized that they had this option. According to Joan, a Beacon student:

> I didn't realize that I could go back 'til a couple of months after I'd been here and I overheard this girl go, "Think I should go back to

[the comprehensive high school] for graduation?" I was, "Hmm." It does say it in the pamphlet [distributed at orientation], but I don't think many people read through the pamphlet. It doesn't really talk about it. It just says, "After completion of one . . . good semester, student can return to previous high school."

The pamphlet did not define a "good semester." This made it difficult for even the most successful to leave. Bob, a Latino with senior credits, had maintained honors status for the semester he was at Beacon, and although he was still shy a few credits, he wanted to return to his neighborhood school. Bob's counselor met with him several times and tried to discourage him. Privately, she told me that his return would "set him up for failure." Bob was able to return only after he publicized his concern and the entire faculty considered his case. He eventually graduated from his neighborhood school, making up the credit difference through a night class.

Third, comprehensive schools had no incentive to accept continuation students back. When they did so and the students had problems adjusting, comprehensive school personnel marshalled this as evidence that continuation education was inferior and only succeeded to the extent that academic and behavior standards were lowered. No transition programs existed to support students as they reentered the more rigid environment.

Many continuation students "choose" not to return. But the fact that such an overwhelming number of students remain in what many perceive as a stigmatized organization cannot be explained simply with reference to individual choice. This choice is shaped by the organizational context in which it is constructed.

MAINTAINING THE CREDENTIAL HIERARCHY BY PUSHING SOME STUDENTS OUT

In short, all three districts contributed to their continuation schools' devalued status by using them as a disciplinary threat and then making them dependent on the comprehensive schools as a base for their nonselective student recruitment. Although many students at Beacon, La Fuente, and Willows were no longer technically involuntary, their choice to attend was often constrained. Further, none offered college preparatory classes, such as a foreign language or advanced math and English, required for entrance into four-year colleges and universities. Over the last decade, however, the schools had sought to bring themselves into closer alignment with the high-status academic curriculum and did award a diploma.

Although many of the people who worked at the continuation schools wanted to provide a safety net for students, it was also true that the schools were not constantly trying to shed stigma. Indeed, by trying to create a safety net for the majority, continuation teachers and administrators sometimes found themselves stigmatizing the most disengaged students as well as the few options left open to them, using those options as safety valves.[2]

In trying to persuade students to reengage, teachers and administrators throughout the educational system often use negative motivations as a last resort. Unwittingly, they reinforce a hierarchy of stigmatized organizations in the students' minds. Many comprehensive staff members cast the continuation school in a negative light in hopes of scaring misbehaving or truant students into changing their behavior. Students who ended up in the continuation school anyway sometimes repeated the horrors they had been told, to the dismay of the staff. Ironically, when continuation staff members' bag of tricks to motivate disengaged students approached empty, they reached for the same "dirty" trick: they disparaged the educational alternatives that remained open, usually adult education, the GED, or independent study—even the continuation school's own afternoon shift in the case of Willows.

The continuation schools had ways of pushing out, or disengaging from, students seen as "troublemakers" or "nonstudents"—including girls but more often boys. Students who did not demonstrate a certain amount of success—measured formally at Beacon, and informally at La Fuente and Willows, by attendance, productivity, and punctuality—were routinely transferred to other alternative programs one rung down the credential ladder. At Beacon, truant or nonproductive students were routinely enrolled in the district's adult education program, which in turn was not required to report them as dropouts if they subsequently left. Of the 70 eventual dropouts from Beacon who were enrolled at Beacon during 1988–1989, Beacon referred 64% to adult education after several months, and most of these students—78% of such referrals—never actually enrolled; three-fifths of the adult education no-shows were male, two-fifths were female. Explained one teacher-counselor at Beacon:

> There is no monitoring once they are at adult ed. It's really the end. They leave saying they'll make it there, but 99% won't. We say, "Yeah, good luck"—sending them out feeling good. But we know they won't make it.

At La Fuente, the independent study program (ISP) served a similar purpose. Out of 350 dropouts from La Fuente High School, 16% had transferred to ISP; almost a third of those were considered no-shows, whereas the rest stayed a couple of weeks or longer before leaving the schooling system altogether.

Increasing gang and drug-dealing activities and the large demand by La Fuente's feeder comprehensive schools—with a combined enrollment of over 20,000 students—to enroll their misfits put La Fuente under pressure to withdraw students who were especially truant, disruptive, or reluctant to work. School staff employed several means of implementing this unstated mandate. First, incoming students had to attend a half-day orientation class for one to three weeks. Among other things, they were told what was expected of a good student. If, after the first day, they came to orientation class late or without a notebook, the teacher—selected for the job because she was well-liked by most students, motivating yet demanding—routinely sent them home:

> Barry appeared at the door around 10 o'clock saying he'd overslept. Ms. Wilson told him to go home. Barry: "At least I made the effort to come." Lance added: "Yeah, if you keep kicking us out, how are we gonna get an education?" Ms. Wilson explained that Barry had to take responsibility for being tardy, and Barry left. (Field notes, May 10, 1989)

If students were frequently absent or reluctant to complete in-class assignments or participate in discussion, they often had to repeat the class for another three weeks. These policies did discourage the most disengaged students: 18% of all eventual dropouts left after 6 weeks or less at La Fuente during 1988–1989. Wrote one student in his journal: "I just got some desturbing [sic] news that I might have to repeat the window. . . . I'm not going to go to the class. I will just get into the GED program." He did not do so while I was at La Fuente.

Another means of disengaging from students deemed marginal was referrals to what was euphemistically called the Responsibility Center. About half the teachers routinely sent tardy and disruptive students there, where they had to copy rules from the student handbook. In interviews, students and some teachers complained that the man in charge treated them harshly. He repeated his philosophy to me several times: "I tell the kids [who come to the Responsibility Center], 'It's like cancer and garbage. You cut one out, and the other you throw out.'" More often than not, girls reported being shocked, upset, and inclined to skip future detention, whereas boys were prone to swear, flee, or challenge the disciplinarian to a fight. As one teacher explained: "The kids [especially boys] who get sent to Mr. Zuniga are at risk of suspension because they're just not as equipped as adults to deal with his abrasive personality. They end up fighting him over piddling offenses like being tardy."

Other teachers and the counselor fully supported Mr. Zuniga's approach; they encouraged one another to deal with chronic absenteeism and other discipline problems through the referral system because this created an official record. At a certain point, students who had built up poor reputations were withdrawn under the code "other"—the largest but least explanatory category of dropouts/pushouts. Sitting in the office on numerous occasions, I witnessed students being quietly withdrawn under the "other" code for smoking marijuana, chronic absenteeism, failing grades, and fighting.

One teacher referred a Latina to the office for chronic tardiness, saying she was "not a serious student" and was just "taking up space in the class." The counselor withdrew her from school that day. I then overheard the girl asking a secretary if she could appeal to the principal—apparently unaware that La Fuente had no principal at that time. A similar pushout practice was observed at Beacon for a Mexican-American boy considered "too disruptive." His teacher-counselor asked that he not be sent registration information, and he was withdrawn under the code "over 18—not reenrolled."

Some teachers at both schools told me they were unhappy with these school-initiated, exclusionary practices. At La Fuente, a group of teachers formally complained to the acting principal that students were being withdrawn before they even knew the students were in trouble. But they hesitated to push strongly for due process unless they felt a particular student had academic potential, was pleasant, if unmotivated, or had participated in school activities.

POLICY IMPLICATIONS

Education options for "at risk" students have grown dramatically over the last 10 years. Besides continuation or "second-chance" high schools, these options include educational clinics, opportunity classes, alternative education and work centers, community schools, adult education, independent study programs, teenage parenting and pregnancy programs, and partnership academies.

Most represent a dual response: (1) to students' need for flexibility and personalization, with the stated aim of "dropout prevention and recovery," and (2) to mainstream comprehensive high schools' need for mechanisms to isolate students identified as discipline problems and to provide specialized services efficiently. In a society stratified by class, ethnicity, and gender, however, these second-chance programs, for structural reasons, usually turn out to be second-rate.

People interested in reforming high schools to incorporate the positive aspects of educational options—flexible scheduling, personalized attention, brokerage of social services—argue that once these reforms are implemented, the need for options outside of the comprehensive high schools will be reduced. But there are reasons to be skeptical; foremost is the imbalance of power and resources that shape the politics of schooling, particularly in large urban districts that draw on a dwindling property and industry tax base for funding. In times of fiscal constraint, dropout programs—which sometimes redirect resources to help those most in need—are among the first items to be cut.

Another problem is that options within a single setting tend to pit various groups against each other over academic and behavior standards, a dynamic which has led administrators to establish alternatives apart from the mainstream. As the various options proliferate, however, problems of communication, coordination, and accountability increase and therefore so does the possibility that students will slip between the cracks.

An examination of the history of continuation education shows that offering options without major reforms both inside and outside the educational system (e.g., job programs, more and better funding for child care, funded access to contraception and abortion services, balanced housing development, social and health services) can simply mean replicating the sorting process pioneered in traditional educational settings. Continuation personnel are under pressure to demonstrate results or face elimination, and consequently some have begun to screen out the most disengaged students, relegating them to other optional programs further down the credential hierarchy.

In the short run, state and provincial governments could increase accountability for retaining and engaging students throughout the education system by requiring schools to track individuals from entry into kindergarten up to age 18 or high school graduation and to calculate longitudinal dropout rates by ethnic group and sex. Currently, California requires schools to report an annual dropout rate; this estimates the number of students who drop out or are pushed out during the school year. A longitudinal rate provides a more accurate and complete picture by estimating the percentage of students in a particular class who drop out or are pushed out between the time they enter and graduation.

The longitudinal rate, and the monitoring system needed to calculate it, would help administrators prevent students from slipping out of the system. At present, students who drop out between school years or in transition from one school or program to another, even within the same district, are sometimes not counted as dropouts. If they are counted, it is often by alternative programs such as continuation or adult education rather than the students' neighborhood comprehensive school; this accounting practice makes the mainstream school's record of retaining and engaging students seem better than it actually is.

Both the comprehensive high school and the options connected to it should take responsibility for students, regardless of where they are within the education system. At the same time, policy makers should recognize that dropout prevention and recovery programs, such as continuation schools, will have a higher dropout rate because they serve many students who have already left once and tend to be seriously behind on credit. Given the extra resources needed to provide these students with a better chance of academic success, funding formulas should provide greater financial incentives for retrieving and retaining dropouts and pushouts.

Are those who push options as a mechanism of public school reform inadvertently helping to lay the ideological groundwork for a private voucher system that, in the end, weakens the idea of the common public school? Or do optional programs help to create openings for the development of curricula that are experimental and more inclusive—that is, responsive to the lives of working-class and ethnic minority girls and boys?

At a time when choice is being offered as a panacea to school administrators grappling with cultural diversity and White, affluent flight versus meeting the needs of low-income people, the context of the debate needs to be broadened. Three lessons can be gleaned from my examination of California's oldest and largest dropout prevention program. First, schooling options should be based on students' current needs, defined and interpreted in sustained consultation with students and family members; change should proceed from the bottom up. Second, administrators and teachers should inform students and parents as fully as possible about the differences in programs and the consequences of the choices open to them within the system. Third, a central forum of accountability within the system must be in place to allow for monitoring of students shifting back and forth between various schooling programs, so that one option does not become a safety valve for another and thus a point of final exit.

NOTES

1. I would like to thank the Spencer Foundation for its financial support.

2. Other continuation schools in California engaged in similar practices. In Ontario, California, for example, continuation administrators have argued: "Many students referred to the program have no positive academic intentions and are simply attempting to continue 'game-playing' and take up space in the program."

As a solution, the district has begun a precontinuation independent study program, which administrators feel has "enhanced" the continuation program because "non-attenders" and "non-productive" students are "redirected without enrollment," thus improving average daily attendance figures and the "academic setting" (Bratta, 1990, p. 8). In Milpitas, California, the continuation school requires students to improve their attendance at the comprehensive school as a condition of enrollment. Not coincidentally, its district uses temporary placement on independent study as a disciplinary threat, reserving the continuation school as a "privilege" (Freedberg, 1985).

REFERENCES

Barr, R. D. (1975). The growth of alternative public schools: The 1975 ICOPE report. *Changing Schools, 12,* 1–15. (ERIC Reproduction Service No. ED 106 898)

Bill, H. (1972). Dropouts: Prevention and rehabilitation. Schools rescue potential failures. In *Education U.S.A.* Washington, DC: National School Public Relations Association. (ERIC Reproduction Service No. ED 065 931)

Bratta, J. (1990, March). Independent study and the continuation program. *California Continuation Education Association Newsletter,* p. 8.

California Legislature, Assembly Committee on Education. (1965). *Staff report on House Resolution 330 (1964) by Assemblyman Beilenson.* Sacramento: California State Printing Office.

California State Board of Education. (1923). *Fifth biennial report, 1920–1922.* Sacramento: California State Printing Office.

California State Department of Education. (1919, June). Part-time compulsory education. *California Blue Bulletin, 5* (2), 3–4.

California State Department of Education. (1920, March). The best way to make citizens of aliens. *California Blue Bulletin, 6* (1), 19–21.

Carnoy, M., & Levin, H. M. (1985). *Schooling and work in the democratic state.* Stanford: Stanford University Press.

Cremin, L. (1964). *The transformation of the school: Progressivism in American education, 1876–1957.* New York: Vintage Books.

Education Code, Statutes of California. (1967). Sacramento: California State Printing Office.

Freedberg, L. (1985, October 31). Teaching success: One school district where suspensions have been suspended. *Pacific News Service,* pp. 4–5.

Goffman, E. (1961). *Asylums.* Garden City, NY: Anchor Books.

Hill, M. L. (1988). *Continuation education programs: Biennial report, 1985–1987.* Sacramento: California State Department of Education.

Jones, A. J. (1907). *The continuation school in the United States* (U.S. Dept. of the Interior, U.S. Bureau of Education Bulletin No. 1). Washington, DC: U.S. Government Printing Office.

Katznelson, I., & Weir, M. (1985). *Schooling for all: Class, race, and the decline of the democratic ideal.* New York: Basic Books.

Kelly, D. M. (1993). *Last chance high: How girls and boys drop in and out of alternative schools*. New Haven, CT: Yale University Press.

Kett, J. F. (1982). The adolescence of vocational education. In H. Kantor & D. Tyack (Eds.), *Work, youth, and schooling: Historical perspectives on vocationalism in American education* (pp. 78–109). Stanford: Stanford University Press.

March, J. G., & Olsen, J. P. (1984). The new institutionalism: Organizational factors in political life. *The American Political Science Review, 78,* 734–749.

Mayman, J. E. (1933, March). The evolution of the continuation school in New York City. *School Review, 41* (3), 193–205.

McDonough, E. M. (1921, June). Organization and administration of a continuation school. *Industrial-Arts Magazine, 10* (6), pp. 203–255.

Page, R. (1987). Lower-track classes at a college-preparatory high school: A caricature of educational encounters. In G. Spindler, & L. Spindler (Eds.), *Interpretive ethnography of education: At home and abroad* (pp. 447–472). Hillsdale, NJ: Lawrence Erlbaum Associates.

Raywid, M. A. (1982). *The current status of schools of choice in public secondary education: Alternatives, options, magnets*. Hempstead, NY: Hofstra University, Project on Alternatives in Education. (ERIC Document Reproduction Service No. ED 242 055)

Shaffer, E. E. (1955). *A study of continuation education in California*. Sacramento: California State Printing Office, for California State Department of Education.

Snider, W. (1989, May 17). Study: Schools violating rights of pregnant girls. *Education Week,* p. 5.

Tyack, D. (1974). *The one best system: A history of American urban education*. Cambridge: Harvard University Press.

Tyack, D. (1978). *The history of secondary schools in delivering social services*. Unpublished manuscript, Stanford University, Palo Alto, California.

Young, T. (1990). *Public alternative education*. New York: Teachers College Press.

CHAPTER 7

What If You Organized a Reform and Nothing Changed? The Fate of Culturally Compatible Curricula in an American Indian Public School District

MARGARET D. LECOMPTE

Recent school reforms in the United States have not greatly changed the overall pattern of activities in schools. In many cases, they have actually exacerbated the very conditions they were intended to correct. Most reform efforts in the United States fail to alter the patterns of power, control, and instruction inside schools; none of them disrupt powerful social, political, and economic factors—including persistent patterns of racism and discrimination—which, although they are external to schools, nevertheless have a profound effect upon the workings of educational systems (see Chafetz & Dworkin, 1986; LeCompte & Dworkin, 1991; Ogbu, 1978, 1987; Sarason, 1971). Similarly, reforms have seldom changed the dynamics at the heart of pedagogy: complex patterns of student–teacher interaction. Even those curricular and pedagogical approaches most salient to dropout prevention, ones that reduce alienation by involving students in their own learning—such as problem solving and discovery learning—necessitate structural changes at the classroom level in how teachers and children relate to each other. These changes are precisely the ones that current educational reforms do not accomplish (Newmann, 1981; Puckett, 1989; Sarason, 1971).

The discussion in this chapter[1] focuses on the impact—or lack of it—of school reforms on the actual teaching and learning experiences of students. My premise is that little enhancement of instruction has occurred, in large part because the planned reforms never become operational. As a consequence, arguments about which reforms are more effective in dropout prevention often are academic. Central to my argument is that while many reforms have been talked to death, few have been implemented solidly enough for assessment by realistic tests, such as the number of students who remain in school until they graduate. Rather than discussion of the merits of hypothetical dropout prevention programs, I believe more attention should be paid to why such programs don't even get off the ground.

I argue in this chapter that school reforms fail to materialize in large part because participants in them resist acquiring the knowledge needed to implement them—or prevent others from acquiring it. Thus, key players never clearly understand what they are to do. Lack of information, created by a variety of obstacles to information flow and communication in complex systems such as school districts, constitutes one reason why understanding is not achieved. More important, and a prior condition to impaired communication, is the degree to which participants in reform attempt to construct understandings about and definitions of the reforms which contradict or are at variance with the original intent of the reform. While an initial consensus on vague goals and objectives can be achieved among a wide variety of often quite diverse constituencies (see, for example, Apple, 1993), the process of implementation often causes the apparent consensus to dissipate and the coalition which supported it to fray.

Diversity in understandings makes consensus creation difficult; it also tends to create warring camps and rigid perceptions. These dynamics are especially salient when consensus needs to be achieved on the importance of someone else's culture. Diversity of culture makes consensus building and resolution of conflicts difficult or impossible, because interaction styles, values, and modes of conflict resolution differ from community to community (see LeCompte & McLaughlin, 1994). When participants are unfamiliar with each others' cultures and resist learning about them, they are often unwilling to enter the world view of their culturally different fellow participants, and they are incapable of constructing meanings together, which might permit them to achieve a new and stable mode of operation. As a consequence, patterns of meaning construction, conflict, and stalemate tend to repeat themselves, and also persist in reflecting existing patterns of cultural power and dominance. In school systems, this means that reform initiatives, in the words of Larry Cuban (1990), occur "again, again, and again." Public school systems in the United States are especially prone to such recycling because the multiple constituencies that they serve have such easy access to and power over educational governance structures; this ensures that conflicts over cultural values attendant to schooling are inevitable.

CULTURALLY COMPATIBLE CURRICULA AS A MEANS FOR DROPOUT PREVENTION

One of the most controversial recent reforms in teaching and learning is the positive or negative effects of students' natal culture on academic achievement. Several theories have emerged which emphasize the relationships—negative and otherwise—between conditions in the home and natal culture and the academic performance of school children. Briefly (and simply), these theories argue that the performance of children can be improved if the disabilities of the home can be overcome or compensated for in school (the "culture of poverty" approach [Valentine, 1968]); if the differences between the home and school can be ameliorated (the cultural differences approach); or if the differences in the home can be understood and adapted for use in the school (the cultural compatibility approach [Erickson, 1987; Foley, 1991; Ogbu, 1987; Trueba, 1988]). The culturally compatible approach is associated with philosophies asserting that language minority, nonmainstream, and poor children have difficulty in school because of incompatibilities, dissonances, or discontinuities between home culture and school culture. The performance of such children would improve, it is argued, if schools could ameliorate these discontinuities, rather than ignore them or make attempts to obliterate them.

Cultural approaches to dropout prevention are controversial because they involve inevitable comparison between cultures—usually the culture of dominant groups, as represented in the governance structure and overall emphases of the schools, and that of subordinate and/or minority groups. They have provided ammunition for separatist groups who argue that nonmainstream children will never be educated adequately in mainstream schools; they also agitate assimilationists who believe that the quickest way to eliminate the problem of minority student failure is to replace the minority child's cultural heritage with that of the mainstream.

The cultural compatibility approach is meliorist—it uses a "least-change" model, which requires the school to make the least change possible necessary to produce the desired result. It neither requires that schools serving minority children adapt completely to the culture of those children, nor does it make nonmainstream children responsible for all accommodation to schooling. Culturally compatible approaches to teaching and learning recognize that schools and homes serve different socializing functions and that all children experience some kind of discontinuity when they go to school (following Durkheimian [1973] arguments; see also LaBelle, 1972). However, the discontinuity is greater for children whose home culture is not reflected in the culture and expectations of mainstream school staff and the larger community. Culturally compatible approaches try to reduce the alienating aspects of going to school by minimizing the negative impact of cultural discontinuity for nonmainstream children. They do so by integrating those aspects of the natal culture that are most relevant to formal instruction into school practice, and by altering or softening aspects of interaction in schools which are most alien to the natal culture of the child. Culturally compatible approaches also are easily sabotaged or ignored, however, simply because they are broad in scope and meliorist.

One of the best known models for such a program was the Kamehameha Early Education Project (KEEP) (Au, 1980; Au & Jordan, 1981; Tharp & Gallimore, 1988). This program, which was based on a five-year ethnographic study of interaction and learning in Native Hawaiian communities, integrated certain characteristics of social discourse and interaction in Native Hawaiian culture into school practice, which either were most dissonant with ordinary interaction in schools, or which were most conducive to learning among Hawaiian children. Most important among these was the use of "talk story," a style of discourse in which stories are mutually constructed by several people talking at once in patterns of overlapping speech, rather than the teacher-controlled patterns of individual turn-taking which characterizes discourse in mainstream classrooms. The Kamehameha Project was piloted with Navajo children at Rough Rock school on the Navajo Reservation, with mixed results that demonstrated the impossibility of transplanting a pedagogical device based on patterns appropriate for one culture into a quite different cultural group (Vogt, Jordan, & Tharp, 1987). A project based upon principles developed in KEEP also is being implemented in a school on the Zuni reservation (Tharp, Dalton, & Yamauchi, 1994; Yamauchi & Tharp, 1995). Because of the success of KEEP in improving the achievement of Native Hawaiian children, administrators in a small rural and extremely isolated public school district on a Navaho reservation were inspired to use it as a model for development of a "culturally compatible curriculum" (Breningstall, 1995; Breningstall & LeCompte, 1992). Their purpose was to reduce the dropout rate in their community.

THE SETTING

This chapter examines the experiences of the school district on the Navajo Reservation in which the author worked as a consultant and researcher.

The district, which is located in the community of Pinnacle,[2] consists of four schools, a primary (K–2), intermediate (3–5), middle (6–8), and high school (9–12). Its enrollment is approximately 97% Navajo, but its teaching staff is predominantly white. At the time of this study, only three administrators were Navajo: the superintendent, Dr. Mason; the director of large special projects, Mrs. Begay; and her assistant, Mr. Laughter. The assistant superintendent, Mr. Aspen, and all the other administrative staff including the staff development team, were white. The primary and intermediate school had a larger proportion of Navajo teachers and a staff of teachers' aides who were Navajo, but even in these schools, the majority of certified staff were white.

In the Pinnacle school district, reform centered on several kinds of educational restructuring, including setting up a "learning community" of teachers and administrators whose purpose was to meet together to introduce and discuss new ideas, including how to implement shared decision making and site-based management, and to introduce a "culturally compatible curriculum." The impetus behind introducing these reforms in Pinnacle was to improve academic performance among the district's predominantly Navajo students and to reduce dropout rates by making classrooms less alienating.

Data were collected by myself and a team of research assistants. We engaged in participant observation and conducted interviews in monthly visits with administrators and teachers over a 4-year period (1989–1993). We also interviewed all the teachers in the middle school (1991 and 1992), conducted two surveys of the high school teachers (1992 and 1993), interviewed teachers in the primary school bilingual program (1992), and interviewed 80 of the 230 high school students who were on academic probation for having failed at least one class (1993). In addition, we used data from a district-conducted survey of parents (1993), and information from district-generated documents.

INTRODUCING CULTURAL COMPATIBILITY IN PINNACLE

The Pinnacle district has tried to become a leader in American Indian education. Movement toward culturally relevant curricula in Pinnacle began in 1989. Pinnacle's superintendent, Dr. Mason, asked Donna Deyhle, an educational anthropologist who has studied the problems of Navajo at risk students since the early 1980s (Deyhle, 1986, 1991, 1992; Deyhle & LeCompte, 1994), to work with the school district to help reduce its dropout rates. Deyhle met with teachers in the high school, who asked her to teach them more about Navajo culture and to help them set up pilot instructional projects using what they had learned in her class. I came to the Pinnacle school district in Fall, 1989, when Deyhle invited me to help the teachers evaluate their projects. Subsequently, I consulted with the district, obtained funding for them to support a number of curricular innovations, and collected a variety of data on the progress of these and other innovations.

Deyhle and I spent Spring, 1990 working one-on-one with a voluntary group of high school and middle school teachers on individual projects associated with the class on Navajo culture. In the fall of that year, the superintendent invited me to give the district-wide fall inservice keynote address, and to elaborate on the kinds of reforms I thought might work best in the district. My talk (LeCompte, 1990) was quite critical of many reforms, including those which simply raised standards or relied on high-tech substitutes for good teaching. It emphasized the need to concentrate on new forms of teaching and thinking about learning that would make an actual difference with students. In particular, I discussed instructional strategies which are constructivist or transactional in nature, and which scaffold (Vygotsky, 1962, 1978; Tharp & Gallimore, 1988) between academic or school-based knowledge and knowledge acquired in and valued by the local community. In Pinnacle, such a pedagogy would require teachers and staff to become more familiar with the culture of Navajo students so they could create the required scaffolds, or bridges, between school knowledge and the home-based "funds of knowledge" (Moll, 1990) which are legitimated by the Navajo community.

Both the superintendent, Mr. Sanders, and the assistant superintendent, Mr. Aspen, wanted a program uniquely designed for the Pinnacle student body. They also sought to avoid adopting programs that are unsuitable for Navajos. Aspen described it this way:

> We have good time on task and good drill on basic skills, but I'm not satisfied with that. And basic skills isn't the way to real literacy, even if it gets good test scores . . . [it's] like standing on the bank of a river watching the dead bodies float by. You don't have time to go upstream to see what's happening to cause the carnage; you just pull out all the live ones you can. It's just damage control. We have to go in and find out how these kids learn. We don't want to adapt anyone else's program. We want to identify the right learning environment for our students and we want to know how Navajo kids learn.

To Aspen, cultural compatibility did not mean "bringing the hogan [typical dwelling of the Navajo] into the classroom." Aspen, Mason, and many of the teachers believed that Navajo parents did not want teachers, especially Anglo teachers, to "teach Navajo culture" to students. Especially with regard to religious beliefs, this was the province of the home. The school staff's stance also acknowledged the considerable diversity within the Navajo community regarding appropriate cultural practices. Notwith-- standing, cultural compatibility meant more to Aspen than what he called "consciousness raising." Teachers couldn't simply know about Navajo culture; they had to use that knowledge to interact more sympathetically and knowledgeably with their students. As Aspen said, "I can walk down the hallways and I can see some classrooms where the kids are really learning, and others where they're just *dying*. It doesn't take any real talent to see the difference. But we have to stop teachers from killing off the kids." While Aspen recognized that there were able and caring teachers in the district, he felt that some teachers "killed off kids": They believed that Navajos just were not capable of success in mainstream curricula. Others, in misguided kindness, "dumbed down" (McNeil, 1988) what they taught in order to avoid damaging students' self-esteem by failure. Even more were ignorant of the culture. For example, one middle school teacher trying to get students to think for themselves demonstrated her lack of awareness of how important sheep are to Navajos by exhorting them not to "act like sheep. You don't want to be a stupid bunch of sheep, do you?" Anglos associate sheep with mindless discipleship. Navajos believe that sheep are a gift from the Holy People. Sheep are crucial to Navajo subsistence and one of the economic and symbolic backbones of their contemporary culture. As the teacher continued her harangue, the students put their heads on their desks and stopped listening. Yet another small but very damaging group consisted of teachers who felt that Navajo culture was a real impediment to school success, and that the sooner students were weaned from traditional beliefs, the more they would improve their performance.

Aspen wanted to develop a curriculum that incorporated indigenous modes of interaction and learning into classroom practice. Like the Kamehameha Project, such a curriculum would draw on those aspects of natal culture most salient for formal education, rather than duplicating local culture in the classroom. Aspen felt this would make going to school less alienating for these nonmainstream children.

Culturally compatible pedagogy generated much discussion among administrators in the district. However, it remained an elusive concept not only for the administrators and teaching staff charged with its implementation, but for Aspen as well. As I will describe, it was difficult to translate the abstract concept of a culturally compatible curriculum from Aspen's vision into concrete reality.

Many Anglos really did not understand what culture meant. Lacking that understanding, they were unable to envision a curriculum informed

by it. In addition, the concept of diversity lacked long-standing and powerful support. Mainstream culture in the United States remains ambivalent
about the value of other cultures, and many educators exercise caution
knowing that significant divergence from traditional assimilationist models of socialization often creates protest from powerful interest groups in
the community. Another problem was the time frame for implementation; Deyhle and I believed that it would take several years to accumulate
sufficient school-relevant knowledge about Navajo culture and to train
teachers to use it effectively—as had been done with KEEP. Although the
administrative team initially supported such efforts, they were dismayed—
as most school administrators would be—when they realized that this
kind of change would be long in coming, and that no real change in
student performance could be expected for quite a while. A major obstacle may have been outright cultural and racial prejudice on the part of
some staff. A final and critical factor was my status as an outsider who
did not really understand the administrative culture of the district. As a
consultant, I stimulated much resistance among the staff developers, who
resented suggestions that they could improve what they were doing to
orient teachers to the culture. These obstacles, which characterize the
institutional culture of all American schools, are difficult for administrators
to overcome—even the able and well-intended administrators in Pinnacle.

For Pinnacle School District, developing and implementing a culturally compatible curriculum meant a complete *conceptual* restructuring of
instruction throughout the district. It also meant restructuring attitudes
about student capabilities and Navajo culture. Cultural compatibility was
one of the most difficult things the district tried to establish, because it
involved changing what is most intractable and least supervised in schools:
teacher behavior, instructional practice, attitudes toward students, and
teacher beliefs about teaching, learning, and what is best for students. Its
difficulty notwithstanding, the effort was worth the trouble, because these
factors lie at the heart of changing the environment in classrooms from
one which produces dropouts to one which inspires academic success
for all.

The Cultural Context of Reform in Pinnacle

It is important to realize that the administrative staff and teachers of Pinnacle School District were familiar with the vocabulary of contemporary
American educational reform. Central office administrators in Pinnacle
had been quick to begin using the terminology of restructuring to characterize both the wholesale reengineering of the educational process, on

one hand, and the general process of any innovative activity, on the other. Although they were not a part of any restructuring schools network or group, Pinnacle administrators and staff began to attend private proprietary and state education agency-run workshops on restructuring in the late 1980s. When he was principal of the high school, Mr. Aspen "restructured" the daily schedule to a four-period day, in large part to force teachers to shift from a daily diet of lectures and worksheets to what he hoped would be more innovative teaching activities. In addition, the primary school principal worked for two years with a consultant from the state university on a variation of shared decision making to substitute teacher governance in curriculum, instruction, and administration of the school for traditional principal control.

Pinnacle administrators and teachers had staff retreats; they also read about and were active in a broad range of professional activities. Unlike many educational CEOs who reserve the privilege of traveling and idea-gathering for themselves, Pinnacle administrators took groups of teachers to meetings and conferences out of state with them. The teachers had received many visits from staff developers—one per building—who worked with teachers to implement changes mandated by the central office. The terms restructuring, empowerment, site-based management, cultural compatibility, and outcomes-based education filled the air around them. All of these activities led the leadership of Pinnacle School District to feel that they were deeply involved in the processes of restructuring and reform.

Two years after I had begun my association with the Pinnacle District, few teachers and no administrators could say they had never heard of the concepts of restructuring, shared decision making, and cultural compatibility, although there was wide divergence in the meanings assigned to them. Under these conditions, one might have expected that some educational ferment would have trickled down to affect the *practice* of teachers and staff—and consequently, might have begun to affect the experience of children. This was, after all, the objective of the reform activity: improvement in the experience, self-esteem, and achievement of students. Optimistically, I had thought that this district might be immune to some of the problems I detail in the next section.

The Learning Community

In December, 1990 I met with all the administrators to find out how they wanted me to help them restructure. They asked that I run a college-level seminar or "learning community" to address what *could* be restructured in school districts, how it could be done, and what should be done in

Pinnacle. They were particularly interested in shared decision making and culturally compatible instruction. The learning community's purpose would be to define what these terms meant and how they could be implemented in Pinnacle. Since the learning community was structured as a graduate-level university seminar for which participants would receive course credit, I assigned readings like those I used in my classes, including Tharp and Gallimore's treatment of the KEEP project (1988) and related readings on innovation and reform in American Indian education.

Problems surfaced almost immediately. The first was attendance. Although all people at administrative rank in the district registered for the class, and Superintendent Mason advocated requiring the class, most participants were too burdened with daily administration to do the reading; none did all of the assignments. One principal assigned his assistant to write the papers for him, after the two of them discussed the questions. The high school principal, newly hired in January, came only once. Mr. Lewis, the middle school principal, was the most candid: "Marki, I have to tell you the truth. I *can't* read this stuff. I get too burned out with the problems of my own school. And then you lay on me a stack of reading *this* high!!"

The second problem was the composition of participants. After a few meetings, where problems in instruction consumed much of the time, one of the staff developers said, "All we do is talk about how we have to get the *teachers* to do things. But we are talking to ourselves, because we don't have any teachers here in this class." So Mr. Aspen, the assistant superintendent, invited three teachers from the high school to join the group; they participated warily (see LeCompte, 1994a). In subsequent meetings, one or two representatives (selected by the principals) from all but the primary school were added to the group. Nevertheless, distrust persisted.

Another sticking point was how to "do" cultural compatibility if it were to mean more than merely a sympathetic stance toward Navajo culture—the "consciousness raising" which Aspen firmly believed was insufficient. Most of the school staff simply did not seem to know how to convert sympathy into instructional practice. Consequently, they leaned heavily on the two Navajo program administrators to tell them what to do. However, since neither of these administrators had strong backgrounds in curriculum development or staff development—and one was lacking both a college degree and teacher certification—they did not feel sufficiently qualified or respected by the other administrators to do so. They also recognized that reforms initiated by the least powerful members of the administrative team had little chance of acceptance. As one of these administrators told me, "If they really are serious about Navajo culture, they should make the changes themselves, and they should hire more Navajo administrators!"

The Construction of Partial and Biased Realities

One of the principal obstacles to development of culturally compatible pedagogy was what I call the Anglo practice of constructing "partial and biased realities" about the Navajo people.[3] Most people employed by the district felt they already knew a great deal about Navajos and how to teach them. In most cases, however, their store of knowledge was partial and biased. Because Pinnacle was profoundly segregated by race, class, housing, and employment, most Anglos had little or no social interaction with Navajos. In the case of the Anglo teachers and administrators, their contact was largely restricted to their students. As a consequence, what many of them knew about Navajos consisted of folk tales and tidbits acquired from other Anglos and atypical individuals in the community— business personnel, school board members, Navajo Mormon converts, and selected district employees, many of whom, while Navajo, did not come from the Pinnacle community. Many Navajos also had little experience with their traditional culture, having been raised in boarding schools or adoptive non-Navajo families.[4] Even Pinnacle students, who might have served as a source of information, often were estranged from their heritage and could not provide details about their culture. Nonetheless, though many acquired more information from MTV and Nintendo than from traditional ceremonies and stories (Deyhle, 1986; 1991), they clearly self-identified as Navajos, and they did not define cultural affiliation solely in terms of how much they knew about or practiced the traditions.

Constraints on the flow of cultural information in Pinnacle were aggravated by the divided and segregated nature of the community. Despite the location of the school district in the heart of the Navajo Nation and the almost totally Navajo student body, many Anglo teachers chose to remain isolated from parents and other members of the Navajo community who might have had a cultural impact on them. While many of the teachers did have Navajo friends, most of those we interviewed had contact with Navajo people only at school in rare parent meetings and during brief encounters in commercial settings, such as the post office and the grocery store. They acquired their knowledge about Navajo people in large part from long-time Anglo residents of the Pinnacle community who professed to "know the Navajo people" and pass this knowledge on to newcomers. Often, this knowledge bore little resemblance to actual life among the Navajo in Pinnacle. For example, many teachers believed that ceremonies were just social occasions, that nobody wanted to learn the language any more, and that the kinaalda, the coming of age ceremony celebrating a young girl's first menstrual period, was no longer practiced. Based upon these beliefs—all erroneous—they could assert that Navajo culture was dying and was no longer a serious influence on the children they teach. Such restrictions on the information base meant that Pinnacle teachers and staff constructed an *appearance* of knowledge about the Navajo people, rather than knowledge based on first-hand experience and solid data. Even among teachers who loved teaching the children and professed appreciation for their culture, knowledge of Navajo culture often failed to permeate deeply or to supplant knowledge acquired in their prior training about children, culture, teaching, or learning.

Because most "multicultural training" in schools of education trivializes the concept of culture (LeCompte & Bennett DeMarrais, 1992), school staff tended to translate culture into mere "do's and don'ts" of interaction—for example, wearing traditional attire, production of artifacts and crafts—rather than recognizing it as a complex, multifaceted, and multileveled way of life. Many Pinnacle staff denied that language was an integral part of culture. Others referred to Navajo religious traditions as stories and myths. Most were unaware of cultural differences in conceptions of the life cycle. Like many educators, both the primary and middle school principals believed that theories of child development were culturally neutral, and that the Eurocentric notions they learned in college were applicable to all cultures (Deyhle & LeCompte, 1994).

These beliefs permitted Anglo educators to decide whether a Navajo was "traditional" or not based upon superficialities, such as how they dressed and talked or how they interacted with white people. Since few Whites had the kind of relationships with Navajos that could counteract the trivializing process, and since few Navajos wore the traditional hair styles or traditional attire—except for ceremonial or festive occasions—teachers could assert that the culture was dying; they could remain unaware that cultures adapt and change, and that practicality dictates that Converse high topped basketball shoes and pickup trucks were as much a part of Indian culture as leather moccasins and horses once were.

Patterns of partial and biased knowledge and the beliefs they engendered allowed many teachers and administrators in Pinnacle to remain oblivious to the issue of cultural compatibility, avoid the need to integrate Navajo cultural knowledge into instruction, and resist attempts to change the way they taught. The staff development team, which was directed to help implement cultural compatibility, concentrated instead on implementing district evaluation procedures and providing curricular resources. While they did an excellent job with issues they understood, such as implementing a program of alternative assessment or mainstreaming handicapped children in regular classrooms, they could not—or did not want—to visualize what they were to do with cultural compatibility. Failing to understand the pervasiveness of cultural influences, they were convinced that cultural differences alone were insufficient justification for a thorough overhaul of instruction, and were unable to initiate a thorough investigation of how cultural practices might be integrated into teaching. Throughout the several years during which cultural compatibility was a focus in the district, staff developers acted as gatekeepers on the flow of knowledge about Navajos to teachers. Except for the initial cultural orientation they provided to new teachers, their inservices only marginally addressed the heart of linguistic or cultural issues, and they resisted introduction of information which might challenge their approach if it came from consultants or other outside sources.

By the end of the 1990–1991 school year, the administrative team—all personnel with administrative rank, program directors, and staff developers—had spent many hours discussing the definition of culturally compatible teaching, how to operationalize it, and what strategies would get teachers to buy into the new philosophy. In Apple's terms (1993), they were able to do so because they achieved a fragile initial consensus on broad, general, slogan-like goals—such as the need for culturally sensitive teaching and a compatible curriculum. However, that consensus unravelled when they faced the hard—and contentious—problem of how to make it operational. They also did not communicate their intentions effectively to the teaching staff.

Interviews with middle school and high school teachers in 1991–1993 indicated that the strenuous and heated discussions which involved the administrators had almost no impact on instruction. Most middle school teachers said they had never heard of the term cultural compatibility before and that they made no adaptations in their instruction to accommodate their Navajo students. The 2 instructors (out of 35) who did say they handled children differently focused on language proficiency or simple social interaction patterns. Some said they had to speak more slowly because the students lacked English language skills; two said that they avoided looking students directly in the eyes or criticizing students in public.

The situation had changed little by the end of the second year. By that time, Mr. Aspen, charged with leadership of curricular change in the face of resistance by staff development, had written a lengthy and thoughtful position paper on an appropriate culturally compatible approach. However, he was still struggling with how the philosophy would look in practice. Given the lack of enthusiasm evidenced by most of his colleagues and the somewhat "hands-off" stance of the superintendent,[5] his reluctance to forge ahead singlehandedly with the implementation was understandable. For example, most teachers in the middle school denied that Navajo conceptions of teaching, learning, growth, and development, had any relevance to their plans for implementing a "middle school concept" (see Deyhle & LeCompte, 1994). This was particularly surprising, since the impetus for creating a middle school in the first place had been the unique developmental needs of middle school children.

By 1992, more teachers had heard of the concept of cultural compatibility than in 1991, but to some extent this can be attributed to the use of the term by staff developers. A bigger influence was the hiring of new teachers, who had heard about cultural differences in college. However, interviews and observations with both old and new teachers indicated little awareness of Navajo cultural conceptions and little change in instructional practice. This is not surprising, since the primary impetus for directed instructional change came from the staff development office. Their orientation program familiarized newcomers with the history of the area and did make them more aware of specifics of Navajo life and behavior. It included workshops on storytelling and outings to the homes of Navajo staff. But it did not go very far to translate awareness into instructional strategies. Rather, it emphasized "do's and don'ts" of interaction and cultural differences in learning style (Rhodes, 1988), rather than specifics of pedagogy.

Responses from the high school were even less encouraging, especially since Mr. Aspen had generated his ideas about cultural compatibility during his four years there as principal and Donna Deyhle and I had taught a class on culture and curriculum to his teachers more than three years earlier. In Fall, 1992 we asked high school teachers whether they noticed anything special about how their students learned. We also asked them what their long- and short-term goals were for teaching. Forty of the 52 teachers in the school listed 250 responses to our questions. But only 11 responses even remotely addressed cultural differences or issues in learning, and those focused on what the teachers wanted to learn, not on how they would change their teaching:

- [I want to] Develop a curriculum that makes sense to bilingual students.
- [I want to] bring more relevant Native American information to the classroom using videos, music, books and poetry as a means of conveying the importance of being a knowledgeable person about things around you and their direct and indirect impact.
- [I want to] show students how to change the system that colonizes them.

- [I want to] Become more knowledgeable in Native American issues, the Navajo culture, building self-esteem through outdoor experiences, like the ropes course trips I take.
- [I want to] be more effective in teaching and working with Navajo people.
- [I want to] study/research more native American historical issues.
- [I want to] learn more about linguistics and language acquisition.

THE CORE OF CONSTRUCTED MEANINGS

Although the administrative staff and the majority of teachers began by supporting the vague concept of "using more information about culture to make kids feel more comfortable in school," after 3 years it was clear that they were at an impasse. Although Aspen and Mason promoted the idea of cultural compatibility with the best of intentions, few other key personnel in the district understood the idea or were willing or able to work with Aspen to make it a reality.

Much of the problem could be summed up by the core of rather deeply held meanings constructed by the staff. These meanings were based upon their own past history, their training and experience in the classroom and community, the conversations they had with other teachers and staff, and a variety of other factors which they brought to the "learning community" with them. These constructed meanings, which impeded implementation of a new curriculum, were variously shared by different members of the teaching and administrative staff. They created a "known world" (LeCompte, 1994b) of partial and biased knowledge which shaped their experience and made them impervious to contradictory or even additional information. I believe that part of the problem is that Anglos in general do not consider *their* beliefs and behaviors to be culturally specific (see Nieto, 1992). Therefore, the "known world" which Anglos in Pinnacle constructed was one in which Anglocentric notions of how the world works were held to be self-evident truths, not cultural constructions. These self-evident truths could be summarized from interviews and survey data as follows:

- We know our Indians. We don't need anyone else to tell us how to act with Navajos.
- Culture doesn't have anything to do with teaching and learning. And anyway, all cultures are more or less alike, except for the ways people dress, eat, and the kinds of crafts they make.
- Navajo culture is dying out.

- Navajo parents don't want their kids to learn Navajo. It interferes with their learning English.
- Language is not part of culture, anyway.
- We know who's qualified to teach us how to teach—and it's not uncertified (Navajo) people and it's not outsiders.
- I don't have time to learn anything new. I'm too overloaded as it is.
- Besides, I know what's best for my students.
- And I already have so much to teach that the state and district requires, that there isn't any room for any frills, like this culture stuff.
- And anyway, Navajo kids learn just like any other kids.

DERAILING INSTRUCTIONAL REFORM

To understand why the teachers remained in the dark about cultural compatibility requires more than an understanding of resistance by teachers and staff developers. A major problem was the discussion of shared decision making which accompanied the debate over cultural compatibility. It illuminated why the teachers and administrators found it so difficult to work together. A second involved the degree to which administrators, consciously or unconsciously, restricted the flow of information in the district, not only laterally within their own ranks, but also up and down the various organizational levels within the system. This made introduction of new ideas difficult, and facilitated the continued construction of partial realities and contradictory activities. A third problem was the centrifugal effect of site-based management, which had been operative in the district for 5 years. Site-based management made it difficult to carry out any district-wide planning or policy making—including policies regarding cultural compatibility.

A final problem was the lack of priority given to planning and the acquisition of new information. In the Fall of 1991, after 6 months of effort, the class with administrators and teachers was discontinued for lack of attendance. However, despite its ineffectiveness in generating a "learning community," it *had* generated a substantial increase in the information about reform available to district administrators. This was digested by Mr. Aspen and turned into summary documents for Dr. Mason's use. New ideas from these summaries gradually filtered down to district level administrators. However, they did not filter down to the teachers, given the difficulty principals had in relinquishing control, the institutionalized pressures for accountability which mitigated against shared decision making, and the constraints administrators experienced against learning about culture and change.

Dworkin (1986) discusses how far more cost-effective it is to teach a few principals new ways of interacting with teachers, rather than change the practice of an entire cohort of teachers. In Pinnacle, even though a principal focus of discussions in the learning community sessions had been how to share ideas about teaching, learning, and governance, information on cultural compatibility was not shared widely with teachers, nor was input solicited from teachers. The stumbling block to which discussions always returned was leadership and the relationship between teachers and administrators: teachers and administrators simply didn't trust each other. In interviews conducted in 1991, middle school teachers asked us to pass on to the principal the following message: "We don't believe you are serious, and we don't trust you. Convince us that this time you really want to share decisions with us. And show us you mean it by not simply giving us more work to do."

The natural operating style of most of the administrators ranged from managerial to autocratic. This could have been predicted from the training school leaders receive in educational administration programs, which is preoccupied with corporate models of leadership.

Such a style proved to be a major stumbling block to reform. Most members of the administrative team showed a remarkable ability to talk lucidly and passionately about sharing and group process without ever demonstrating either activity among themselves—except in occasional exercises organized by consultants for that specific purpose. Several of the principals even seemed oblivious to their need to initiate the process themselves.

A second-year survey of middle school teachers demonstrated more consensus on what shared decision making, cultural compatibility, and site-based management meant. Unfortunately, fewer teachers believed that these reforms would give them increased voice in governance of the school district. With few exceptions, those who said that the school *was* site-based spoke of increased autonomy in their own classrooms. Lacking real power in the school, they lowered their sights to the classroom level and left other kinds of decisions, including what to do about cultural compatibility, to the administration.

Although administrators sometimes were painfully aware of their own roles in perpetuating the mismatch between reality and the appearance of reform, they continued to develop perceptions of themselves, the teachers, and the way their work needed to be done which were diametrically opposed to the conceptual shift which shared decision making and cultural compatibility would require. This in turn made implementation of a culturally informed curriculum impossible, because it obviated the prior collaboration between teachers and staff which a new curriculum neces-

sitated. The "known world" (LeCompte, 1994b) that administrators constructed was based upon a justification for doing things the way they
always had been done. These justifications often were framed in the technical discourse of bureaucratic rationality and hierarchical control which
suffused the culture of school administration and their earlier training.
They were at complete variance with discourses prevalent in the Navajo
community (LeCompte & McLaughlin, 1994). Some of the meanings
which drove administrator behavior could be paraphrased as follows:

- Teachers really can't be trusted to do a good job of making decisions, so you have to keep tabs on what they're doing all the time.
  If they do it wrong, you have to overrule them and take over.
- It's good to have input from community people, but when a job
  has to get done, you need real expertise.
- Long-term planning is great, but hey! Who's got time? I've got to
  run this building (department, program, workshop . . .).
- Our own staff can do training (planning, teaching, budgeting, etc.)
  better and cheaper than outside consultants. And they know our
  kids and our teachers.

THE CONSEQUENCES OF MEANING CONSTRUCTION

Pinnacle's experience is not unique, and in many ways it illustrates some
of the key problems of school reform. Even with well-intended efforts
within the district, external pressures mitigate against change. Contradictions between the ideal of diversity and the reality of deeply entrenched
racial and cultural prejudice meant that Pinnacle administrators had little
support to legitimate their efforts. In addition, the inconsistency between
conceptions of leadership in which administrators have been trained, internalized, and consequently practiced, and conceptions of "democratic"
leadership (see Goodlad, 1983; Sizer, 1984–1985) make it difficult for
them to implement many of the current trends in school reform. Few
school administrators have been trained in democratic leadership. As a
consequence, administrators—and often teachers—continue to use old
practices in new situations, whether or not it is appropriate and even
when what they know best is incompatible with or irrelevant to the innovations they are trying to adopt.

Site-based management aggravates this situation. Often it can be used
by top administrators to avoid responsibility; the act of making difficult
district-wide choices is passed to principals. This places final accountability for success or failure—whether from staff or students—squarely on

the shoulders of principals, regardless of their training and expertise. Principals are given so many duties that little time remains for them to acquire the knowledge base necessary to confidently introduce new ideas or programs to the teaching staff. As a result, terminology is misused and misconstrued, difficulties are minimized or oversimplified, and meanings are trivialized. Principals often arrange or provide for teacher training that is inadequate or not germane to the topic. This was a particular problem with information about Navajo language, patterns of learning, culture, and bilingualism, since such information was not valued by many of the Anglo staff.

Establishing a learning community to build collegial relationships, acquire new information, and provide a forum for new ideas proved unworkable without a change in the way it was structured and integrated into everyday school life. In Pinnacle, such a change did not take place, and the superintendent's verbal support and requirements for attendance were not compelling. As a consequence, administrators did not have time to do the reading, school-based emergencies always took precedence over discussion, and teachers found it difficult to participate and were suspicious when they did.

Finally, changing instructional strategies and teacher attitudes about appropriate ways to teach, the capabilities of their students, and precisely what, outside of the classroom, is relevant to teaching and learning, proved elusive. Administrators were not able to translate their ideas into practice, and they were equally unable to model what they expected teachers to do. Cultural compatibility did not just "trickle down"; the attitudes of most Pinnacle teachers resembled those of high school teachers who said:

- Navajos are just like any other group of people. Some prefer to work alone, some in pairs, and some in small groups.
- I don't believe there is such a thing as Navajo learning style.

CONCLUSION

A partial and biased notion of culture formed the basis for the inability of Pinnacle School District to implement a culturally compatible curriculum. Although a culturally compatible curricula was not developed and implemented in Pinnacle, some reforms occurred. In other writings, I have discussed a number of the innovations which took place in the district during my stay there; other articles are underway at the time of this writing. However, the district found initiating a culturally sensitive strategy for reducing school failure to be the most difficult of the reforms they tried. Their failure is instructive, especially since, as I have written elsewhere (LeCompte, 1994a; LeCompte & McLaughlin, 1994; LeCompte & Wiertelak, 1994), Pinnacle seemed to be the "if it can't happen here, it can't happen anywhere" case with regard to reform in general and culturally informed curricula in particular. Its staff had strong motivations and the appropriate context for instituting such a program. Thus, the district's saga—and failure—provide a cautionary tale to other districts, especially since cultural approaches currently are widely advocated for dropout prevention.

Pinnacle staff were not able to devote sufficient time to learn about cultural approaches to teaching and learning, much less plan for and develop the program by themselves. Individual teachers and principals did, in fact, implement curricula and instruction which closely followed the principles of the KEEP project, but no district-wide curricular reform was produced. The consultants Pinnacle hired—including the author—could not deliver such a curriculum in what district administrators felt to be a timely manner, in large part because prior time was needed to gather information about which aspects of Navajo culture to integrate into instructional interaction and delivery. Since the consultants could not deliver, the district moved on to quite different innovations which were more mainstream and came with a preestablished structure. Most school districts—including Pinnacle—simply do not have the staff or resources to do much research and development—and a KEEP type of project required a great deal of initial research and development. Typically, the reforms districts adopt are those which come prepackaged, and a prepackaged cookbook was what the consultants could not deliver in a timely fashion.

School districts also are more likely to adopt those reforms which least disrupt existing cultural systems and patterns of meaning and power. The meaning systems which drive change processes must be responsive to or at least hospitable to the new notions being introduced; if they aren't, or if they can't be induced to be so, reform efforts will fail. Cultural approaches to instruction, in particular, are problematic because they call into question the values and beliefs of all involved in the process—especially the Anglos who control the schools. The difficulty is that the power structure in school districts is unlikely to give up control easily. It is easier to deny that culture is relevant than to admit that cultural approaches to instruction generate power struggles between culturally informed vested interests and then cope with the ensuing conflict. This is a principal reason why a reform such as a cultural approach to learning, which was at variance with belief systems and power structures in Pinnacle, simply didn't happen.

Time frames also proved to be a major obstacle; districts want to see results in a hurry, and the timeframe required for the kind of change which cultural approaches required was insufficient—even though Pinnacle devoted 3 years to it, which is a very long time for a school district to keep the faith. It would have taken a very long time, given the well-established patterns of power, resistance, and information control in the district, for cultural approaches to acquire more legitimacy, although they probably would have achieved the results that the Pinnacle staff desired. As a young Navajo teachers' aide in The Learning Circle, a culturally sensitive afterschool program in Phoenix, said:

> If there'd been more programs like Learning Circle when I was a kid, it would have been easier for me. The kids in this program really feel wanted and proud of who they are. And they know about other Indian kids, too. If they'd have been in Learning Circle when they were kids, maybe my brothers wouldn't have dropped out.

NOTES

1. The author gratefully acknowledges the support of the Metropolitan Life Foundation, whose School District/University Partnership provided funds for the researcher's activities during a portion of the study, as well as the University of Colorado's IMPART program, which provided release time for the research. Deep appreciation is owed also to the staff of "Pinnacle" School District, who, although they must remain anonymous, continue to work hard for Navajo children and made this project possible.

2. "Pinnacle" is a pseudonym, as are all other names used in the article, except for that of the author and nationally known figures.

3. As Braroe (1975) points out, construction of partial and biased realities is reciprocal; Indians also construct them about Whites.

4. The Church of Latter Day Saints home placement program, in which Navajo children are adopted by Mormon families so that they can be raised in the LDS Church.

5. Even though Dr. Mason fully supported the notion of cultural compatibility, he was often absent from the district and couldn't give it full attention. He was embroiled as a lobbyist for the district in battles between the state and federal governments over revenue, which kept him in the state capital, working with the state education agency and tax lawyers. As a consequence, the day-to-day operation of the school district was left to Mr. Aspen, but the limits of his authority

were unclear. As a new assistant superintendent, he was reluctant to overstep boundaries, especially when he didn't know where they were.

REFERENCES

Apple, M. W. (1993). *Official knowledge: Democratic education in a conservative age.* New York and London: Routledge.

Au, K. H. (1980). Participation structures in a reading lesson with Hawaiian children: Analysis of a culturally appropriate instructional event. *Anthropology and Education Quarterly, 11,* 91–115.

Au, K. H., & Jordan, C. (1981). Teaching reading to Hawaiian children: Finding a culturally appropriate solution. In H. Trueba, G. P. Guthrie, & K. H. Au (Eds.), *Culture and the bilingual classroom: Studies in classroom ethnography* (pp. 139–152). Rowley, MA: Newbury House.

Braroe, N. W. (1975). *Indian and White: Self-image and interaction in a Canadian Plains community.* Stanford, CA: Stanford University Press.

Breningstall, O. E. (1995). *Matching school and learning: Cultural compatibility at Long View Middle School.* Doctoral dissertation, School of Education, University of Colorado.

Breningstall, O., & LeCompte, M. D. (1992, December). *Constructing success, constructing failure: Culture, achievement and identity among Navajo adolescents.* Paper presented at the meetings of the American Anthropological Association, San Francisco.

Chafetz, J. S., & Dworkin, A. G. (1986). *Female revolt: Women's movements in world and historical perspectives.* Totowa, NJ: Rowman and Allanheld.

Cuban, L. (1990, January). Reforming again, again, and again. *Educational Researcher, 19,* 3–11.

Deyhle, D. (1986). Break dancing and breaking out: Anglo, Ute, and Navajos in a border reservation school. *Anthropology and Education Quarterly, 17,* 111–127.

Deyhle, D. (1991). Empowerment and cultural conflict: Navajo parents and the schooling of their children. *Qualitative Studies in Education, 4* (4), 277–297.

Deyhle, D. (1992, January). Constructing failure and maintaining cultural identity: Navajo and Ute school leavers. *Journal of American Indian Education,* 24–47.

Deyhle, D. M., & LeCompte, M. D. (1994, Summer). Cultural differences in child development: Navajo adolescents in middle schools. *Theory Into Practice, 33* (3), 156–166.

Durkheim, E. (1973). *Moral education: A study in the theory and application of the sociology of education.* New York: Free Press.

Dworkin, A. G. (1986). *Teacher burnout in the public schools.* Albany: State University of New York Press.

Erickson, F. (1987). Transformation and school success: The politics and culture of educational achievement. *Anthropology and Education Quarterly, 18* (4), 336–355.

Foley, D. E. (1991). Reconsidering anthropological explanations of ethnic school failure. *Anthropology and Education Quarterly, 22,* 60–86.

Goodlad, J. I. (1983). *A place called school.* New York: McGraw-Hill.

LaBelle, T. J.(1972). An anthropological framework for studying education. *Teachers College Record, 73,* 519–538.

LeCompte, M. D. (1990, October). *School reform in the 1990s: What's hot and what's not.* Keynote speech presented at the district-wide inservice of "Pinnacle" Unified School District.

LeCompte, M. D. (1994a, Summer). Defining reality: Applying double description and chaos theory to the practice of practice. *Educational Theory, 44* (3), 277–298.

LeCompte, M. D. (1994b, July 28). *How to build a dropout: New perspectives on at-risk students.* Address presented at the Educational Leadership Institute, Nova Southeastern University, Ft. Lauderdale, FL.

LeCompte, M. D., & Bennett DeMarrais, K. B. (1992, Summer). The Disempowering of Empowerment: Out of the revolution and into the classroom. *Educational Foundations, 6* (3), 5–33.

LeCompte, M. D., & Dworkin, A. G. (1991). *Giving up on school: Teacher burnout and student dropout.* Newbury Park, CA: Corwin Press.

LeCompte, M. D., & McLaughlin, D. (1994). Witchcraft and blessings, science and rationality: Discourses of power and silence in collaborative work with Navajo schools. In A. Gitlin (Ed.), *Power and method: Political activism and educational research* (pp. 147–166). New York: Routledge.

LeCompte, M. D., & Wiertelak, M. E. (1994). *Constructing the appearance of reform: Using chaos theory to analyze site-based management, restructuring and shared decision-making.* 1994 revision of a paper presented at the American Educational Research Association Meetings, San Francisco, CA, April 1992.

McNeil, L. M. (1988). *Contradictions of control: School structure and school knowledge.* New York: Routledge.

Moll, L. C. (1990). *Vygotsky and education: Instructional implications and applications of sociohistorical psychology.* Cambridge: Cambridge University Press.

Newmann, F. M. (1981). Reducing student alienation in high schools: Implications of theory. *Harvard Educational Review, 51,* 546–564.

Nieto, S. (1992). *Affirming diversity: The sociopolitical context of multicultural education.* New York: Longman.

Ogbu, J. U. (1978). *Minority education and caste: The American system in cross-cultural perspective.* New York: Academic Press.

Ogbu, J. U. (1987). Variability in minority school performance: A problem in search of an explanation. *Anthropology and Education Quarterly, 18* (4), 312–334.

Puckett, J. L. (1989). *Foxfire reconsidered: A twenty year experiment in progressive education,* Urbana, IL: University of Illinois Press.

Rhodes, R. W. (1988). Holistic teaching/learning for Native American students. *Journal of Navajo Education, 27* (2), 21–29.

Sarason, S. B. (1971). *The culture of the school and the problem of change.* Boston: Allyn and Bacon.

Sizer, T. R. (1984–1985). *Horace's compromise: The dilemma of the American high school.* Boston: Houghton Mifflin.

Tharp, R. G., & Gallimore, R. (1988). *Rousing minds to life: Teaching, learning and schooling in social context.* Cambridge, MA: Cambridge University Press.

Tharp, R. G., Dalton, S., & Yamauchi, L. (1994, August). Principles for culturally compatible Native American education. *Journal of Navajo Education, 11* (3), 21–27.

Trueba, H. T. (1988). Culturally based explanations of minority students' academic achievement. *Anthropology and Education Quarterly, 19* (4), 270–285.

Valentine, C. A. (1968). *Culture and poverty: Critique and counter proposals.* Chicago: University of Chicago Press.

Vogt, L. A., Jordan, C., & Tharp, R. G. (1987). Explaining school failure, producing school success: Two cases. *Anthropology and Education Quarterly, 14,* 277–286.

Vygotsky, L. S. (1962). *Thought and language* (Eugenia Hanfmann & Gertrude Vakar, Eds. and Trans.). Cambridge, MA: Massachusetts Institute of Technology Press.

Vygotsky, L. S. (1978). *Mind in society: The development of higher psychological processes* (M. V. John-Steiner, S. Scribner, & E. Souberman, Eds.). Cambridge, MA: Harvard University Press.

Yamauchi, L. A., & Tharp, R. G. (1995). Culturally compatible conversations in Native American classrooms. *Linguistics and Education, 7,* 349–367.

PART III

REFRAMING THE ISSUES: SPEAKING FROM ELSEWHERE

Those interested in critical, feminist, and antiracist pedagogy are on a search for means to counter dominant ways of speaking about stigmatized groups such as early school-leavers. Some see promise in attempts to reformulate the dominant public discourse by starting with the experience of those on the margins, rather than starting at the center of the policy discourse. There is a substantial tradition in the sociology of knowledge pointing to the importance of "standpoint" in understanding, and to the "epistemological privilege" of the marginalized. Marxist traditions as well as the feminist ones articulated by, for example, Sandra Harding and Dorothy Smith, make the argument that those outside the relations of ruling can see most clearly how work gets done and how social relations are organized. The implication for seeing the dropout problem clearly is to start outside the dominant discourse. How do the marginalized see the problems of school and work? How do they understand the issues involved?

But it is not a simple matter to start our thinking from elsewhere, for every place is subject to dominant modes of speaking and conceptualizing, even if the discourse is refracted through different interests, different beliefs, and different cultures. We speak using the "master's language," to a large extent. There is a danger in seeing the experiences of marginalized groups as somehow more authentic and transcendent of the dominant discourse to a new point of clarity.

We also need to attend closely to the context in which marginalized groups make their voices heard. Writing about the discourse of survivors of incest, rape, and sexual assault, Alcoff and Gray point out:

> Before we speak we need to look at where the incitement to speak originates, what relations of power and domination may exist between those who incite and those who are asked to speak, as well as to whom the disclosure is directed. (1993, p. 284)

With these caveats in mind, is it possible for marginalized groups to counter the dominant discourse? How might such change come about? According to Scott (1991), "change operates within and across discourses": "Subjects are constituted discursively, but there are conflicts among discursive systems, contradictions within any one of them, multiple meanings possible for the concepts they deploy" (p. 793). In other words, marginalized groups interested in reframing the dominant discourse may employ at least two strategies. They may use one discourse against another, and they may take advantage of the contradictions within the dominant discourse in an effort to forge a positive identity for themselves.

The ultimate success of their efforts, though, depends on whether members of a marginalized group are able to fashion a reasonably coherent representation which they recognize as their own, and this in turn would involve coming to terms with differences within the group and even with shifting self-identities (Kelly, 1993b; Kelly, in press, 1996). More importantly, it would depend on others adopting their way of speaking (Davies, 1991, p. 52). In the 1960s, for example, critics of exclusionary schooling practices, such as long-term suspension and expulsion, began using the term *pushout* to describe the early school-leaving phenomenon. The protest movements against racial injustice and the war in Vietnam lent support to the notion that institutions, not individuals, had failed; for a time, public support rallied around the idea of looking at the so-called dropout problem institutionally (Kelly, 1993a, pp. 57–61).

If we do not want obsession with global competitiveness to dictate educational policy, then we need some utopian thinking that would help people imagine alternatives to comprehensive high schools as the solution to our economic problems and also help them re-imagine the conditions under which learning takes place as well as the main purposes and meaning of public schooling.

Self-conscious reflection on our language and theory as well as careful attention to the experience of "other voices" can help us rethink the issues involved in dropping in and out of school, and perhaps start the conversation on a different footing. The chapters in this section take up the challenge of starting from elsewhere, from outside the dominant policy perspective outlined in Part I. They reflect on the possibilities and limitations of doing so, and ask about the implications for curriculum, for schools, and for researchers and public policy.

In Chapter 8, Leslie Roman considers the difficulties of transgression in a world of repression. She names a crisis of representation in a time of "moral panic" and explores the conditions necessary to make criticism and counterhegemonic consciousness possible. Inclusion alone is not enough. A radical democratic politics of speaking with youth can only emerge with shifts in power.

George J. Sefa Dei (Chapter 9) starts with the views of Black youth in Toronto, specifically with their concern to be taken seriously. He questions concepts like self-esteem and participation, which are often used in the literature to explain the phenomenon of dropping out of school. Black youth, he points out, think well of themselves and participate in school and community, but on their own terms. The process of reviving the discourses of these youth is complicated by the way they are the "products of ideological conditioning" and the way they are treated in and "betrayed by" the school. Dei ends with reflections on critical pedagogy and its place in the school.

Shauna Butterwick's (Chapter 10) research starts with the experience of women who have dropped back into the educational system by enrolling in a job training program. She explores what it would mean to have a policy discourse that allows women to interpret their own needs, and the research that helps them to do so, by getting close to the experience of reentry women and trainers and asking how they construe the needs of women. Using Nancy Fraser's analysis of the politics of need interpretation, she contrasts the understandings of the students with the understandings implicit in the Canadian Jobs Strategy, which is the government-run program that funds the training. The program is premised on the assumption that women who are out of work need training and job experience, but Butterwick finds these women articulate their needs in more complex and varied ways. She sees research as part of the struggle for a new articulation of women's needs.

We end, then, on a hopeful note. Research can be part of the solution, not part of the problem. It is situated within the same power relations as the schools, and is by no means simply emancipatory, but it can begin to imagine and rearticulate the meaning of schooling for all young people, and the many roles education can play in their problems and in their growth.

REFERENCES

Alcoff, L., and L. Gray. (1993). Survivor discourse: Transgression or recuperation? *Signs*, *18*(2), 260–290.

Davies, B. (1991, December). The concept of agency: A feminist poststructuralist analysis. *Social Analysis, 30*, 42–53.

Kelly, D. M. (1993a). *Last chance high: How girls and boys drop in and out of alternative schools.* New Haven, CT: Yale University Press.

Kelly, D. M. (1993b, Spring). Secondary power source: High school students as participatory researchers. *The American Sociologist, 24* (1), 8–26.

Kelly, D. M. (in press, 1996). Warning labels: Stigma and the popularizing of teen mothers' stories. *Curriculum Inquiry.*

Scott, J. W. (1991, Summer). The evidence of experience. *Critical Inquiry, 17*, 773–797.

CHAPTER 8

Debating "Dropouts": The Moral Panic and the Spectacle Over "Youth at Risk"

LESLIE G. ROMAN

The commonly repeated admonition "Don't make a spectacle of your-self!" functions as one of the ordinary discursive contradictions youths face when they attempt to enter the symbolic and political order called adulthood. The moment of their contested entrance into civil society, with its attendant rights, privileges, and enfranchisement, is commonly represented in various forms of official discourse as a moment of both transgression and repression.[1]

In the best of times, the category "youth" gets articulated as an absent presence. In times of moral panic,[2] however, youth is "known to" adults as a visible spectacle, invoking either a familiar nostalgia for the times of "outlandish fun"[3] and "momentary but irresponsible abandon" or a strange iconography of late modern society in crisis (Hebdige, 1988). Lately, this articulation of the discursive category of youth functions in particular reified representations as a metaphor for the alleged lack of stasis in the family, the school, the inner city, and/or the nation.

Youth is a landscape for journalists, social workers, media, social scientists, and educators and, simultaneously, an inaudible if not totally repressed voice in public debates over concerns that crucially affect their conditions of existence and, hence, the quality of their lives. The missing presence of youths themselves (as speakers with political legitimacy and unique epistemic standpoints) from most forums in which they are the literal, metaphorical, and political subjects should not go unremarked. The "dropout" debates are no exception. That youth functions as a signifier and a subject of much speculation, research, theory, and social concern raises important ethical, methodological, and political questions for all (myself included) who have benefited either from theorizing about "the youth question" or from playing the role of political pundit in the latest moral panics over youth at risk (e.g., for dropping out, teen pregnancy, teen suicide, spectacular youth subcultures, gang violence, juvenile delinquency, or becoming latch-key kids).

Yet merely including youths at the table during state policy debates will not necessarily resolve the crisis of representation raised by the issue of their politically disenfranchised, trivialized, or silenced voices. Those questions, which are mystified by the moral panic of youth at risk, are not answered simply by suggesting that youths advocate or speak for themselves, since being taken seriously as legitimate speakers requires conditions of enunciation, addressivity,[4] and audience that make criticism and counterhegemonic consciousness possible (McGee, 1992, p. 121).

Researchers, relative to many other agents of the state and private-sector actors (including local governments, businesses, and/or multinational corporate interests) may have little power to make "real" things happen in the "real world" of policy debates. But if researchers hope to challenge the paternalistic illusion that those adults (including ourselves) empowered as civil servants or other agents of the state really do know best, and if we refuse to demystify the discourses of official policies that function as moral panics that construct youth, then are we not reinstituting the hierarchy between legitimate knowledge and transgressive spectacle? It might be argued that such a hierarchy is an inevitable outcome of age-related power differentials. Such an argument, however, does not address the ethical consequences of researchers of youth failing to clean up the "adult mess" of the ideologies underlying official discourses (J. Willinsky, personal communication, 24 September 1994).

Within the contested space of unequal power among the various parties of the state, researchers have an ethical responsibility—however contradictory and complex—to call into question the position of agents of the state (i.e., the position that makes the official spokesperson of the youth at risk moral panic possible in the first place). It is one thing to participate as an analyst, researcher, or policy maker who largely accepts the terms of the debate as they are constructed in official discourses; it is quite another to participate while thinking against the grain.

By thinking against the grain, I mean developing the epistemic, methodological, and political stances to alter, as well as challenge, official policy discourses that naturalize the spectacle of youth at risk. I argue that, when researchers and policy makers create youths as subjects at risk, they also become subjects of blame and pathology and thus are constructed as deserving of particular paternalistic state interventions (see Chapters 3, 5, and 6; Goode & Ben-Yehuda, 1994; and Lipsitz, 1994). Such constructions not only trivialize or silence the voices of youth altogether, they also distract from the larger structural realities of late capitalism and longstanding inequalities of distributive and social justice which are the real and complex culprits with respect to the problems young people face today (Fine, 1991, 1993; Lesko, 1992).

To put it another way, no matter how much any of us might strive to include the actual voices of youths—a step some might argue is worth taking in books such as this—inclusion alone is insufficient to prepare the ground for radical democratic empowerment of youth's voices. Critically deconstructing moral panics about youth is one necessary (but insufficient) condition of enfranchising young people. It is a first step toward overcoming institutional deafness. In this chapter, I sketch what is involved in taking such a step. I offer some provisional ways of semiotically critiquing the moral panic over the "youth at risk of dropping out of school" debates and acknowledge the ethical and methodological dilemmas involved in the interaction between research on youth as the voice of critique and research as the voice of adult paternalism. I turn my attention to one specific example of a contemporary moral panic: the moral panic over youth at risk for dropping out of schools as evidenced in *A National Stay-in-School Initiative* (Employment and Immigration, 1990), hereafter referred to as the *Initiative,* sponsored by Employment and Immigration Canada (EIC). This moral panic attempts to secure public consent for what I call ideological and textual closure with respect to how the problem is framed. In the conclusion, I will discuss some implications that follow from the provisional framework for the semiotic analysis of moral panics developed in this chapter. I will show how such an analysis is a necessary but insufficient condition for enabling academic researchers to forge a radical democratic politics of speaking with youth (Roman, 1993a; 1993b, 1993c, p. 82).[5]

TOWARD A SEMIOTICS OF MORAL PANICS

The power of moral panics comes from an ability to create imaginary positions that redefine and rearticulate popular common sense, particularly through linguistic or discursive invocations of identities. Indeed, "the public" or "the people" have been well discussed by both cultural studies analysts and feminist analysts in relation to grand-scale discourses such as Thatcherism (Hall, 1984, 1988) or Reaganism (Apple, 1993), and the backlashes they have produced against the gains of progressive movements (Faludi, 1991; Fraser & Gordon, 1994).

Far from being immune from recent backlash discourses, youth have been at the center of them: they are pejoratively constructed in both the popular media and academic research as subjects of "raging hormones," adolescent transgression, and perpetual infantalization (Lesko, 1992; G. Lipsitz, 1994; Whatley, 1988). Yet such discourses often belie the material realities of the 1990s brought on by global "restructuring"—a euphemism for the effects of de-industrialization which result in poverty, power-lessness, and mass unemployment among significant sectors of youth (Gaines, 1994; J. Lipsitz, 1991; G. Lipsitz, 1994).

This raises the following question: How do discourses over youth at risk work to construct social subjects in particular contexts? While youth per se are not the subjects of Hall's analysis of the ideological workings of Thatcherism discourse, his historically specific approach to the processes of ideological articulation and rearticulation is germane. For example, Hall (1984) argues that Thatcherism fractured public support for the wel-fare state and a social democratic consensus by rearticulating demands for law, order, social discipline, and a Keynesian free-market, demand man-agement economy, as well as a virulent racism and ethnocentric national-ism directed against Black immigrants. He shows how Thatcherism did so: through a populist discourse and program that strung together several problematic and often contradictory imaginary positions for people to take up (or refuse): "The self-reliant and self-interested tax payer—the Possessive Individual Man [sic]; or the concerned patriot or the subject passionately attached to individual liberty and passionately opposed to the incursions . . . of the state; or the respectable housewife; or native Briton" (Hall, 1984, p. 15). Using Laclau's (1977) notion of "condensed connota-tions," he shows how these imaginary positions trigger and connote one another in a chain of linked interpellations which constitute the "imagi-nary"—the so-called unity of the discourse, linking the speaker to the spoken, as well as one site to another: "The liberty-loving citizen is *also* the worried parent, the respectable housewife is *also* the careful manager of the budget, the solid citizen is *also* proud to be British" (Hall, 1984, p. 15 [Emphasis in original]). Hall argues that subject positions are neither fixed nor free-floating; thus, they can be fought by taking consciously counterhegemonic standpoints (Hall, 1984). He does not treat ideologies or discursive subjects as preestablished or as unified by an uncontradictory set of ideas, thus pointing us away from the static, deterministic, and uni-versalizing tendencies of most approaches to "youth" and "adolescence."

His largely Gramscian reading of ideology and its discursive functions invites us to examine not only the general features of moral panics over youth as ideological discourses, but also to examine how these features are transformed by the "historical specificity of the contexts in which they become active" (Hall, 1986a, p. 23).

One critical dimension of Hall's conceptualization is undeveloped. Although he uses the language of subjects taking up subject positions, which is suggestive of the actual performative dimensions of discourses, he does not develop this point in relation to his discussion of the articulations of Thatcherism as an ideological discourse. In other words, he does not show how, semiotically, Thatcherism performs these subject positions. This undeveloped dimension of Hall's work takes center stage in the work of many feminists and cultural studies analysts (Alcoff, 1991/92; Butler, 1992; de Lauretis, 1984 & 1987; Fraser & Gordon, 1994; Roman, 1988; Roman & Christian-Smith with Ellsworth, 1988; Roman & Stanley, 1994).

As poststructural feminist Judith Butler (1992) argues so persuasively, the material or linguistic assertion of identity is an occasion for the performative invocation of an identity. Invocations of identities in discourses produce occasions for the enunciation and enactment of desires for community, affiliation, recognition, and commitment, while at the same time they articulate the terms of marginalization and exclusion. This kind of approach to discourse points to the strategic value of analyzing official policies as occasions for the invocation of youth as a category. It also legitimates the urgent need to deconstruct semiotically how categories such as youth are operationalized in state policies which are, after all, a kind of official performance. Semiotic analyses are significant to the process of showing how such categories evoke particular affective investments, memories, and ideologies of what it means to be constituted as "youth," while at the same time these categories totalize and render essential the differences within them that are troubling to them. I now turn to the semiotics of moral panics as a particular set of discursive performative conditions.

I outline several identifiable semiotic features that appear to function in moral panics as performative conditions for establishing modes of voice, addressivity, and enunciation. To win people's hegemonic consent to particular notions of society, moral panics must create an affective identification between the text and those who interact with it. By modes of voice, I refer to something more than genres, styles of speaking, or discursive production; I mean the manner in which the form of the discourse stages and sets epistemic limits on how a particular discourse (in this case, a moral panic) establishes its authority to create a sense of social crisis, as well as how it can be spoken, heard, and responded to by those it attempts to inscribe as its subjects. I argue that these features operate more generally to distinguish moral panics from other discursive formations.

THE SEMIOTICS OF AFFECTIVE CONSENT

What makes a discourse official has a great deal to do with how the bounds of dominant and subordinate knowledge are defined, legitimated, and transformed in struggles for hegemony. In several respects, moral panics can be regarded as a subset of official discourses. First, both official discourses and moral panics may emerge in the context of state policy making. Second, both kinds of discourse may share some similar features and codes in terms of how they work ideologically. For example, as James Donald (1981) observed,[6] following many of the insights of Frank Burton and Pat Carlen (1977) who extend Barthes's (1974) analysis of textual codes, official discourses rely on two codes that move their interested knowledge claims toward their apparently inevitable conclusion:

> The proiaretic composes the text into already known narrative patterns; the hermeneutic constantly reformulates the problem that is the impulse of the narrative, poses and reposes the teasing enigma which must finally be resolved. These two codes create a discourse of tautology which appropriates the problem in three stages—i) it theorizes a beginning; ii) it structures an argument; iii) it attempts a resolution. (Burton & Carlen quoted in Donald 1981, p. 105)

It is safe to assume that moral panics, like other official discourses, follow the progression of formulating a problem, theorizing its beginning, and moving toward its apparently inevitable resolution. This pattern, Donald shows, will often be repeated in sections of policy documents covering topics other than those presented in their main argument. The purpose of such a progression (as well as the codes) is to begin with "apposite history, which establishes when the debate began and who has the authority to initiate it" (1981, p. 105). Not every official discourse, however, rises to the emotional or affective tenor of a moral panic. It is thus important to determine under which conditions official discourses become moral panics and how their discursive forms may vary from those of other official discourses.

THE SEMIOTICS OF FEAR

Moral panics can be distinguished from other official discourses in that they produce subjects which are to be the focus of fear and moral consternation—this is a prelude to such subjects being objects of state intervention/explanation. For moral panics to be successful, first they have to engage people's attention and they then have to create for them polysemic possibilities for identification with the named "crisis" (Fiske, 1987; 1989a & 1989b). In short, they must scare people, and they do this by creating "others" who are constituted as fundamentally different from the "official" voice.

One common semiotic feature of moral panics is the reification of the supposed differences between those constructed as other and those so constructing them. Another common semiotic feature of moral panics has to do with keeping the other the subject of pathology, deviance, or blame so as to render it constantly and irredeemably alien. Of course, the flip side of this practice normalizes those in power by regularizing their so-called positive attributes of character, demeanor, cultural and socio-economic background, and so on.

But even moral panics are not free of contradictions both within and in relation to other competing discourses.[7] Moreover, it is difficult to identify with constantly dehumanizing language. For moral panics to be successful in many diverse contexts, they must be inspired by personalism, as is evidenced by first-person narrative styles of authority (e.g., Reagan's fireside chats, or heated exchanges between Canada's liberal leader and former Prime Minister Mulroney, who was accused of selling out the country by supporting the North American Free Trade Agreement). They can even become confessional and evoke what I call a secular evangelical mode of address, which obscures or mystifies the material location of the speaker/addressor, causing listeners, readers, or viewers to distrust the truth-value or epistemic status of the speaker's claims.[8]

MORAL PANICS AT THE CROSSROADS OF HISTORY AND POWER

My argument about the semiotics of moral panics is necessarily provisional because moral panics do not articulate the same content or take the same form transhistorically; rather, they occur at the crossroads of historical contexts and are embedded in particular power relations. Thus, I do not lay claim to an exhaustive or absolutist explanation of the semiotic features of moral panics, since these occasions are historically constructed in the dynamics and relations of everyday institutional practices. However, in moral panics, as in all performances of discursive and ideological practices, located and interested speakers make claims to represent the "real" or "reality" (whether through a discourse defining the subject's "needs" or "social problems") and thus become part of a broad struggle for hegemony. As it is also the case with other ideologies, the discursive operations of moral panics make it possible for people to "make sense" of their everyday experiences, to frame their options, and to learn (or be mystified by) other ways of acting upon the world (Hall, 1986a; Rizvi, 1993).

At any historical juncture, the context for enacting a particular moral panic takes on its own distinctive moments of articulation even as it may rearticulate residual elements of common sense. For example, as Phil Cohen (1987) observes, popular racism in its modern form no longer requires people to express the stigmatizing references to visible color differences or alleged physiological differences between so-called races—expressions that characterized the nineteenth century biodeterministic discourse of popular racism. Instead, new emergent references to alleged "cultural deficits" or "differences" can now do the same job: "[n]ames and modes of address, states of mind, clothes and customs, every kind of social behavior and cultural practice have been pressed into service to signify this or that racial essence" (1987, p. 14). Thus, if articulations of moral panics share some semiotic features of past discourses while articulating contemporary or emergent ones, then it makes sense to turn our attention to the operations of one such panic—the construction of youth at risk, which in some general way is as old as the invention of adolescence itself, but recently has even been seen as a metaphor for a nation at risk in a global economy (Enright, Levy, Harris, & Lapsey, 1987; Offer & Schonert-Reichl, 1992).[9]

Noise of Moral Panic: National *Stay-in-School Initiative*

To challenge the truth of the *Initiative* (Employment and Immigration Canada [EIC], 1990) is not to assert that it is all lies or a conspiratorial imposition of dominant groups' interests. Instead, to challenge its truth is to demonstrate how it works as text. This means challenging the conditions, definitions, effects, and legitimacy of its knowledge, and examining the institutional context in which it was produced, regulated, distributed, and circulated. In what follows, I offer some tools for a reading that goes against the grain of the *Initiative*. I provide examples of how, in the written text, youths are constructed as metaphorical, literal, and political "problems" for the state. I show how Canada rearticulates its status as a nation-state in the context of a post-Cold-War global economy, primarily by making youth a metaphor for socio-economic dysfunction partially arising out of late capitalism.

One way of demonstrating this last point about the referential context for the discursive construction of Canada as a nation-state is to analyze how the apparently benign words "I," "we," and "our" function in the construction of "truth." Let us examine one strategic occasion for the invocation of an invisible "we." For example, at first glance, the *Initiative's* foreword concludes in a straightforward manner. It is signed by Barbara McDougall (Minister of Employment and Immigration in 1990), clearly naming her the author of the comments: "I urge your support and participation. Our youth and our education system deserve it" (EIC, 1990, p. 3). The use of the first-person pronoun, "I" exemplifies the mode of the personalistic mode of voice and appears to be quite straightforward if taken only on its own; this is the voice of the Minister of Employment and Immigration. But this voice and its exhortation must not be taken to signify only Barbara McDougall, since the comments preceding it in the foreword authorize not just her personal voice but the body politic. In other words, the "we" signifies particular linked interpellations of author and reader, state and citizen, adults and youth, state and youth, and so on in specific connotations. These connotations imply that various normative subject positions endorse the specific way in which "reasonable citizens," "concerned parents," and, perhaps most important, those who are members of a "nation that cares" should respond to the alleged crisis of increasingly high dropout rates among teenagers in Canada: "No nation that cares for its youth and its future can be indifferent to thousands of teenagers dropping out of high school in times like these" (EIC, 1990, p. 1).

Indeed, this last quotation begins with what Laclau (1977) calls a "condensed connotation" (i.e., the "caring nation"). The caring nation is composed of citizens who are not "indifferent to" youth—citizens who are also concerned school officials, fearful parents, and responsible professionals in business, welfare agencies, and labor who rise to the challenge of "attacking" the alleged crisis of youths who drop out of school "by the thousands" (EIC, 1990, p. 3). The caring nation is also composed of adults who can see through "times like these," thus signifying an imaginary "we" who must now prepare for the uncertainties of Canada's future in the 1990s.

The vague temporal reference to "times like these" evokes the fear surrounding the present economic recession, even as it suppresses any concrete evidence of the latter's effects on different social classes, genders, and racial groups of youths. Indeed, the recession is an absent presence within the text, functioning as its background, justification, and validation. The important point about the vagueness of such expressions as "times like these" is not merely their lack of concreteness: It is that they refer to a "common-sense reality" outside the text that an implicit "we" (as readers) are presumed to share.

This vague temporal reference is followed immediately by an urgent call to Canadian citizens to seize the present moment, which is erroneously and dramatically presented as a time without historical precedent.

Continuing the oblique reference to the present economic crisis of recession, the *Initiative's* foreword states:

> *As perhaps never before,* Canada in the 1990's needs well educated, well trained people in large numbers. They are indispensable to the productivity gains that our industry must achieve to survive and thrive in a highly competitive world. Yet as matters stand, we could see one million young people abandon secondary school over the next 10 years, seeking to enter the labour market that increasingly views them as functionally illiterate, largely untrainable and mostly unemployable.
>
> *We must act, now.* This paper outlines an initiative by the government of Canada for attacking the dropout problem in partnership with provincial governments, the business community, labour, welfare agencies, parents and youth. (EIC, 1990, p. 3, emphasis added)

The recession's daily structural realities form the missing backdrop that enables the imaginary "we" and "our" to play upon the commonsense anxieties of the subject positions which the text creates for the imaginary citizens which it constructs—imaginary citizens with whom actual readers may finds points of fearful identification. The significance of such phrases is that their naturalizing language invites readers into what Barthes (1974, pp. 97–98) identifies as the "cultural code"—the things and experiences that everybody knows, converting them into "proverbial statements" (1974, pp. 98, 100) or maxims whose repetitions function without question.

The unity of the *Initiative's* discourse works to redefine schools for certain instrumental goals to suit a particular representation of the nation's industrial economic needs, which reifies the category of "youth" as "indispensable" to the "productivity gains of our industry" (EIC, 1990, p. 3). The "caring nation" is one in which the federal government forms "partnerships" with "provincial governments, the business community, labour, welfare agencies, parents, and youth" (EIC, 1990, p. 3). By implication then, the others of this normalizing discourse place Canada at risk of losing not only its economic productivity, but also its moral authority as a caring nation. Objectifying and reifying stigmas get attached to many of the epistemic locations from which the constructed citizens, schools, parents, and, most significantly, youths themselves as "dropouts" might critique their representation. Youths are "viewed" from the labor market, gazed upon as culturally and educationally deficient: they are objectified as "functionally illiterate," "ill-educated," "largely untrainable," and "mostly unemployable" (EIC, 1990, p. 3). From this viewpoint, youth is constituted not only as metaphorical spectacle but also as economic liability.

Hence, the power of the state to speak for youth comes from the effort to "combat the unacceptable dropout rate" (EIC, 1990, p. 9).

This pattern of discursive codes and formulations to both construct and resolve the problem continues throughout the rest of the *Initiative;* its proiaretic and hermeneutic codes have been established in the foreword. Thus, it is not surprising that in subsequent sections which repose the dilemma, youths are the objects of the gaze from the labor market. Indeed, the gaze is explicitly stated as coming from "industry" itself, which represents youths as "trapped in cycles of unstable work and dependency, a situation that will perpetuate low self-esteem, and one that invites increasing problems with illiteracy, innumeracy and poverty" (EIC, 1990, p. 7). But for youth, the price of stigmatization is more than bearing derogatory labels. To understand what other ideological effects are the product of objectification, othering, normalization, and reification, a return to the analysis of the relations among "I," "we," and "our" is necessary.

"We" and "our" do not signify the author of the *Initiative* as individual subject inviting individual readers into a personalized relationship. It is probably safe to presume that when it was circulated, the *Initiative* was redrafted, commented upon, and/or revised by civil servants and politicians, in addition to McDougall herself. Furthermore, given that in some sense it speaks in the name of the Ministry of Employment and Immigration, what is at stake is more than the literal relations between McDougall and individual readers (whether "you," "me," or "the prime minister," for example).

What provides coherence to this unity of "I," "we," and "our" is the shifting conception of the state and its relation to youth, which in turn changes the geography on which youths are charted as discursive subjects. I have quoted instances of a *depersonalized mode of voice,* in which the "we" is present as a subject of enunciation and authority from the state itself, as well as instances of a *personalized mode of voice,* in which the state is made invisible and only Barbara McDougall, as an actor, becomes its nominal subject.

At other times, the state is mentioned explicitly (but only in the passive sense) to indicate that the time has come for some sort of action or leadership: the state is a voice enacted to perform its moral authority in some cloudy but evocative temporal context. The actors within it become token agents superseded by the call for *responsible action, duty, initiative, and leadership.* For example, in the conclusion's framing of "the dilemma," the state is presented as a community of Canadian citizens who are called to redress the risk to the nation that will be brought about by the state of its dropout youth: "*Unchecked,* the current dropout rate implies an unacceptable loss of human potential, higher social costs, and a serious deficit in the supply of skills needed to expand employment, productivity and incomes for *all Canadians*" (EIC, 1990, p. 7, emphasis added). As Donald (1981, p. 104) argues, the fact that the state implicitly signifies "our people" is tautological—the imaginary ideal of the communality of the government and the governed is expressed in the phrase "all Canadians."

To complicate matters further, the call to action at times specifies interests in which the state apparatus is represented in the plural form (*governments*) as one among many implicitly and purportedly equal parties participating in "collective action," deemphasizing its hegemonic role: "Collective action is necessary, now, by governments, educators, the business and academic communities, labour, social agencies, parents and youth" (EIC, 1990, p. 7). At other times, however, the tautology of the collectivity of the governed and government dissolves into one agent— the Government with a capital "G," as vested in the federal government's "national responsibility" to take certain action: "The Government of Canada has a national responsibility to initiate co-operative, consultative action to deal with this labour market problem, taking care always to respect the province's fundamental responsibility for education" (EIC, 1990, p. 8).

The moral agency of the state, however, is not just its performative voice as call to action, social responsibility, duty, accountability, and leadership. In Donald's (1981, p. 104) words, the moral authority of the state mediates two moments of its agency and, I would add, voice: it represents and reproduces its policy making role for the bureaucracy, and its hegemony by constructing the needs of Canada as both (1) the juridically defined state and (2) the "public." Thus, the hegemonic job of the moral category of the state is to sanction the actions of those it nominates as its legitimate spokespersons. This goes a long way in explaining why youths can simultaneously be symbols of the nation's moral and economic future and paternalized discursive subjects of blame, pathology, and deviance.

There is plenty of evidence throughout the *Initiative* of the state endorsing the actions of its apparatus, invoking them as one united voice working "towards a collective solution": "The Government believes this threat [referring to the alleged threat that the presumed secondary school dropout rate "poses to the future of productivity of the Canadian economy"] can best be met through a spirited, imaginative collaboration of many partners in one national enterprise" (EIC, 1990, p. 14). The three-part national initiative (which actually entailed four separate efforts) articulates the state's moral authority to ratify its own actions by expanding the role of business and private enterprise in "partnerships" with local and provincial governments, labor, and others encouraged to participate in efforts to foster "student retention" (EIC, 1990, p. 14). Projected expenditures for a 5-year program included efforts and monies to be directed to the following areas: $166.3 million for the design, assessment, and delivery of counseling and labor market program services at the local level, including consultations of the Canadian Labour Market and Productivity Centre in which "social assistance" recipients, in particular, "could explore possibilities for reinforcing a stay-in-school theme" (EIC, 1990, p. 15); $76.6 million for the mobilization of a nonprofit institution to collaborate with business, labor, the academic community, and education ministries (EIC, 1990, p. 17); $53.5 million for an information campaign targeted at "raising public awareness about the dropout problem" and focusing on "at-risk youth and their parents" in order to develop "realistic career options and the fundamental values of a high school education" (EIC, 1990, p. 17).

A fourth and final effort was the *School Leavers' Survey* (1990, p. 19) conducted after the fact by Statistics Canada (1991) (which was under contract to EIC). The intent of the survey was to estimate for the first time the national magnitude of the "dropout problem," and it served as validation for the *Initiative,* providing both the naturalization of "the reality of a dropout problem" and the means to solve it. Ironically, this effort appears almost as an aside, even though its exaggerated estimates of the dropout rate in Canada served as post-hoc justification for the entire *Initiative* (see Chapter 5). As Donald (1981) argues, the survey is invoked as a "sleight of logic, as both the outside cause of the text and also its guarantee" (p. 105).

The document's final "we" is implicit and thus highly ideological. It relies on a *normalizing mode of voice,* first turning back to Canada as a "nation" and then gazing upon "these youth[s]" who put it at risk. It draws all the dissonant modes of the state's voice and agency which speak on behalf of youth—from the personalistic, to the reifying, to the normalizing—into an imaginary coherence (and possibly into political consensus and collusion): "Canada cannot afford to remain indifferent to the wasted human potential represented by so many young people abandoning their basic high school education" (EIC, 1990, p. 18). In contrast to the previous passage, which gives voice to the "we" as the unified nation, this one, which immediately follows it, acknowledges some vague anxieties that improving retention rates for high-school students might not solve such economic problems as the long-term effects of recession or mass youth unemployment. Although these problems are never mentioned specifically, the state as a moral authority unified in the voice of the "nation," appears to anticipate something less than a Canada that can create full employment for all. It obliquely registers that a caring nation might be at risk for failing some of its youths—"these youth[s]"—more than others. It is safe to say, though, that the discourse works to pull those anxieties out of the light of exposure and to push them into the darkness of a depersonalized implicit "we," as evidenced in the call to "imperative" action on behalf of "these young people": "It is imperative to do everything possible to give *these young people a realistic view of the labour market* and to promote their individual participation and fulfillment" (EIC, 1990, p. 18, emphasis added). The use of the definite article "these" to modify "young people" signals more than youth as a general spectacle for an unspoken national economic recession. It singles out specific youths, those whom "everybody knows" have been constructed earlier in the document as being at risk for poor education and training, for failing to understand the importance of getting a basic high school education (presumably as a result of coming from having had to rely on social assistance), and so on.

Through the condensed connotation of "these youth[s]," certain youths become a voiceless spectacle in the adult world of real policy making and state building. They are represented at once as an economic drain on the economy and as a symptom of an indifferent nation. Tautologically and ideologically, "they" are both the *cause* for the nation's problem and a *symptom* of the problematic nation: they are both those "we" fail and those who are about to fail or already have failed "us." Hence, the noise of moral panic over "youth at risk of dropping out" cannot completely suppress the fact that, as a late capitalist society, Canada is in a state of crisis.

Noise of Moral Panic: Will It Strike a Chord and with Whom?

The *Initiative* appears to speak to its readers in a single unified voice, as if inviting them into the auto-referential terms of the debate. It is crucial to ask what subject has the authority to speak of the "caring nation" as one that presumes that there is a "dropout crisis among youth"? What subject can allege that the job of schools is to define narrowly the purpose of education as training for the labor market and thus negate the value of critical thinking in favor of vocational and technical skills? What subject has the authority to replace the purpose of a liberal education with a technocratically driven education? What subject has the authority to displace onto schools late capitalism's legitimation crisis (which is what results in mass youth unemployment)? What subject has the authority to speak of "our youth," "our education system," "our future," and "our nation" as requiring a purportedly *new and equal* partnership among business, labor, welfare agencies, parents, and youth?

Each articulated combination of signifiers can have different connotations in the text (as well as in the context in which they are read by differentially located readers). On the one hand, "our future" and "our education system" can represent not only the social democratic ideal of a society that belongs to all of its citizens, but also as a society whose institutions are responsive to all its citizens' needs and to whom all its institutions belong. On the other hand, it can also signify the struggles among such conflicting interests as capital and labor; differentially located groups of youth, parents, and schools; and/or welfare agencies and the private sector. In other words, it can exemplify how conflicting and unequal interests can be incorporated into a new discursive unity that unsettles the old social democratic consensus in Canadian education and attempts to win popular support for the economic and political priorities of a new corporatist state.[10]

To ask academic researchers whether the *Initiative* strikes or will strike a chord (and with whom) is in part to engage in debate over how the document is positioned and critiqued, as well as to ask what alternative accounts of it may be offered. It is to ask thorny and difficult questions about the fears and desires to which it may speak about the material contexts that might give it credibility. It means researchers of youth must think contextually about our choices of language, positioning the "I," "we," and "our" within larger visions of social justice, thus making their means and ends explicit. In other words, each occasion for rereading and reframing the *Initiative* can produce opportunities to critique the authority of the speaker and the spoken—each is an opportunity to provide alternative accounts of young people's varied relationships to schooling, domestic and paid labor, and/or unemployment. What language and modes of voice do we use to position our authority and/or that of youths as subjects of our texts? It is to take the risk of speaking differently than do the moral panics about youth at risk to audiences of official power in the state, while realizing that as researchers we cannot speak effectively on behalf of youths without learning (from them) of their various material/political contexts.

CONCLUSION: THE RISKY BUSINESS OF CREATING COUNTERHEGEMONIC INSTITUTIONAL MEMORY

Throughout this chapter, I have argued that researchers of youth have an important role to play in critiquing and demystifying contemporary moral panics that discursively position youth in a struggle that ultimately has material/political, as well as symbolic, consequences. By redirecting our gaze from the spectacle of youth at risk and to both ourselves and to the material/political contexts that produce particular moral panics about youth, we can (however modestly) begin to alter the terms through which public memory is constructed in official policies. The value of such an analysis is ultimately tested in its usefulness in altering the terms of the dropout debate by asking new questions.

What does it mean to speak about or "reframe" youth through existing moral panic discourses? Are there alternative ways of speaking about youths that do not invoke them as spectacle? How can official categories such as "dropouts" be used without lending further credibility to the various institutions and bureaucrats of the state whose documentary evidence often denies the specificities of the local, national, and global economic realities as well the specific differential interests within various groups of youths? What does it mean to be able to speak to those who are agents of the ideological discourses that produce moral panics about youth without succumbing to their language and terms of debate? Will they listen if "we" do not use their language? Can our texts have appeal if we do not use the already familiar rhetoric of "at-risk youth"? How can research about, on, or with youth have empirical credibility in the spheres of the powerful without reproducing the technologies of surveillance and neutral-sounding languages of documentary realism mobilized by the media and bureaucrats? On the other hand, how can our analyses avoid what I have called "discourses of horror and redemption" (Roman, 1993b, p. 214) or (as exemplified in Oprah Winfrey, Geraldo, and so many confessional television shows) the affectively engaging and yet mind-numbing forms of secular evangelism? (Roman, 1996). What can we researchers learn from the popular appeal of such discourses that might make our own critical analyses engage broader audiences? Who is our audience when we enter the murky and contested arena of youth and state politics?

To call our attention to the semiotic features inventing and positioning specific groups of youths in the contest among ideological discourses, policies, and practices is to call into question the role of adults as agents of the state to limit or, worse yet, to deny them opportunities to speak and to be heard in ways that affect positive social change. It is to place ourselves squarely in the adult mess of the ideologies that separate adults from youth (J. Willinsky, personal communication, 24 September 1994). Is debating about dropouts just another occasion for empirical voyeurism, with the primary question being how many "kids" belonging to particular groups are dropping out? Or is it a genuine invitation to open the public debate to youths themselves by laying some of the groundwork necessary for their voices to be taken seriously?

If "we" accept the proposition that when youths make a spectacle of themselves by going out of bounds or out of control that they are doing something more than making interesting or bizarre fashion statements, then we must consider the possibility that such transgressions may represent challenges to particular notions of civility, belonging, and voice. By making a spectacle of themselves, youths make their presence known to the adult world, to those who possess the power to define their needs as well as to limit the effectiveness or deny the legitimacy of their moral and political voices.

Going out of bounds in schools (or quietly leaving them) can take many different gendered, classed, racial, and sexually oriented forms, but as Dick Hebdige (1988) so aptly reminds us, "there is a logic to transgression" (p. 18). Youths become the subjects of consternation, outrage, concern, explanation, and, not inconsequentially, commodification and appropriation. Whether vilified or applauded, philanthropized or harassed, jailed or held out as the hope for the future of their families, schools, and generation, they are exerting the only real power they have in a public debate which simultaneously makes them visible as spectacle and inaudible as serious voices. The net effect is that transgression and youth are rendered as nearly synonymous, thus ironically and all too often ensuring that young people's voices do not get heard in official places of power, where they might contribute to systemic change. When youths are made spectacles by adults as agents of the state, they become subjects of transgression and normalization—subjects to be brought back into the official discursive gaze of counseling and adjustment, law and order, and, finally, civility and normalcy.

To talk about reframing the dropout question for the purpose of more adequately addressing the needs of specific groups of youths requires a shift from constructing youth as spectacle to drawing attention to the ideological workings of moral panics that so position youths. Ultimately, this may mean altogether abandoning uncritical talk of dropouts. Ongoing deconstruction of the discourses that locate youth (as well as adults and other institutional agents of the state) is one way of going beyond both the liberal empirical and the neoconservative discourses which, ironically, unite at this historical juncture to position youths as subjects of blame, deviance, and pathology.

But deconstruction is not an end in and of itself. Critical researchers will have to offer alternative accounts that have explanatory power and that appeal to broad audiences. At this historical juncture in late capitalism, it is politically important to locate what we say about youths in the context of the specifics of a welfare state roll-back and a backlash against the gains made by new social movements. Talk of youth putting the nation at risk of losing its competitive edge in the global economy is emblematic not only of the appeal of the new corporatist state and the authoritarian populism of the Right, but also of the failure of the Left to offer what Hall and Jacques (1990a) call a "popular modernizing rhetoric" to capture public disenchantment with some aspects of the social democratic welfare state in order to inaugurate a new phase of socialist (and I would add feminist) development and an alternative economic strategy (p. 31).

Although moral panics inescapably define all of us in the play of ideological discourses, they have the most powerful effect on those with the least power—youths themselves. These questions remain: Are we, as researchers, prepared to think and act against the grain? Will we join with progressive social movement activists to make some counterhegemonic noise in contexts that reach broad audiences of policy makers and official agents of the state?

NOTES

1. I would like to acknowledge the encouragement and comments given on various drafts of this essay by Lesley Andres, Deborah Britzman, Pam Courtenay-Hall, LeRoi Daniels, Jane Gaskell, Roger Simon, Tim Stanley, Charles Ungerleider, and John Willinsky. Special thanks are also owed to the members of the Gertrude Stein Salon, whose insights sharpened my thinking. A longer and significantly different version of this essay has been accepted for publication in *Educational Theory*. See Roman (1996).

2. The commonly used term in cultural studies for manufactured crises that alter public common sense is "moral panic." It originates in the work of Stan Cohen (1980), who used the term to break away from traditional criminology and sociology of deviance and is further developed by Hall, Critcher, Jefferson, Clarke and Roberts (1978). For Cohen, moral panics were periodic campaigns to regulate various working-class youth subcultures by personifying them in the media or other agencies of social control as the latest "folk devils" of society. My own use of the term draws upon the later work of Hall (1984; 1991; 1992b) and Hall and Martin Jacques (1983; 1990b) who widened the concept to include the articulation of the contradictory interests of gender, sexuality, and nation (along with race and class) as part of the process of ideological commonsense making in both official and popular culture. This formulation provides the basis for my own conceptualization of moral panics, because it is capable of addressing the articulation of a range of conflicting interests within and across such diverse sites as the family, national policies, the welfare state, and the lived cultural formations of particular groups.

3. I note that this expression carries the geographical specter of a transgressive politics of pleasure. See Dick Hebdige (1988) for an analysis of youth as transgressive spectacle vis á vis the notions of trouble and fun (pp. 17–37).

4. "Addressivity" is James Donald's (1981) term for conditions of address and now is widely known in semiotics as a performative condition of speech in different contexts.

5. Elsewhere (Roman, 1993c), I argue that in contrast to the dominant

meaning of "speaking for," which implies that one group's voice can replace and stand for another's, the concept of speaking with others conveys the contradictions of voices in dialogue. Dialogue can occur either through direct interactions with one another or indirectly in a discourse that articulates them as related subjects. I emphasize the conjunctive "with" to suggest that these voices are not necessarily reducible to the same voice or epistemic standpoint and to convey the possibility of shifting alliances between speakers from different and unequal located groups that may or may not create conditions for effective coalitions and positive social transformation.

6. I am indebted to Donald's (1981) semiotic approach to analyzing official policy documents as exemplified in his own deconstruction of the Green Paper, which crystallized the British Right's call to restructure education through identification of an "educational crisis" in the late 1970s.

7. For example, the recent Canadian moral panic over invasion by particular immigrant groups is challenged by countervailing discourses of liberal humanism and multiculturalism, both of which articulate the ideologies of tolerance and respect for cultural differences. Of course, the balance of ideological power is tilted to the right in the context of neoconservative gains and economic retrenchment. For more on these points, see Roman and Stanley (1994).

8. Secular evangelical modes of address denote the powerful effect of testifying in a secular context (such as some television talk shows) as one would in a church or before a religious congregation. Such performances may evoke references to Biblical stories or the language of persecution and redemption. Elsewhere (Roman, 1996), I develop and elaborate this concept more fully by analyzing, among others, one powerful discursive example of secular evangelism witnessed by millions in North America during the televised spectacle of U.S. Supreme Court confirmation hearings of Clarence Thomas.

9. See Enright et al. (1987). They show that during times of economic depression theories of adolescence portray teenagers as immature, psychologically unstable, and in need of prolonged participation in the educational system; whereas during times of war, the psychological competence of youth is emphasized and their need for education is downplayed.

10. In future work, I intend to demonstrate the forging of the new consensus of state corporatism.

REFERENCES

Alcoff, L. (1991/92, Winter). The problem of speaking for others. *Cultural Critique, 23,* 5–32.

Apple, M. W. (1993). Constructing the "other": Rightist constructions of common sense. In C. McCarthy & W. Chrichlow (Eds.), *Race, identity, and representation in education* (pp. 24–39). New York: Routledge.

Barthes, R. (1974). (R. Miller, Trans.). *S/Z.* New York: Hill and Wang.

Butler, J. (1992, Summer). Discussion. *October, 61,* 108–120.

Burton, F., & Carlen, P. (1977). "Official" discourse. *Economy and Society, 6* (4), 377–407.

Cohen, P. (1987). *Racism and popular culture: A cultural studies approach.* London: University of London, Centre for Multicultural Education.

Cohen, S. (1980). *Folk devils and moral panics: The creation of the Mods and Rockers* (2nd ed). Martyn Robertson: Oxford.

de Lauretis, T. (1984). *Alice doesn't: Feminism, semiotics, cinema.* Bloomington: Indiana University Press.

de Lauretis, T. (1987). *Technologies of gender: Essays on theory, film and fiction.* Bloomington: Indiana University Press.

Donald, J. (1981). Green paper: Noise of crisis. In R. Dale, G. Esland, R. Fergusson, & M. MacDonald (Eds.), *Education and the state: Vol. 1. Schooling and the national interest* (pp. 99–114). Basingstoke, UK: The Falmer Press with Open University Press.

Employment and Immigration Canada (EIC). (1990). *A national stay-in-school initiative.* Ottawa: Minister of Supply and Services.

Enright, R., Levy, Jr., V., Harris, D., & Lapsey, D. (1987). Do economic conditions influence how theorists view adolescents? *Journal of Youth and Adolescence, 16* (6), 541–559.

Faludi, S. (1991). *Backlash: The undeclared war against American women.* New York: Crown Pub., Inc.

Fine, M. (1991). *Framing dropouts: Notes on the politics of an urban high school.* Albany: State University of New York Press.

Fine, M. (1993). Making controversy: Who's "at risk"? In R. Wollons (Ed.), *Children at risk in America* (pp. 91–110). Albany, NY: State University of New York Press.

Fiske, J. (1987). *Television culture.* London: Methuen.

Fiske, J. (1989a). *Reading the popular.* Boston: Unwin Hyman.

Fiske, J. (1989b). *Understanding popular culture.* Boston: Unwin Hyman.

Fraser, N., & Gordon, L. (1994). A genealogy of dependency: A keyword of the U.S. welfare state. *Signs, 19* (2), 309–336.

Gaines, D. (1994). Border crossing in the U.S.A. In A. Ross & T. Rose (Eds.), *Microphone fiends: Youth music & youth culture* (pp. 227–234). New York: Routledge.

Goode, E., & Ben-Yehuda, N. (1994). *Moral Panics and the social construction of deviance.* Cambridge, MA: Blackwell.

Hall, S. (1984, July). *Thatcherism and the theorists.* Paper presented at the conference "Marxism and the Reinterpretation of Culture," Urbana, IL.

Hall, S. (1986). Gramsci's relevance to the analysis of racism and ethnicity. *Journal of Communication Studies, 10* (2), 5–27.

Hall, S. (1988). The toad in the garden: Thatcherism among the theorists. In C. Nelson and L. Grossberg (Eds.), *Marxism and the interpretation of culture* (pp. 34–57). Urbana: University of Illinois Press.

Hall, S. (1991). Old and new identities, old and new ethnicities. In A. D. King (Ed.), *Culture globalization and the world-system* (pp. 41–68). London: Macmillan.

Hall, S.(1992a). Cultural studies and its theoretical legacies. In L. Grossberg, C. Nelson, & P. Treichler (Eds.), *Cultural studies* (pp. 277–294). New York: Routledge.

Hall, S. (1992b). The West and the rest. In S. Hall & B. Gieben (Eds.), *Formations of modernity* (pp. 275–331). Cambridge: Polity Press.

Hall, S., Critcher, C., Jefferson, T., Clarke, J., & Roberts, B. (1978). *Policing the crisis: Mugging, the state and law and order.* London and Basingstoke: MacMillan Press Ltd.

Hall, S., & Jacques, M. (1983). *The politics of Thatcherism.* London: Lawrence & Wishart.

Hall, S., & Jacques, M. (1990a). From the manifesto for new times. In S. Hall & M. Jacques (Eds.), *New times: The changing face of politics in the 1990s* (pp. 23–30). London: Lawrence & Wishart.

Hall, S., & Jacques, M. (Eds.). (1990b). *New times: The changing face of politics in the 1990s.* London: Lawrence & Wishart.

Hebdige, D. (1988). *Hiding in the light: On images and things.* London: Routledge.

Laclau, E. (1977). *Politics and ideology in Marxist theory.* London: New Left Books.

Lesko, N. (1992, October). *Mind over matter: Towards a postcolonial theory of adolescent 'development.'* Paper presented at the Curriculum Theory and Classroom Practice Conference, Dayton, OH.

Lipsitz, G. (1994). We know what time it is: Race, class, and youth culture in the nineties. In A. Ross & T. Rose (Eds.), *Microphone Fiends: Youth music & youth culture* (pp. 17–28). New York: Routledge.

Lipsitz, J. (1991). Public policy and young adolescents: A 1990s context for researchers. *Journal of Early Adolescence, 11* (1), 20–37.

McGee, P. (1992). *Telling the other: The question of value in modern and postcolonial writing.* Ithaca: Cornell University Press.

Offer, D., & Schonert-Reichl, K. A. (1992). Debunking the myths of adolescence: Findings from recent research. *Journal of American Academy of Child Adolescent Psychiatry, 31* (6), 1003–1014.

Rizvi, F. (1993). Children and the grammar of popular racism. In C. McCarthy & W. Chrichlow (Eds.), *Race, identity, and representation in education* (pp. 126–140). New York: Routledge.

Roman, L. G. (1988). Intimacy, labor and class: Ideologies of feminine sexuality in the punk slam dance. In L. G. Roman & L. Christian-Smith with E. Ellsworth (Eds.), *Becoming feminine: The politics of popular culture* (pp. 143–184). London: Falmer Press.

Roman, L. G. (1993a). Double exposure: The politics of feminist materialist ethnography. *Educational Theory, 43* (3), 279–308.

Roman L. G. (1993b). "On the ground" with anti-racist pedagogy and Raymond Williams's unfinished project to articulate a socially transformative critical realism. In D. Dworkin & L. G. Roman (Eds.), *Views beyond the border country: Raymond Williams and cultural politics* (pp. 158–214). New York: Routledge.

Roman, L. G. (1993c). White is a color!: White defensiveness, postmodernism, and anti-racist pedagogy. In C. McCarthy & W. Chrichlow (Eds.), *Race, identity, and representation in education* (pp. 71–88). New York: Routledge.

Roman, L. G. (1996, Winter). Spectacle in the dark: Youth as transgression, display, and repression. *Educational Theory 46*(1), pp. 1–22.

Roman, L. G., & Christian-Smith, L., with Ellsworth, E. (Eds.), (1988). Introduction. In *Becoming feminine: The politics of popular culture* (pp. 1–34). London: Falmer Press.

Roman, L. G., & Stanley, T. (1994, April). *Empires, emigrés, and aliens: Young people's negotiations of official and popular racism in Canada.* Paper presented at the conference of the American Educational Research Association, New Orleans, LA.

Statistics Canada. (1991). *School leavers survey.* Ottawa: Ministry of Supply and Services.

Whatley, M. (1988). Raging hormones and powerful cars: The construction of men's sexuality in school sex education and popular films. *Journal of Education, 170* (3), 100–121.

CHAPTER 9

Black Youth and Fading Out of School

GEORGE J. SEFA DEI

> I know we [Black youth] have been saying some of these things about
> the school system for a while now and no one has listened to us. I am
> not sure it is because no one seems to care. Why do you think people
> will take seriously what we say to you now? Maybe I'm a skeptic. I
> personally don't like the term dropout, but we can discuss my reasons
> later. What I want to know is what do we get for speaking out? What
> would come out of your work? . . . Some more silence and denial
> . . . ? (June 12, 1992).[1]

This quote is from a conversation with a Black male who left the
Ontario public school system about 6 years ago over his frustrations with,
as he put it, "what was going on and my desire to regain control over my
life." His comments were made in the course of my explanation of the
objectives of my study about the experiences of Black youth in the school
system and, particularly, why some youth drop out of school. For me, his
comments are significant for the underlying frustrations that he speaks
about, the fact that society in his opinion is not listening to the voices of
its youth.[2]

In June 1991, a confidential study by the Anti-Racist Directorate of
Ontario's provincial Ministry of Citizenship was released to the press. The
report indicated that Black students are dropping out of the provin-
cial school system in much greater proportion than other minorities and
Whites. This study, entitled *Report of the Sub-Committee on Racial Minority
Youth and Visible Minority Youth,* explored the issue of education of racial

minorities and found an overrepresentation of Blacks in vocational schools and an underrepresentation in advanced level programs.[3]

The findings are not unique to Ontario and Canada (see Ontario Ministry of Citizenship, Visible Minority Youth Project, 1989; Pollard, 1989). In fact, it is frequently asserted that one of the most crucial issues facing North American educational systems is the dropout problem (see Conference Board of Canada, 1991; Cadieux, 1991; King, Warren, Michalski, & Peart, 1988). Currently in Canada, it is widely believed that 30% of students do not finish school and that at the present dropout level as many as one million undereducated and untrained youth will have entered the Canadian labor market by the year 2000 (Canadian Association of University Teachers, 1991, p. 5).[4] Many Black Canadian parents and educators have become increasingly concerned about the dropout problem and its effects on their communities (see Toronto Board of Education, 1988). Community leaders point to the disturbing trend of downward mobility among some Black youth as the latter underachieve compared to their first-generation immigrant parents (Editorial, 1991).

Many factors have been suggested as influencing student dropout, ranging from streaming in the schools, poverty, Eurocentrism, White male privilege, and discrimination (Ontario Ministry of Citizenship, 1989; Pollard, 1989). However, many of the analyses overgeneralize without delving into the specifics concerning various social groups in the education system. They fail to adequately explore the questions of class, gender, race/ethnicity, power, and history in the discussion of dropping out, and particularly how students' lived experiences and social reality have contributed to compound the problems of minority education.

As Lawton (1992) points out, much work needs to be done by way of re-theorizing and re-conceptualizing the whole phenomenon of school dropouts. We must move away from the simplistic cause and effect models of behavior in which correlation implies causation. Instead, we need a grounded theory based on students' articulation of their lived experiences and a good conceptual analysis of how the diverse experiences of students inside and outside the school system contribute to dropping out (see also Dei, 1992).

Although I focus on students' subjective lived experiences, I am also interested in the role social structure and culture play in shaping those experiences. By analyzing the subjugated knowledge and discourse of students, I believe we can obtain alternative perspectives on the dropout phenomenon. In providing alternative explanations of how and why the school system produces dropouts, it is necessary to focus on the power asymmetries of relationships structured by race, ethnicity, class, and gender that Black and other minorities experience in the wider society.

It is generally known now that in some Ontario schools a disproportionate number of Black students (both immigrant and Canadian-born)
are assigned to the lowest academic tracks. The practice eventually re-
stricts their educational opportunities and socially segregates them from
mainstream society (see Radwanski, 1987; Solomon, 1992, p. 92). If the
majority of these students in lower academic tracks have relatively "weak
academic abilities" and/or have accumulated fewer credits than other students, what are the structural causes for this?[5] Can any of the causes be
explained by ideological, institutional, or social structural factors? What
do the causes tell us about society, culture, social and individual responsibilities, accountability, and future educational practices? What can the
narratives of students themselves tell us regarding the role institutional
practices like streaming, academic failure, in-grade retention, and biased
curriculum play in students fading out of school?

METHODOLOGY

Since May 1992, with the assistance of four OISE graduate students, I have
interviewed over 150 Black students. This figure includes 22 school dropouts and youths designated "at risk" of dropping out identified through
our ties to the Black/African-Canadian community groups in and near
Toronto, as well as 25 students from various Toronto high schools whom
we interviewed over the 1992 summer holidays. A few of the dropouts
have actually dropped back into school. In September 1992, we began a
series of student interviews with Black youths in four selected Toronto
high schools. The schools were chosen from two school boards to reflect
racial/ethnic position of students and their family socio-economic backgrounds. Within each school, students were selected to provide a representation of male and female students from general and advanced-level
programs, and to include grade 10 and 12 students. The project has also
included an ethnography of the school and a survey. I have sat in classroom
discussions and hung around school compounds and hallways to observe
the varied interactions that take place in the daily life of a school.[6]

Among the students and the actual dropouts interviewed, 145 also
completed a survey which sought firm responses to certain basic questions. The responses of students and dropouts were obtained prior to beginning the in-depth, individual interviews. Of completed surveys, 80
said they were born outside of Canada. Among these, 64 were born in
the Caribbean, 11 in Africa, and 5 elsewhere; 71 came to the country
after 1980. From the total 145 students surveyed, 97 speak English only;
43 students speak additional languages. Sixty-five students took advanced-

level courses. The majority of the students and the "dropouts" (93) do not live at home with both parents. Among the students in the survey, the majority (95) said they knew someone who had dropped out of school. Finally, 47 students admitted they had considered leaving high school.

ON THE CATEGORY OF "BLACK"

"Black" has been defined in this study as students who are of African descent and who identify themselves as such. Since this project began, I have often been asked two questions: Why I am focusing on Black students, and do I see Black students as a homogeneous group? One can interpret these questions as contradictory. Firstly, there is an implicit and mistaken assumption that the dropout issue and the factors that account for it may be uniform for all students. There is a substantial body of literature that emphasizes obvious differences between the educational experiences of Black and non-Black students (see Fine, 1991; Garibaldi, 1988; Goodlad, 1984; Jaynes & Williams, 1989; Kozol, 1991). Second, although Black students are not a homogeneous group, I do believe that there are some commonalities in the educational experiences of students born in Africa and in the Diaspora, or those of mixed parenthood (Black and non-Black). Many of the educational issues these students contend with may stem from the dynamics and the disjunctures of being Black in a White-dominated society (see also Henry, 1992).[7]

(RE)CONCEPTUALIZING SCHOOL "DROPOUTS"

Dropping out is related to the structure, culture, and politics of schooling in our society. To understand this phenomenon, we have to critically explore the intricate link between the social and historical forces of institutional power and how these forces intersect with class, gender, race, and the power relations in school and society.

The school system, as a whole, is filled with dominant group norms and values, stringent policies, and codes of conduct that emphasize student subordination to power structures. Powerful economic, political, and ideological forces influence the schooling processes of subordinate groups in society, relegating them to a marginalized social status (see also Apple, 1989, p. 207). Mainstream society imposes both positive and negative sanctions to induce patterns of behavior that support social and economic systems of inequality. The behavior demanded by the school's social norms sometimes clashes with the behavioral patterns which emerge transpersonally from students who do not identify with the school system.

Some Black students react negatively to the institutional power structure of the school and its rationality of dominance. They employ behavioral tactics that constitute part of an antischool "culture of resistance." It is not coincidental that many students who fade out of school also exhibit what the school system sees as "problem behaviors" (e.g., truancy, acts of delinquency, or disruptive behavior). Rizo [pseudonym] is a middle-aged Rastafarian who dropped out of high school. He is a widely read individual who gave me a lecture on Marxism and economics at the start of our interview. He jokingly pointed out that since I have a grant for my research, I should be paying people for their knowledge and information. Like many other dropouts, (see also Fine & Rosenberg, 1983, p. 6), Rizo is being critical of society and the public school system when he says:

> To me the school typifies everything that goes on in our White-controlled society. The people running the system have an idea as to how people should behave if they want to be part of their buddy–buddy [system]. Those who go astray are pushed aside and made to feel it is their fault or some personal weaknesses in character. There is no serious effort to find out why some of us behave contrary to what is expected of us. (July 7, 1992)

To find out why some Black students see the school as part of White dominance is to understand the "culture of the school" and why certain students resist this culture by acting up or opting out. School "culture" embraces a unique set of core norms and values, well-defined hierarchies of authority, and definitions of what is knowledge, what is good pedagogy, and how students are best assessed and rewarded. Conventional norms about schooling rest on assimilationist assumptions (Solomon, 1992).

To challenge their marginalization and exclusion, and to assert their legitimacy and presence in the school, some students find ways to antagonize and manipulate the authority structures which are perceived as working against their interests. The school system, on the other hand, cannot tolerate any challenge to its established authority and power structures. To do so would be to diminish the school authority's credibility and legitimacy. To counter the threats of rebellious behavior, the school enforces its norms, rules, and regulations. Students who have a hard time identifying with school see its actions as authoritarian and as further evidence of their institutionalized marginalization. Disenchanted with the whole process of schooling, eventually "rebellious" students fade out.

Thus, dropping out becomes, in a sense, a reflection of the student's failure to adapt to the exclusive control over the school by the authority structures. In this context some students explain their leaving school prematurely as the actualization of a desire to be in charge of their own destinies and to confront some of the basic contradictions in society.

Leah is a very articulate youth, born in Canada to parents who came from the Caribbean. In 3 years she was in three different high schools, never finding what she wanted. As she says, "I was looking for something in particular which I never found." Eventually she faded out. Like Rizo, dropping out was to her a political act of resistance to the public school system and its reproduction of Black marginality in the wider Canadian society. She is philosophical about the denial of power to Black people. She talks about the silencing of her political voice in school. She also insists the Canadian state has denied Blacks "strategic resources" either to influence the structures of schooling or to question their marginalization and exclusion from mainstream White society. She talks about her lack of connectedness to the school and the authority structures which contribute to her separation and alienation. She is adamant that a school system, which she sees as a privileged institution, is intended to produce graduates who will be slotted into stratified positions in the workplace and in society in general. Discussing the reasons she left high school, she laments:

> I believe high school, especially, is a processing plant. You walk in there and you're about to be processed and in the end you come out a product, for lack of a better word. Any Black youth will tell you the school atmosphere lacks respect, principle, values, and invades everything about one's character. If you permit it, it totally breaks down and reconstructs another character. . . . I personally think it is wrong. And you never leave high school the way you entered it. A lot of people call it maturity . . . they call it leaving with a greater education. But I don't think so. I think, as a Black person, you leave high school stripped and a part of you does feel raped to a certain point. And I couldn't just deal with that. I could not deal with that. I felt, grade after grade, level after level, something was being chipped away and what was being replaced wasn't great enough. And personally, I just figured I wasn't going to let it happen to me. I could not speak to anyone about it . . . not anyone who had the means to do something. And so I left. (November 26, 1992)

Leah is very philosophical when asked if she regrets dropping out of school:

All I will tell you is that, as a Black student, it [the school system] kills your character, your inner strengths, it kills certain abilities in order to reincarnate you, to turn you into something totally different. It either leaves you with a complex, or a chip on your shoulder . . . whether it be a mental or physical disorder or emotional disorder. It literally takes what used to exist and terminates it. It takes a strong Black person with inner strength to see what the current education system does to you and to leave it. (November 26, 1992)

Leah's sentiments and feelings are typical. One picks up similar concerns in interviews with other Black students about their schools. Black youth will talk about the fact that classroom discourses occasionally spoke to their lived experiences—the fact of being Black, a Black woman, poor, or any form of a minority living in Canadian society. Black students yearn for the schools to reflect the communities in which they live and vice versa, and are very frustrated because this is not happening. Added to these pressures and frustrations is the constant struggle of students to maintain their individual selves and group cultural identities. Students attribute the struggle to negotiate their individual self and group cultural identity to a very narrow school curriculum. Michael, a 19-year-old general-level student, came to Canada from Jamaica nearly 9 years ago. The frustrations and the emotions with which he speaks about the deprivileging of Black peoples' history and contributions to society throughout his public schooling cannot be lost on the astute listener:

I only know about Canadian history, which is White history. I did not learn anything about Black people. And then, probably in the past two years, I would say, we have improved in our geography, but we don't really learn about the cultural background, we just learned about . . . not even the people, but just the city or the country. Basics, nothing deep. Is it tough? I mean, I would like to know more about my history, yes. A lot more. I think I need to know a lot more than I know. (November 15, 1992)

The point worth emphasizing here is that we cannot divorce these experiences of Black students from such behaviors such as truancy, questioning of authority, disrespect for institutionalized power structures, and other rebellious acts which tend to land students in trouble with school authorities. As the school enforces its rules without a simultaneous attempt to address pressing and legitimate student concerns, students lose faith in the system and eventually fade out.

From Leah and Michael we learn that dropping out of school can be a resolution to the deep inner conflicts felt by Black students who feel betrayed by the school system which promised to develop their academic potential, raise their self-concept and self-worth, and build their confidence. At the same time they witness how the system marginalizes their experiences and alienates them with rigid institutional structures. Students exercise every option to respond to the often conflictive relationships to the authority structures of the school. Dropping out is, therefore, seen as breaking out of the shackle of institutional dominance and school control. To some students it is part of the incessant struggle to extricate themselves from a disadvantaged position. School dropouts like Leah see themselves as those who broke their culture of silence, perpetrated through the use of institutionalized power.

Black youth articulate their anger and disappointment in particular at the failure of school authorities to help students facing family and personal problems in the home. Paulette, a mature student now in the final year of her undergraduate university program, dropped out of high school a few years ago. Upon her graduation she intends to do graduate work. So far she has managed to pull herself up through the cracks, thanks in part to an innovative bridging program offered by her university. The program assists mature, disadvantaged, and visible minority students achieve higher education. Although she attributes her decision to "step out" of school to "family and cultural problems," she faults the school for its inability to help her in times of personal crisis. She questions the false separation between school and home, and sees the lack of space for students to talk openly about their personal and home problems as part of a process of silencing students (see also Fine, 1991, p. 77). The narrative of her lived experiences shows that dropping out from school can be related to the political and cultural asymmetry between home and school, and community and schooling. Paulette asks why school has been structured in ways that do not accommodate students experiencing family and personal problems, and argues that the responsibility of the school must not stop at the exit door:

> I was an abused child and I remember running away from my foster parents to hang out with friends and roam the streets. I didn't think it was advisable for me to bring my personal problems to the authorities at school. There was an unwritten code that the school was separate and distinct from the home and that you leave your home problems outside the gate of the school. Sometimes too, because the school system has such low expectations of Black students, you say to yourself, "Why bother?" Discussing your personal problems won't convince anyone that it has a bearing on your academic progress.

Some teachers still see us [Blacks] as innately dumb. . . . (August 31, 1992)

Jermaine, born in the Caribbean, will be finishing high school this school year and plans to go on to university. He thinks he will be successful, and the fact that he is in the advanced-level program has helped. He has also accumulated the required credits. He attributes any success to personal hard work, his parents, and his teachers. But he is critical of one prior experience with a guidance counselor. To him that experience confirms what most Black students say that the school system has very low expectations of them. Jermaine speaks about what might have been:

The advice from the counselor nearly broke my back. I could not believe it. She said I should be making choices guided by what my capabilities are and that she didn't think I can compete in the advanced stream. I will be left behind. I wanted to hear something like: "You can make it just like all the other students there. But you must be prepared to work hard because all those who succeeded worked hard. And I know you can." When I told my mother she was furious and she said, "If that's where you want to be, you damn sure you will be there." (October 20, 1992)

The impact of teachers' low expectations of students must be emphasized. Dennis is an 18-year-old 12th grade student who was born in South Africa but grew up in Canada with foster parents. He discusses how the school's low expectation of Black students can affect the thinking of the students themselves via negative peer pressure (see Fordham & Ogbu, 1986). He argues that negative peer pressure tends to diminish Black students' propensity to succeed academically. For those who beat the odds to do well academically, there can be an emotional and psychological cost. Dennis points out that the achieving student, who hits the books at every opportunity, runs the risk of ridicule from his or her peers because "[they] think I want to be accepted by my teachers or I want to impress them."

Elaine is a 12th grade student who was born in Guyana. She laces her discussion of teachers' low expectations of some students with comments on sexism at her school:

I think in our school . . . especially . . . where the field is more dominant in men, and when a woman goes in and tries to succeed, it's pretty hard. Because . . . I experienced it [male teacher bias against female students] when I was in Grade 10 math . . . if I recall correctly, I was probably the only Black girl in this math class, advanced. And,

I used to always put up my hands to ask the teacher a question, because I don't think whatever he did was correct. And I would have
my hands up for, like five minutes, and somebody else at the back of
the room would have their hands [up] for, like [snaps fingers], just a
minute or so, and it's a male, doesn't matter whether it's Black or
White, but he [the teacher] would prefer going to that person. (February 25, 1993)

BLACK YOUTH AND CRITICAL CONSCIOUSNESS

Black youth share the aspirations, hopes, and dreams of many Canadians:
to be what they want to be and to be respected and acknowledged by
family, school, and society. Many of them espouse high educational aspirations when asked to reveal their life goals and ambitions. Unfortunately,
there is a feeling of dissonance as students question whether these aspirations are attainable at all, particularly if things remain the way they are.
This is, in part, because everyday messages and commonsense ideas con-
veyed to Black youths by various institutions of society make students feel
marginalized. Thus, to understand dropping out from school is also to
problematize social structural conflict. Current harsh economic realities
mean that students who find jobs want to hang on to them and continue
to work while going to school. Although it is possible that the current
unfavorable economic climate may influence a few students to stay in
school longer or to drop back in, there are many students who find de-
plorable economic conditions legitimate grounds on which to question
the relevance of education.

Julian, 17, a Grade 10 and 11 student, struck me as a student who did
quite a bit of reading. He too epitomized the deep internal conflicts of
Black students in the inner city who come to grips with economic hard-
ships while still at school. I will always remember his powerful response
to my question as to where he got his ideas from. He told me simply: "I
live it":

Sometimes I think about leaving school, because really what's the
point? You can go to college and get educated—I know people like
that—and they don't have a job. So sometimes they just want to go
and make money, you know, but . . . I don't think I'm serious about
leaving school. Sometimes I say, yeah I'm going to quit school when
I get pissed off at my teachers or something. But I don't think seriously about it . . . 'Cause all the time we're in school, we're not making any money. And just because you're in school it doesn't mean that
you stop eating while you're going to school. So you know? If people

were paid to go to school, a lot more people would be in school right now. Because they wouldn't have had to leave school to find a job so that they could take care of themselves and so on. A lot more people would still be in school, you know. (August 27, 1992)

The fact that high school dropouts usually develop what Fine (1991) characterizes as a "budding, confused, and critical social consciousness" (p. 126) has been observed by many others (see Weis, Farrar, & Petrie, 1989). But what accounts for this critical (and sometimes conflicting) consciousness? Questions of compliance to the whims of mainstream society, and the low expectations that some in society and in the schools have of Black students, both account for the critical consciousness of students who drop out of school. The rich narratives of their lived experiences reflect how their ideological conditioning is "out of sync" with social reality. As Fine and Rosenberg (1983) pointed out in another context, when school dropouts launch a powerful critique of the school system, they are fully aware of the contradictions between their academic learning and actual lived experiences, and specifically, of the fact of being Black in a White-dominated society.

Many studies show that immigrant Black youths from low-income households have internalized the folk theory of education and the achievement ideology more than any other groups in society (see Fine, 1991, p. 181; James, 1990; Solomon, 1992, p. 94). Education is generally seen as driving social and economic mobility (see Kluegel & Smith, 1986; Marable, 1985; Ogbu, 1978). Many Black students and parents, therefore, have positive educational aspirations (see Garibaldi, 1992, p. 7). Yet Black students disproportionately drop out of the school system. Does this puzzle anyone?

For many Black youths, it is a daily struggle to respond to the contradictions in the achievement ideologies transmitted by the school and the social reality. Although students realize education is essential, they have the idea that in a society structured by racial, ethnic, class, and gender oppression, education may not be sufficient for advancement. Students who are significantly influenced by such thoughts may decide to devote some of their energies to "more rewarding" out-of-school pursuits as alternative strategies for social advancement and survival (see Solomon, 1992).

CONCLUSION

When Black youth are allowed to define and talk about themselves, and to articulate problems in their own language and according to their experiences in the schools, they construct self-identity and give meanings to events that shed light on the dropout dilemma. The narratives of Black youth point out that the search for an understanding of the school dropout dilemma must be rooted in the institutionalized policies and practices of exclusion and marginalization that organize public schooling and characterize the out-of-school environment of many students. This observation calls for a critical analysis of the institutional power structures in which learning, teaching, and administration of education take place in the public school system, and how these structures function to alienate some youth while engaging others.

When Black youth speak of being bored, frustrated, and alienated from the school system, they are referring indirectly to social structural conditions. We must be critical of attempts to view dropping out from a "pathological perspective" and to "individualize" the problem (see also Lomotey, 1990; Trueba, Spindler, & Spindler, 1989). Such approaches legitimize a view that it is students and dropouts, rather than the processes of schooling, who must change. These approaches consequently suggest that schools and society have to be absolved of any responsibility for the conditions that make dropping out a viable option for students. As Fine (1991) has rightly pointed out, there is a powerful message for educators when students fail to do homework or pay attention in class, when students prefer to hang out in the hallways instead of being in class, when students skip classes, when students show a general lack of respect for school rules and regulations, when students cannot connect or identify with the school. We need to view these behavioral patterns and strategies critically as students' ways of questioning the very foundations of schooling in our society.

Elsewhere (Dei, in press), I have critiqued conventional theories and models of school dropouts. For instance, I critique Finn's (1989) frustration-self-esteem model and participation–identification model, and Le-Compte and Dworkin's (1991) deviance theory of dropping out for their failure to focus on the actors' viewpoints and lived experiences. These studies also fail to situate these experiences within the broader framework of the institutionalized structures in which learning, teaching, and the administration of education take place in schools (see also Manski, 1989; Stage, 1989; Bickel & Papagiannis, 1988).

Student narratives provide us with alternative perspectives on why some youth easily disengage from school. Although students' explanations of dropping out may not fit neatly into theoretical boxes, it is clear that their "bodies" are deeply implicated in the processes of public schooling. Previous theoretical models of school dropouts have a reified notion of social reality. Students are presented as "disembodied." Particularly for minority students, the issues of gender and family socio-economic background present additional challenges of intersecting and shifting marginalities in the school environment. Black youths are continually negotiating and contesting their marginality in the mainstream culture of the school. For some youths and school dropouts, leaving the school system prematurely must be understood from the marginalized resistance viewpoint. Leaving constitutes resistance to students' marginality and peripherality, defined by the intersections of race, gender, and family economic status.

The narratives of Black youth suggest the need for alternative teaching and learning practices in the schools as a possible solution to the problem of students' marginality in the schools. The question is: How can critical progressive forms of education assist in searching for answers to practical questions about the schooling of Black youths in the Canadian society? At a general level, we need to develop alternative strategies for cooperative education, and emphasize collaborative group learning among students and teachers. Furthermore, teaching an inclusive curriculum as praxis would allow students to examine their own educational histories, and the experiences of living in their communities. Teachers could lead the way to resurrect the subordinated knowledge of their students. Progressive educators would have to redouble their efforts to challenge how and why alternative and oppositional viewpoints, perspectives, and discourses within the schools are made peripheral. Critical pedagogues should ensure that Black students' voices and experiences are brought from the margins to the center of mainstream knowledge. Educators must value all ways of knowing and affirm every student's ability to make sense of her or his world. Educators must also engage students to speak from their respective social locations and to articulate emancipatory discourses to provide counterdefinitions to those portrayed in the curriculum (see Estrada & McLaren, 1993). Educators should also continue to search for ways to develop a suitable match between youth cultures and the culture of the school (see also Nieto, 1992).

Specifically, I believe schools should explore ways to incorporate African-centered perspectives and other forms of cultural knowledge in the education of youth. Educators must target both the official and the unofficial school curricula for meaningful changes that reflect the diverse cultural and historical experiences of the student population. Canadian students must learn about more than simply the contributions and achievements of non-Europeans in world civilization. For example, they must learn to value African cultures and histories in their own right. The schools could teach about the cultural heritage of all students and about the values of human coexistence with nature, group unity, mutuality, collective work, and social responsibility (see Dei, 1994a). This is essential if we are to build a community atmosphere in the schools where there is mutual respect for all members. In line with the proverbial African saying that it takes a whole village to educate a child, an African-centered pedagogy should stress the role and importance of the "community" in the education of all children. We should thus promote the active involvement of the community in the schooling process (see Asante, 1991; Henry, 1992; Karenga, 1988),[8] and work hard to ensure that our schools become "working communities."

NOTES

1. Unless otherwise identified, quotations in the text are from interviews and field notes from research conducted during the period from May 1992 to February 1993 with actual school "dropouts," youths designated "at risk" of dropping out, adult learners, and high school students.

2. This paper discusses the preliminary findings of an ongoing 3-year study examining Black students' perspectives on school dropout. The project has been using the narratives of the experiences of students and dropouts in a Canadian inner-city public school system to explore the influence of race/ethnicity, class, gender, power, and social structures on dropping out of high school. Students' narratives and ethnographic observations of the schools suggest that our understanding of the school dropout dilemma must be grounded in the institutionalized policies and practices of exclusion and marginalization, which organize public schooling and structure the out-of-school environment of some students. Black students view dropping out as both a response and a solution to social structural contradictions.

I would like to acknowledge the assistance of the many graduate students at the Ontario Institute for Studies in Education (OISE) who are working on various aspects of this longitudinal study: Deborah Elva, Gabrielle Hezekiah, Nigel Moses, Anita Sheth, Jennifer Pierce, Elizabeth McIsaac, Josephine Mazzuca, Thato Bereng, Rinaldo Walcott, and Bobby Blanford. I am particularly grateful to Deborah Elva, Nigel Moses, Anita Sheth, and Bobby Blanford for their critical comments on an earlier draft of this paper. This research project is being funded by the Social Sciences and Humanities Research Council of Canada (SSHRC), and the Ontario Ministry of Education and Training (Transfer Grant to OISE).

3. In 1993, the Ontario Ministry of Education and Training abolished the practice in the public school system where students entering 9th grade were placed in one of three different course levels, based on ability: the basic or vocational level, the general four-year level, and the advanced level, which includes courses leading to university entrance. This is a process referred to as "streaming."

4. It has been pointed out that all this should be placed in the context of the fact that more than 60% of new jobs being created in Canada need at least a high school education (Conference Board of Canada, 1991; Cadieux, 1991, p. 1).

5. To illustrate with a specific case, what seemed to have been sidestepped in

the furor following Radwanski's (1987) report was a critical questioning of the processes and procedures through which students are assigned to the various tracks in the schools.

6. In subsequent phases of the project we have been interviewing parents, teachers, school administrative staff, and a small sample of non-Black students as a way to cross-check what the main interviewees have said to us.

7. As I have pointed out elsewhere (Dei, 1994b), a critical examination of the school experiences of Black/African-Canadian youths show that students' concerns vary to some extent. For example, Continental African students have concerns around broad issues of language, religion, and culture. Students who have been schooled in the Caribbean complain about the "social labelling" of Black male youths as "troublemakers." Questions of identity are raised by students born here in Canada and in particularly to mixed parents. Students who speak with different accents and dialects point to intragroup discrimination and prejudices among their peers. But it is noted that concerns around the lack of representation of Black/African perspectives, histories and experiences, the absence of Black teachers, and the prevailing culture of White dominance in the mainstream school system, are shared by all Black youths.

8. However, it is extremely important that an African-centered pedagogy is not pursued by marginalizing or degrading other groups' perspectives, histories, cultures, and traditions. Such pedagogy should not romanticize or unduly glorify the African past. It must not deny European influences on African peoples or completely reject the intellectual validity of European culture and scholarship on the development of African-informed epistemology.

REFERENCES

Apple, M. (1989). American realities: Poverty, economy, and education. In L. Weis, E. Farrar, & H. Petrie (Eds.), *Dropouts from school* (pp. 205–223). Albany: State University of New York Press.

Asante, M. (1991). The Afrocentric idea in education. *Journal of Negro Education, 60,* 170–180.

Bickel, R., & Papagiannis, G. (1988). Post-high school prospects and district-level dropouts. *Youth and Society, 20* (2), 123–147.

Cadieux, P. H. (1991). The stay-in-school initiative: A call to action. *Equation: The Newsletter of the Stay-In-School Initiative.* Ottawa: Ministry of State for Youth.

Canadian Association of University Teachers. (1991, August). The high school dropout rate. *University Affairs,* p. 5.

Conference Board of Canada. (1991). *Profiles in partnerships: Business-education partnerships that enhance student retention.* Ottawa: Author.

Cummins, J. (1989). Education and visible minority youth. In *Visible minority youth project* (pp. 1–59). Toronto: Ontario Ministry of Citizenship.

Dei, G. J. S. (1992, May–June). *The school dropout dilemma.* Paper presented at the luncheon round table of the Canadian Sociology and Anthropology Association, Learned Societies' Meetings, University of Prince Edward Island, Charlottetown.

Dei, G. J. S. (1994a). Afrocentricity: A cornerstone of pedagogy. *Anthropology and Education Quarterly, 25* (1), 3–28.

Dei, G. J. S. (1994b). Examining the case for African-centred schools in Ontario. *McGill Journal of Education, 22*(3), 179–198.

Dei, G. J. S. (in press). Is anyone listening to these voices? *Our Schools/Ourselves.*

Editorial. (1991, October 15). *Share*, p. 8.

Estrada, K., & McLaren, P. (1993). A dialogue on multiculturalism and democratic culture. *Educational Researcher, 22* (3), 27–33.

Fine, M. (1991). *Framing dropouts: Notes on the politics of an urban public high school.* Albany: State University of New York Press

Fine, M., & Rosenberg P. (1983). Dropping out of high school: The ideology of school and work. *Journal of Education, 165,* 257–272.

Finn, J. D. (1989). Withdrawing from school. *Review of Educational Research, 59* (2), 117–142.

Fordham, S., & Ogbu, J. U. (1986). Black students' school success: Coping with the burden of "acting white." *The Urban Review, 18,* 176–206.

Garibaldi, A. M. (1988). *Educating black male youth: A moral and civic imperative.* New Orleans: New Orleans Public Schools.

Garibaldi, A. M. (1992). Educating and motivating African-American males to succeed. *Journal of Negro Education, 61,* 4–11.

Goodlad, J. (1984). *A place called school.* New York: McGraw-Hill.

Henry, A. (1992). *Taking back control: Toward a Black woman's Afrocentric standpoint on the education of Black children.* Unpublished doctoral dissertation, Ontario Institute for Studies in Education, Toronto.

James, C. E. (1990). *Making it.* Oakville, ON: Mosaic Press.

Jaynes, G. D., & Williams, R. M. (Eds.). (1989). *A common destiny: Blacks in American society.* Washington, DC: National Academy Press.

Karenga, M. (1988). Black studies and the problematic paradigm. *Journal of Black Studies, 18,* 395–414.

King, A. J. C., Warren, W. K., Michalski, C., & Peart, M. J. (1988). *Improving student retention in Ontario secondary schools.* Toronto: Ontario Ministry of Education.

Kluegel, J. R., & Smith, E. R. (1986). *Beliefs about inequality: Americans' views of what is and what ought to be.* New York: A. de Gruyter.

Kozol, J. (1991). *Savage inequalities: Children in American schools.* New York: Crown Publishers.

Lawton, S. B. (1992). *Dropping out: A literature review, 1988–1992.* Unpublished manuscript, Ontario Institute for Studies in Education, Toronto.

LeCompte, M. D., & Dworkin, A. G. (1991). *Giving up on school: Student dropouts and teacher burnouts.* Newbury Park, CA: Corwin Press.

Lomotey, K. (Ed.). (1990). *Going to school: The African-American experience.* Albany: State University of New York Press.

Manski, C. F. (1989). Schooling as experimentation: A reappraisal of the post-secondary dropout phenomenon. *Economics of Education Review, 8,* 305–312.

Marable, M. (1985). *Black American politics: From the Washington marches to Jesse Jackson.* London: Verso.

Nieto, S. (1992). *Affirming diversity.* New York: Longman.

Ogbu, J. U. (1978). *Minority education and caste.* New York: Academic Press.

Ontario Ministry of Citizenship, Visible Minority Youth Project (1989). *Child, youth and family project. Report of the sub-committee on racial minority youth and visible minority youth.* Toronto.

Pollard, D. S. (1989). Against the odds: A profile of academic achievers from the urban underclass. *Journal of Negro Education, 58,* 297–308.

Radwanski, G. (1987). *Ontario study of the relevance of education, and the issue of dropouts.* Toronto: Ontario Ministry of Education.

Solomon, P. (1992). *Black resistance in high school.* Albany: State University of New York Press.

Stage, F. K. (1989). Motivation, academic and social integration, and the early dropout. *American Educational Research Journal, 26,* 385–402.

Toronto Board of Education. (1988). *Education of Black students in Toronto: Final report of the consultative committee.* Toronto: Author.

Trueba, H., Spindler, G., & Spindler, L. (Eds.). (1989). *What do anthropologists have to say about dropouts?* Basingstoke: Falmer.

Weis, L., Farrar, E., & Petrie, H. G. (Eds.). (1989). *Dropouts from school.* Albany: State University of New York Press.

CHAPTER 10

Government Funded Job-Entry Programs for Women: Whose Needs Are Being Addressed?

SHAUNA BUTTERWICK

They [the government] say isn't it wonderful that 80% of the women got jobs that paid six [dollars] per hour. Are we doing them [the participants] a favor? Are we just allowing companies and employers to exploit the women? I think it's far worse and detrimental to those women being underemployed, not unemployed. There's nothing as demeaning, as depressing, as awful as that. (lifeskills instructor, women's job-entry program)

There is one woman who is very bright, she's got a quick mind, a good personality, energetic. Her career goal is to clean houses. But she's capable of so much more. We try to recognize what their talents are and not try to fool them, that they don't have their limitations. (coordinator, women's job-entry program)

There's no way we can go back to the old ways. It's better to move on and live in White society. (participant in job-entry program)

These quotations are taken from interviews I conducted while studying a government funded job-entry program for Native women, run by Native women. These remarks illustrate the tensions and contradictions I found in this program and two other government-funded programs for women that I studied in 1990 and 1991. In the following discussion, I focus on the program for Native women and draw attention to the contested terrain of "needs talk," which was part of the everyday interactions among participants, staff, and government policy.

The staff in the program resisted the government's "get a job—any job" agenda, which they believed reinforced the participants' economic oppression. In a similar vein, they challenged the participants' stated desires for work, particularly when it was for low-waged, entry-level jobs. They wanted the participants to imagine more for themselves. In turn, the participants also challenged the staff. Some resisted the staff's efforts to build a curriculum which reinforced the value and contribution of Native heritage and identity. Others resisted the staff's emphasis on further education and the development of a career, and in this way their desire for entry-level work matched the government's emphasis to "get a job—any job."

I believe that this analysis of a women's reentry program can contribute to rethinking the issue of dropping out. I argue here for an approach oriented to political discourse, one in which the focus is not on "needs" alone, but on the political process of interpreting needs. Just as my study of women's reentry programs pointed to the dominant interests of government and the ways in which staff and participants contested these interests, similar research on dropping out can focus attention on how "needs talk" is central to the current policy discourse. Whose interests dominate this discourse? What kind of needs talk is produced by those on the margins— students who have dropped out or who are thinking about dropping out? What social and institutional relations organize the production of this needs talk?

My focus on the contested terrain of needs talk has been informed by Nancy Fraser's (1989) analysis of social welfare policy and programs. Fraser has drawn attention to the "politics of need interpretation," that is, a process characterized by unequal access based on gender, race, and class. I expand on Fraser's work later in this chapter.

I first observed this struggle over the interpretation of women's "needs" when I worked as a research assistant and did fieldwork in a government-funded reentry program for women, which was part of a larger study of how women learn to be office workers (Gaskell, 1992). I also participated in *constructing* this needs talk (i.e., what it is that women *really need* to enter the labor market) as a member of a feminist advocacy group. The focus of this group's efforts was to change government policy related to women's access to training, education, and paid work. Most members of the group worked in nonprofit agencies and organizations, which received government money to run reentry programs for women.

Thus, my study grew out of my work as an activist and researcher attempting to make sense of and influence labor market policy and the creation of high-quality job-training programs to help women find paid work that gave them a living wage and opportunities for advancement. I began my research with a critical examination of the larger policy context in which women's reentry programs were structured, paying specific attention to the needs talk of the Canadian Jobs Strategy (CJS)—a labor market policy initiated by the Canadian federal government in 1985 under which women's reentry programs were funded. My fieldwork included studies of the Native program already mentioned and of two other CJS-funded reentry programs for women that welcomed my research.

The official CJS policy interpreted women's needs rather simply—to successfully make the transition from home to the labor market, women need to gain more recent work experience and to improve their skills. In many situations this makes sense. This interpretation, however, neither includes nor reveals the circumstances of poverty, violence, sexism, classism, and racism that have created obstacles to women's successful participation in reentry training and in the paid work force. My own observation of these CJS-funded programs revealed that the participants had needs far more complex and diverse than those suggested by the rather simplistic, individualized interpretation outlined in the official policy. Thus it was not surprising that, as stated previously, there were many moments of resistance by both staff and participants.

The women who staffed these programs played a key role in mediating between the participants and the government. The staff produced a needs talk, which at times challenged government demands and at other times reinforced the government's interpretations. This contradictory needs talk must be understood within the structures and constraints of the everyday world of running CJS programs, which were short-term and given limited resources.

Before discussing in more detail the needs talk of the policy and of the staff and participants, I begin this chapter with a discussion of the methodological and theoretical framework that helped me make sense of what I was observing, reading, and hearing. The chapter concludes with a discussion of the contribution this framework can make to research, policy, and program development in relation to the discourse on dropping out and reentry.

RESEARCH FROM THE MARGINS

My study was an alternative to "top-down" policy analyses, which often fail to challenge the assumptions informing policy, in that it employed a critical discourse oriented approach focused on the providers (and to a lesser extent, the participants) of the reentry program. A critical discourse oriented approach helps to reveal how practitioners interpret and operationalize policies in the course of their daily work (Finch, 1986). I also wanted my research to explore and place in context the everyday world of women's experience; I was following Haraway (1991), who has argued for "politics and epistemologies of location, positioning, and situating, where partiality and not universality is the condition of being heard to make rational knowledge claims" (p. 595).

Dorothy Smith's (1987) work was also particularly useful in shaping the method of this inquiry. Smith has criticized mainstream social science research and its objectification of women, and argues that what is needed is research "for" women rather than "about" women. She has developed a method of study which begins with the everyday world of women and which illuminates women as knowledgeable agents. In this method, the focus is not limited to the everyday; rather, attention is also given to how women's everyday worlds are organized and determined by social relations immanent in and extending beyond the everyday. Smith calls this approach "institutional ethnography" and contrasts it with standard ethnographic research, which describes a local setting as if it were a self-contained unit of analysis. Instead, Smith argues for inquiries that locate the dynamics of local settings within the complex institutional relations that shape the local dynamics.

Smith has been particularly interested in how power, organization, and regulation are pervasively structured. She identifies the "ruling apparatus" as a complex of organized practices, such as education, that take the particular and construct it into the abstract and generalized. In my inquiry, the official policy discourse reflects such a ruling apparatus in its construction of abstract and generalized notions about women's training needs, as I later discuss in more detail.

My study was also organized around my interest in outlining both the constraints and possibilities of reentry programs and policies, as well as my desire to avoid constructing women as passive victims (Acker, 1988; Anyon, 1983; Davies, 1983). I wanted to illuminate women's agency through the active role they play in negotiating their needs, and to do so while considering their work as historically and contextually situated (Gaskell, 1983; Wharton, 1991).

ANALYZING NEEDS TALK

Nancy Fraser's (1989) exploration of the discourse of the welfare state in advanced capitalism spoke directly to my experiences as an advocate and to what I was hearing and observing in the reentry programs. Fraser insists that feminists must directly challenge the discourse of the welfare state in the current "welfare wars":

> Because women constitute the majority of social-welfare program recipients and employees, women and women's needs will be the principal stakes in the battles over social spending likely to dominate national [U.S.] politics in the coming period. . . . And the fiscal crisis of the welfare state coincides everywhere with a second long-term, structural tendency: the feminization of poverty. (p. 144)

Fraser suggests a different approach to analyzing policy. She calls for attention to "the politics of need interpretation," that is, to the political struggle over the interpretation of needs, particularly women's needs. Starting from the experience of marginalized women, Fraser shows how participation in the political process of interpreting needs is limited and structured around unequal access to resources based on gender, class, race, ethnicity, and age—and how little opportunity women have to influence the process.

According to Fraser, most policy analyses do not focus on the politics of constructing need; as a result, they ignore the fact that the interpretation of people's needs is itself a political matter. By focusing on the politics of need interpretation, the relational structure of needs claims are brought into view: that is, who (A) needs what (B) in order to do what (C). Fraser suggests that when discussions about needs are at a "thin" level, there are few problems. For example, when discussing the needs of the unemployed, most would agree that they need jobs or they need help reentering the work force. The relational structure of such needs claims goes like this: "People who are unemployed need help to reenter the labor market in order to avoid poverty/the problems of unemployment." But when the discussion moves to why people are experiencing unemployment, to what kind of jobs, and to how unemployed people are to be assisted to find jobs—that is, to a "thick" description of needs—the claims become more contested and controversial. Fraser emphasizes that this approach to policy analysis deals less with the needs themselves than with the discourses about them that various groups produce. Fraser's approach must also be understood as different from the common understanding about the politics of needs, which focuses on the distribution of resources.

In her study of the politics of need interpretation, Fraser identifies three analytically distinct but practically intermingled struggles. These are: (1) politicizing a need, (2) determining how to satisfy the need, and (3) democratizing the process of decision making about the need, so that those whose needs are involved can participate. Struggles to politicize a need, that is, to secure or deny the political status of an issue, often involve efforts by oppositional social movements. To position a particular need on the public policy agenda, such social movements as feminism must challenge commonplace understandings about what is a public policy matter and what is a private/domestic issue. The issue of child care exemplifies this struggle. Some argue that child care is a public matter, that the government and citizens of a nation must all take responsibility for the care of children; others claim that it is a private matter, better left to the domestic realm of families, most often mothers.

A second struggle revolves around the satisfaction of a need once it has secured some status on the public policy agenda. Here, the challenge for social movements and those arguing for a public policy response ensures that their perspectives on how to satisfy the need will be considered. Again, take the example of child care—advocacy groups in Canada have been successful in pushing this issue onto the federal policy agenda but the government's response (i.e., the government's interpretation of how to satisfy the need for child care) has been very limited. This is an example, I would argue, both of keeping child care within the private domestic sphere and maintaining old boundaries between the public and the private.

The third aspect of the politics of need interpretation is the democratization of decision making and policy making, which empowers those individuals and groups whose needs are in question to determine their own needs and the satisfaction of those needs. If we think again about the example of child care, children, parents, and child care workers are rarely at the public policy table. Democratization would seek to change this situation.

Another significant contribution of Fraser's work is her identification of three main discourses about needs that emerge in these three areas of struggle. She has termed these "oppositional," "reprivatization," and "expert/public policy" discourses. Oppositional needs talk is often found when needs are being politicized. As mentioned previously, this politicization entails challenging old boundaries and offering alternative interpretations. Feminist and other social movements have played a major role in creating oppositional needs discourses. Reprivatization needs discourses are often constructed in reaction to oppositional discourses and are attempts to maintain previous boundaries and to depoliticize the needs identified by social movements. Expert or public policy discourses emerge during discussions about the satisfaction of needs. This kind of talk involves taking the needs that have found their way onto the public policy agenda and translating them in such a way that they can now be satisfied through state intervention. Expert or public policy discourses are often found in private or semiprivate agencies of the state.

Again, taking the example of child care, the "needs talk" of advocacy groups could be considered oppositional discourses as they struggle to place child care on the public policy agenda. The government's response to child care issues, for example—the establishment of child tax credits—could be considered a reprivatization discourse because child care is still characterized as a private concern. Expert or public policy discourse has also developed as various agencies become involved in the debate about child care.

Fraser has also developed a model of social discourse in which she outlines the discursive resources different groups use when making claims. Fraser wants to avoid reinforcing a simply pluralist notion of communication and to emphasize the multivalent and contested character of needs talk. Her model identifies five key elements (pp. 164–165). First, there are the "officially recognized idioms used to press claims" (e.g., needs, rights, or interest talk). Second, there are the "vocabularies available for interpreting and communicating one's needs" (e.g., therapeutic, administrative, religious, feminist, or socialist vocabularies). Third, there are the various ways in which conflicting needs claims are dealt with (e.g., drawing on scientific expertise, making compromises, voting, or privileging certain groups over others). Fourth, there are the "narrative conventions available for constructing the individual and collective stories that are constitutive of social identities." Fifth, there are the "modes of subjectification," that is, how different discourses position people and endow them with specific capacities for action (e.g., normal or deviant, freely self-determining or victims, passive recipients or potential activists).

Fraser emphasizes that these means of communication are not part of a coherent web. Rather, they are multiple and diverse, "stratified and differentiated by unequal status, power, and access to resources, and organized unequally along lines of class, gender, race, ethnicity and age" (p. 165). Fraser's model reveals the emergence of different types of needs talk from struggles among groups which have unequal access to the process itself and to the resources which might enable them to participate in it. Fraser calls for research which distinguishes between discourses that are hegemonic and part of "societal patterns of domination and subordination" and those that are "nonhegemonic, disqualified and discounted" (p. 165).

Given this overview of the background to my study of women's reentry programs, I turn now to an analysis of how women's needs were interpreted within both the official CJS policy and the needs talk of the women working in the CJS reentry program for Native women.

THE POLICY CONTEXT OF WOMEN'S REENTRY PROGRAMS

The Canadian Jobs Strategy was introduced in 1985 by the Canadian federal government. One objective of this policy initiative was helping those "most in need" to gain access to the labor market. A previous Royal Commission had identified women, people with disabilities, Aboriginal peoples, visible minorities, and the long-term unemployed as disadvantaged groups when it came to labor market participation (Abella, 1984). Specific program areas described as "entry" and "reentry" were created under the CJS umbrella to assist these groups.

According to a 1988 government information package provided for prospective training coordinators (Employment and Immigration Canada, 1988), the objective of the CJS reentry program was "to provide on- and off-the-job training and work experience for women who have difficulty making the transition from home to work" (p. 20). Eligible participants are those women "having difficulty making a successful transition into the labour force, i.e., obtaining employment that realistically meets both their expectations and the local labour market needs, due to lack of adequate training and/or work experience" (p. 20). Support for these women was given "through the provision of financial assistance to co-ordinators for operating and training costs and allowances for participants" (p. 20).

This policy was unique in its attempt to address both social equality and economic concerns (Prince & Rice, 1989). But there were other concerns, in addition to helping those "most in need," which played a dominant role in the government's development of CJS. These included the desires to reduce government spending, to supply the market with workers, and to have a better match among training programs, the needs of employers, and the changing labor market. In this respect, CJS was a market-driven or supply-side policy, one in which the need of employers for skilled workers dominated.

There were many critiques of this policy by educational, labor, community, and women's organizations (e.g., Association of Canadian Community Colleges, 1986; Association for Community-Based Training and Education for Women, 1986; Canadian Labour Congress, 1985 and 1987; Canadian Congress for Learning Opportunities for Women, 1987; Community Coalition on the CJS, 1987). A recurring issue was that training had become the focus of labor market initiatives without a concomitant strategy for economic development and the creation of jobs. "Training for what?" was a question commonly posed by many groups, including labor groups, women's organizations, and educators, who argued that the government should be focusing on job creation as well as training (Jackson, 1992). There were also challenges to the government's desire to restrict spending at a time when there was more demand for programs. Thus, serving more trainees with limited and decreasing funds created what Jenson (1988) has termed the "fast food" approach to training—billions served at the cheapest prices.

My analysis, employing Fraser's model of social discourse, revealed the contested and problematic nature of the interpretation of women's needs within the official discourse of CJS. CJS could be seen as a policy based on a rather "thin" interpretation of women's needs: that is, women's lack of training and job experience. This interpretation decontextualized women's experiences, and constructed abstract and generalized notions—a process documented by Smith (1987) as a technique of the "ruling apparatus." The structural inequalities of the labor market and the interlocking nature of women's oppression based on gender, race, and class were ignored.

In the official policy discourse of CJS, the formally recognized idiom used to press claims was *needs* talk rather than *rights* or *interests* talk. CJS represented a policy that privileged the concern of supplying the changing labor market with workers and the policy of fiscal restraint over the "needs" of women and other disadvantaged groups.

The vocabulary employed within the official policy discourse could be described as therapeutic and administrative. It was therapeutic in that women, not the structure of the labor market, were constructed as the "problem" and as having to be "fixed." The dominance of administrative vocabulary was evident in the concern expressed with the finances and responsibilities of coordinators. For the most part, the dominant discourse constructed women as passive recipients of programs, not as active agents who could determine their own needs.

It is important to place the CJS policy in some historical and political context. CJS was initiated at a time when significant restructuring of the economy was taking place, a time when most job growth was in the low-waged service sector (Economic Council of Canada, 1990). As previously mentioned, government was particularly concerned with reducing spending and meeting local labor market needs. These economic and political realities, together with an individualistic and simplistic interpretation of women's needs, had significant structural implications. For the most part, programs for women were relatively short-term and had limited resources. As a result, they assisted women to find only entry-level, low-waged work. There was also an emphasis on "on-the-job" learning, which translated into some participants spending over half of the program time with their "host-employers," where there was limited opportunity for the government to monitor the quality of training being provided. Concerns were raised by both labor and women's organizations that this emphasis on on-the-job learning, without proper monitoring, led to exploitation of the participants as a source of cheap labor.

CJS was a policy that attempted to serve what appear to be conflicting interests. Serving those "most in need" was difficult, if not impossible to do, given the economic and political context. With fewer jobs, increasing unemployment, a desire to reduce government spending, and the growth of labor markets offering predominantly low-waged, entry-level work, the needs of disadvantaged groups can be only minimally addressed. The challenge for policy makers, researchers, and advocates is to create policies and programs that serve what appear to be competing goals: efficiency and equity.

LONG-TERM CAREER PLANNING OR GETTING A JOB—ANY JOB?

The women who participated in the job-entry program for Native women had diverse and complex needs that the official policy ignored. They struggled with histories of violence, ongoing poverty, racism, sexism, and substance abuse. According to the official policy, their difficulties arose out of a lack of job skills and recent work experience, a rather "thin" discussion of women's needs compared to a much more "thick" understanding of the complexities of their struggles.

The program for Native women was run by an all-Native nonprofit society established in 1985. The mandate of the organization was to "prepare Native women to participate fully in society and achieve and secure employment in an urban environment." The agency, located in a large Canadian city, had been offering government-funded, job-entry programs for 6 years. Their programs were funded under a specific CJS category— "severely employment disadvantaged." An eligible participant for this program was considered to be severely disadvantaged for employment if they faced "significant barriers to securing and maintaining employment for such reasons as poor work habits; attitudinal or motivational problems; a serious lack of education/training; functional illiteracy; prolonged periods of institutionalization; a history of drug or alcohol abuse; or lack of ability to communicate in either official language" (Employment and Immigration Canada, 1988, p. 20).

At the time of the study, the agency was offering three programs each year for 15 weeks each: 5 weeks in the classroom where the trainees received life skills instruction; 4 weeks with host employers; 1 week back in the classroom; another 4 weeks with host employers; and a final week back in the classroom. Seventeen women were participating in the program; most of them were on social assistance. Their educational backgrounds ranged from completion of 6th grade to high school diploma, with the majority having left school before completing 12th grade. Most trainees had children, with half either married or living with a partner and the remaining half single mothers. A few participants were single women with no children. Altogether, they represented a wide variety of Native nations and they had a variety of urban and rural experiences.

Consent for the research project was given by the board of directors and the staff. Although I was welcomed by the board, staff, and participants, I was acutely aware of being an outsider, a temporary visitor. The privileges afforded to me as a White, well-educated, middle-class, straight woman were in stark contrast to the poverty, violence, and racism that many in the program had experienced and were continuing to deal with. I interviewed and had many informal discussions with all the staff of the project. I also interviewed one member of the board of directors, and spoke informally during and between classes with the trainees. I examined program documents including the proposal made to the government, program recruitment flyers, and curriculum materials. I also observed the life skills training component for several weeks.

The curriculum in many ways challenged the official policy discourse. There was a clear emphasis on building self-esteem and creating a positive sense of Native identity. During the life skills classes that I visited, the classroom activities were organized around the medicine wheel, with attention given to the spiritual, emotional, and physical as well as the cognitive aspects of the participants' lives.

I found that the staff were committed to the participants, passionate about their work, and frustrated with the constraints of the policy. They had to work both with the government and the opportunities provided by the CJS policy and against the narrow interpretations of the policy framework. As one member of the board for the agency indicated, they had little choice but to use the policy to provide services, given that there was almost nothing else available: "We must use [the policy] to provide programs . . . because we see what the women struggle with; we see the cultural differences and help women get through. Because we're it, the only opportunity."

The instructors also recognized the contributions the program had made to the community and expressed concern with their dependence on government funding. As one said, "I think it's a really good thing that this program exists. I really believe in it. This organization's done a lot of good for women; it would be a terrible thing if they ever stopped funding it."

All of the staff believed the government had little understanding of what the women were up against and unrealistic expectations of what could or should be accomplished within the boundaries of the program. Women needed much more than the program could offer:

> What they [Canada Employment] are failing to recognize is who we're dealing with here. We're dealing with a very abused population of women and what that means. They don't understand what that means . . . all they [Canada Employment] care about is the goal of getting a job.

The staff went on to challenge the official position that success meant getting jobs for the trainees. In their experience, it was a major accomplishment simply to have the women maintain attendance and finish the program. They believed that building self-esteem was the biggest task, and one that would not be accomplished in 15 weeks:

> The part they don't get is that, number one, just keeping them in the program—secondly, recognizing the issues, for them [the participants] to even have to begin to have any self-esteem, it's such a complicated thing. It's not going to happen in this program; it may do if they go to 5 years of therapy.

The board member shared this view and felt that the government's approach to these programs was too rigid: "Building self-esteem is one of the most important issues, but the government doesn't see it as part of the formula."

The staff felt that the focus on "getting a job—any job" reinforced exploitation and underemployment which, they argued, was far worse than unemployment. The senior life skills instructor argued similarly that getting a job at the end of 15 weeks of training was not necessarily the best outcome. She believed that helping women develop long-term and sustainable goals was more important:

> One of the things that I like to stress is they can actually have a career and not just go out and get a job—any job. I stress that because we'd like to see them working years from now and being happy with it and I know that unhappy people don't stay working. So we think that it's better to give them a little bit of extra time for them to figure out, when they get going, what direction they want to take . . . it gives them a sense of the long term.

Expansion of the resources (financial, material, and human)—for example, improved computer software—for the program was a central negotiating issue between the staff and the government. Of particular concern was the need for an in-house psychologist or counselor. Although the staff provided counseling and support throughout the program and often on their own time, they argued that they were not adequately trained to do this. Given the seriousness of some of the participants' problems and the staff members' other responsibilities, they could provide only minimal support. They also felt it was unfair to send the participants to yet another new agency for counseling. The senior instructor expressed dismay with the government's resistance to this request:

> We've asked for a half-time psychologist. It would cost them too much money so they wouldn't give that. It's like saying Native women aren't worth it. We have to fight for every little thing we get, whether it's a cost-of-living increase, whether it's more office supplies or updating the computer.

In an effort to respond more appropriately to participants' needs, the staff developed curricula that addressed more than specific job-finding skills. Discussions of Native issues and Native heritage were a significant part of the classroom activities and, as mentioned earlier, the medicine wheel was used to develop the life skills curriculum. The fact that the staff and participants in the program were all Native created a unique learning context for many of the women. Said one instructor, "We have comments from many of the women that they're really very happy that there's a Native program because so often they'll feel out of place. So at this most basic level, it is healing."

The staff were also aware that there were many nations represented in the group and they wanted to avoid reinforcing the mainstream notion that there existed a unitary Native culture:

> We try to be very sensitive to the fact that many of these women were not raised traditionally and they're really not terribly comfortable with Native ways per se. And there's the other issue that Native is not homogeneous, it's many different nationalities and they are not the same.

The staff's approach to attendance posed another challenge to official policy. The government's rule was that training allowances would be withheld if participants were absent. At the beginning of the program all participants signed a contract which outlined some basic requirements for participation, including attending all classes, and abstaining from alcohol and other drugs. When problems did arise, the staff worked hard to keep the women in the program:

We try to review these expectations at least once a week. Try to keep reminding them, and doing it in an orderly way, not just coming down on them because someone's been bad. One woman has had some serious problems. She missed four out of eight days but when we were able to welcome her back and not make her feel guilty and bad and judge her, she's been here every day since.

In another attempt to move beyond simply imparting job-finding skills and information, the staff introduced the participants to other resources, particularly those serving the urban Native community. For example, they arranged to have visitors from different agencies, took the trainees to visit other services and organizations, and encouraged the women to learn for themselves by visiting other resources in their communities.

Apart from the staff's struggles, the participants faced dilemmas of their own. The program was both an opportunity to create better lives for their families and a source of conflict. When talking about their motivation for participating, many of the participants spoke not so much about their own goals and aspirations, but about their children's futures:

It was big thing to come here and show my daughter that going to school is a good thing and that encouraged my daughter to go back to school, which she did. I want to be something for my daughter and granddaughter. That's what keeps me going.

Yet, the women who wanted to set examples for their children also found that there were negative outcomes to their participation. One participant found that her family and friends were distancing themselves from her because she was attending the program and changing: "It makes me mad that I'm all alone and don't have friends. It's either one thing or another. You have to make new friends or have everybody reject you."

Another participant found that attending the program was a major event in her marriage. Her husband expressed both concern and pride about her participation

He sees me dressed up in the morning. Then I'm gone all day and he wonders where I really go. I phone him at the break. He was really upset the other day—worried that I'll leave. He also feels proud of me. . . . He's really scared that I'm going to change.

An important part of the program was valuing and acknowledging the participants' life experiences and homemaking skills, and translating these into labor market skills. One woman who had a lot of experience caring for sick and elderly family members wanted to work in the health sciences and knew that the first step was finishing high school: "I want to work in a health area, visiting people, advising them. I want a challenge, and if it takes more training I'm willing to do it."

As outlined before, the fact that the program was for only Native women and run entirely by Native women was a unique learning context for many participants. Many of the women had lived mainly in urban centers, had never been on a Native reserve, and had little experience of working with other Native women. One admitted: "I never spend time with Native women. It's good to see that there are good Native women and beautiful Native women and powerful Native women."

Not all the participants readily accepted the staff's interpretations of their "needs." Some were resistant to learning about traditional Native culture; they had not lived on a Native reserve nor in a Native urban community. For them, the only way to survive was to blend completely into the White dominant culture: "There's no way we can go back to the old ways. It's better to move on and live in White society."

Others felt strongly that they wanted to find work right away, even if it meant low-waged jobs. This was a big enough change for them, and they found the idea of going back to school for several years unrealistic.

At the end of the program, the majority of the women went back to school to complete 12th grade. Many of these women also planned to go on for further training in such areas as the health sciences and office automation. Most of these participants continued their education at a local Native-run postsecondary institution. Three participants found jobs following the program, one as a sales clerk and two in clerical positions. Three did not complete the program and the remainder neither found work nor continued with their education.

SEVERELY EMPLOYMENT DISADVANTAGED OR SURVIVORS OF COLONIALISM

The staff had established a relationship with the government funding agency and had created a curriculum that in many respects challenged the government's interpretation of the needs of "severely employment disadvantaged" participants. In their negotiations with government and with participants, the staff were engaged in a struggle that could be characterized as a politicization process. At times, they employed an alternative and oppositional interpretation in contrast to the narrow interpretation in the official policy, using a variety of oppositional, reprivatization, and expert discourses. In some respects, the staff employed feminist and antiracist interpretations, insofar as they argued for some understanding of the abuse the participants had suffered as a result of poverty, violence, racism, and sexism. In other ways, however, the staff employed an "expert" kind of discourse, translating the needs of the students in ways that could be taken up by the state.

For example, when staff argued that the participants needed counseling and therapy, they were translating issues of abuse and violence into the need for intervention, which focused, not surprisingly, on the individual rather than on social structures and practices. In other respects, this demand for counseling resources and the claim that the participants needed years of therapy could be considered a kind of "reprivatization" discourse because it focused on the individual and in a sense maintained old boundaries between public and private. On the other hand, counseling and therapy could help the women become aware of and understand how their difficulties of abuse and violence relate to their social/political oppression. All the staff, to some degree, challenged the main goal of CJS to get women jobs—any jobs. Although the staff contested the narrow official interpretation, they were constrained in their challenges and tended to construct the trainees as "needing to be fixed."

The contested terrain of needs talk also existed in the relationships between staff and participants and was influenced by their similarities in race and differences in class. As Native women, the staff and participants were positioned in similar ways relative to colonial practices of the market, the Canadian state, and the church (Herbert, 1994). The fact that this was an all-Native program was a unique experience for many participants and provided a context which drew attention to their Native heritage. The staff and participants were also from different Aboriginal communities, with different urban and rural experiences, and different experiences of living both on and off reserve. To some extent, the staff could be described as middle class and the participants as working class or poor. It may be that the staff's aspirations for the participants and their desire to have the participants think beyond getting a job reflected a desire to have the participants reach a class status like their own. Thus the everyday struggles in this program were the result of complex and shifting relationships, at times reflecting solidarity between staff, board members, and participants, and at other times reflecting conflicts emerging out of differences in experience and class.

The providers of such programs were positioned as mediators between the participants and the government, reinterpreting official policy discourse and calling for more complex understandings and different curriculum and resources. Their challenges, however, had contradictory outcomes. Sometimes they brought an oppositional and politicized interpretation of the participants' needs, and at other times they had to translate these politicized interpretations by using therapeutic and individualistic discourse.

DROPOUT AND REENTRY: IMPLICATIONS FOR RESEARCH AND ADVOCACY WORK

In this final section, I want to move from a focus on the Native women's program to a discussion of research and advocacy for both reentry women and youth who have dropped out of school. I suggest that for both groups there are benefits to employing a political discourse-oriented approach. I also argue that there are significant parallels between these two groups. Both groups are the "targets" of recent government initiatives, and have emerged as categories of the state in times of economic restructuring and fiscal restraint. Also, both groups have been marginalized from decision making and are viewed as needing to be "fixed."

As both Smith and Fraser argue, policy discourse often decontextualizes and depoliticizes the everyday reality of those groups whose needs are being addressed. By examining how the "ruling apparatus" produces a generalized, abstract notion of reentry women or dropout youth, our attention shifts to what is often hidden by such discourse—the social relations and structures which are immanent in and extend beyond the everyday. What is often ignored are the systemic societal inequalities which push students out of school and prevent women from becoming economically independent. To create a deeper understanding of these inequalities we need research which starts with the everyday world of these groups and individuals and which also examines the social and institutional relations organizing the everyday.

The research must also attend to the ways in which the interlocking nature of oppression works to create barriers to students finishing school and women reentering the paid work force. One must resist the tendency to view these individuals and groups as homogeneous and instead work toward understanding how gender, race, and class shape their experiences.

Fraser's model of social discourse can also help draw attention to the different discursive resources being used in government policy. Needs talk, rather than talk of rights or interests, appears to be the dominant vocabulary used to press claims. Government also tends to construct a moralistic narrative that often describes what students and reentry women "should be doing." The dominant vocabularies that are used to interpret needs appear to be therapeutic and administrative, with little feminist or socialist talk showing up in policy discussions. Conflicting needs claims are settled frequently by privileging certain groups over others, with little input from those whose needs are being discussed. The narrative conventions that are used to construct social identities are frequently abstract and generalized, with few actual stories told by students and women themselves. Finally, the individuals who are the focus of the discussion are positioned as deviant rather than normal, and as passive recipients and victims rather than as self-determining individuals.

Fraser has outlined three struggles within the politics of need interpretation: politicizing a need, satisfying a need, and democratizing the need interpretation process. Politicizing the issue of dropping out and women's reentry requires that an oppositional kind of discourse be employed, one which challenges the assumptions of current discussions put forward by government. It could be argued that the dominant interpretation of the "problem of dropout" and of reentry women has been constructed according to the needs of the state and capitalism, and not the needs of the marginalized. Like the CJS policy that funded the Native women's reentry program, recent policy papers such as *Dropping Out: The Cost to Canada* (Conference Board of Canada, 1992), support the view that fiscal restraint is the central issue driving the government's initiatives. Helping students finish high school often requires that governments spend money outside of the regular school system. Including basic education in the government's economic agenda can be viewed as an example of old boundaries being challenged as new needs are put on the public policy agenda. Including services such as counseling in women's reentry programs and other resources requires some recognition by government of the complexity of needs and also requires a fiscal commitment to responding to these needs.

Another significant struggle in the politics of dropping out and reentry is maintaining an oppositional stance during discussions about satisfying certain needs. Rather than emphasizing that students should "stay in school," which is the title of the current Canadian federal initiative (Employment and Immigration Canada, 1990), or that women should "get a job—any job," the education system could become more flexible and a system for truly lifelong education, so that students and reentry women have a wide variety of options and a significant voice in deciding the kinds of educational services that will help them return to school. For the third struggle, that of democratizing the need interpretation process, students who are thinking about dropping out or who have already dropped out and women struggling to reenter the paid work force must be included in the politics of need interpretation.

Research that captures the perspectives of students, teachers, counselors, and policy makers can help to illuminate this contested discourse. There is no straightforward solution, however, to the question of whose interpretation should be taken up. As Fraser (1989) has argued, "to say that needs are culturally constructed and discursively interpreted is not to say that any need interpretation is as good as any other" (p. 181). She goes on to say that it is not simply a matter of finding the interpretation that accurately describes the "true" nature of the need, nor of epistemic superiority—of locating the group which has the privileged view. What kind of interpretive justification should be employed?

Fraser suggests that attention should be given to the procedures and consequences of the social processes through which different need interpretations are produced. Procedurally, the best approach is one that works toward the goals of democracy, equality, and fairness. When considering the consequences of different need interpretations, the better approach is that which does not disadvantage one group in relation to another. The challenge is to translate these notions into guidelines for the discussion about dropping out and reentry.

It appears that "needs talk" is here to stay for some time as the "discursive coin of the realm" (Fraser, 1989, p. 183), therefore, those who bring an oppositional perspective must learn to work critically in this discursive arena. Fraser has suggested that orienting the discussion away from needs toward talk about rights could help to overcome "some of the forms of paternalism that arise when needs claims are divorced from rights claims" (p. 183). What are the rights of students who have dropped out of the school system? What are the responsibilities of researchers and educators and policy makers? What are the rights of Native women who have suffered as a result of the colonial practices of the Canadian government, the market, and the church? What are the rights of women who face barriers to their economic independence as a result of the structural inequalities of the educational system and the labor market?

Fraser (1989) cautions that it is important to understand that needs talk is neither "inherently emancipatory nor inherently repressive" (p. 183), but that it is contested and multivalent. I hope that this review of my study of a women's reentry program has helped those working on the issue of dropping out to take an alternative approach. To summarize, I urge advocates, educators, and researchers to recognize "the emancipatory from the repressive possibilities of needs talk" (p. 183).

In closing, I would like to give the last word to one of the instructors in the Native program. Her comment, I believe, captures her passion for and commitment to the participants, and speaks of the struggle to bring a long-term vision to a policy context which often addresses only short-term interests:

I try to be caring and honest and humble and happy and have a good sense of humor. I mess up all the time but you don't fail unless you quit. I see myself as a spiritual being first. We are all children of our ancestor's dreams. We need to live our lives not just for ourselves but how it is going to affect the seventh generation. I feel that I've been able to contribute in a small way to keep things going.

REFERENCES

Abella, R. (1984, October). *Report of the Commission on Equality in Employment.* Ottawa: Employment and Immigration Canada.

Acker, S. (1988). Teachers, gender and resistance. *British Journal of Sociology of Education, 9,* 307–322.

Anyon, J. (1983). Intersection of gender and class: Accommodation and resistance by working-class and affluent females to contradictory sex-role ideologies. In S. Walker & L. Barton (Eds.), *Gender, class and education* (pp. 19–37). Sussex: Falmer Press.

Association for Community-Based Training and Education for Women. (1986, October). *The Canadian Jobs Strategy: An overview* (Prepared by Terry Dance, member of ACTEW). Toronto: Author.

Association of Canadian Community Colleges. (1986, November). *Brief on the Association of Canadian Community Colleges Report on Practical Experiences With the Canadian Jobs Strategy.* (Presentation to the Hon. Benoit Bouchard, Minister of Employment and Immigration, by the ACCC Task Force on the CJS). Toronto: Author.

Canada Employment and Immigration. (1985, February). *Employment opportunities: Preparing Canadians for a better future.* Tabled at the First Ministers' Conference, Regina, Saskatchewan.

Canadian Congress for Learning Opportunities for Women. (1987, February). *Presentation of CCLOW to the Standing Committee on the Secretary of State* (Presented by Martha Calquhon, President, and Aisla Thomson, Executive Director). Toronto: Author.

Canadian Labour Congress. (1985, May). *Response to the Government of Canada's Consultation Paper on Training.* Report No. 85–5670. Ottawa: Author.

Canadian Labour Congress. (1987, January). *Position paper on Canadian Jobs Strategy.* Ottawa: Author.

Community Coalition on the Canadian Jobs Strategy. (1987, February). *A community critique of the Canadian Jobs Strategy: Proceedings of the Community Conference on the Canadian Jobs Strategy.* Toronto: Author.

Conference Board of Canada. (1992, May). *Dropping out: The cost to Canada* (Synopsis). Ottawa: Author.

Davies, L. (1983). Gender, resistance and power. In S. Walker & L. Barton (Eds.), *Gender, class and education* (pp. 39–52). Sussex: Falmer Press.

Economic Council of Canada. (1990). *Good jobs, bad jobs: Employment in the service economy.* Ottawa: Supply and Services Canada.

Employment and Immigration Canada. (1988, July). *Working opportunities for people: Canadian Jobs Strategy and other programs and services.* Ottawa: Supply and Services Canada.

Employment and Immigration Canada. (1990). *A national stay-in-school initiative.* Ottawa: Minister of Supply and Services.

Finch, J. (1986). *Research policy: The use of qualitative research methods in social and educational research.* London: Falmer Press.

Fraser, N. (1989). *Unruly practices: Power, discourse, and gender in contemporary social theory.* Minneapolis: University of Minnesota Press.

Gaskell, J. (1983). Education and women's work: Some new research directions. *Alberta Journal of Educational Research, 29,* 224–241.

Gaskell, J. (1992). *Gender matters from school to work.* Toronto: OISE Press.

Haraway, D. (1991). Situated knowledges: The science question in feminism and the privilege of the partial perspective. *Feminist Studies, 14,* 575–599.

Herbert, E. (1994). *Talking back: Six First Nations women's recovery stories from childhood sexual abuse and addictions.* Unpublished master's thesis, University of British Columbia, Vancouver.

Jackson, N. (Ed.). (1992). *Training for what?* Toronto: Our Schools/Our Selves Educational Foundation.

Jenson, J. (1988). The limits of "and the" discourse. In J. Jenson, E. Hagen, & C. Reddy (Eds.), *Feminization of the labor force: Paradoxes and promises* (pp. 155–172). New York: Oxford University Press.

Prince, M. J., & Rice, J. J. (1989). The Canadian Jobs Strategy: Supply side policy. In K. A. Graham (Ed.), *How Ottawa spends: The buck stops where?* (pp. 247–287). Ottawa: Carleton University Press.

Smith, D. (1987). *The everyday world as problematic: A feminist sociology.* Toronto: University of Toronto Press.

Wharton, A. S. (1991). Structure and agency in socialist-feminist theory. *Gender and Society, 5,* 373–389.

About the Contributors

Lesley Andres is an assistant professor in the Department of Educational Studies at the University of British Columbia. Her research and teaching interests include the sociology of education, foundations of higher education, issues of inequality and access, and quantitative and qualitative research methods. She has previously published under the name Lesley Andres Bellamy.

Paul Anisef is an associate professor in sociology at York University in Toronto. For well over a decade, Professor Anisef has conducted extensive research on the topics of accessibility to Canadian higher education, the transition from school to work at the secondary and postsecondary levels, and careers for Canadian youth. This research has resulted in three books: *Losers and Winners,* Butterworths, 1982 (with Norman R. Okihiro); *What Jobs Pay,* Hurtig Publishers, 1984; and *Transitions: Schooling and Employment in Canada,* Thompson Educational Publishers, 1993 (with Paul Axelrod). A fourth book, entitled *Learning and Sociological Profiles of Canadian High School Students* was published in 1994 by Edwin Mellen Press.

Shauna Butterwick is an assistant professor in educational studies at the University of British Columbia. She brings a critical feminist approach to her teaching and research interests with a focus on women's experiences in adult education and the labor market. She remains active in the feminist community, advocating for change to government job training policy.

Kari Dehli is an associate professor in the Department of Sociology in Education at the Ontario Institute for Studies in Education. She teaches courses in feminist theory, cultural studies, educational policy making, and school–community relations. Her publications include papers on parent–school relations, educational policy, feminism in the academy, and the historical sociology of gender, class, and schooling.

George J. Sefa Dei is an associate professor in the Department of Sociology in Education at the Ontario Institute for Studies in Education. His teaching and research interests are in the areas of antiracism, education, development education, and international development. In addition to his recently completed study, which appears in this collection, he has received a new grant from the Ontario Ministry of Education and Training to conduct an in-depth study of "Best Practices of Inclusive Schooling" in Ontario Public Schools.

Michelle Fine is a professor of psychology at the City University of New York, Graduate Center, and the Senior Consultant at the Philadelphia Schools Collaborative. Her recent publications include *Chartering Urban School Reform: Reflections on Public High Schools in the Midst of Change* (1994), *Beyond Silenced Voices: Class, Race, and Gender in American Schools* (1992), *Disruptive Voices: The Transgressive Possibilities of Feminist Research* (1992), and *Framing Dropouts: Notes on the Politics of an Urban High School* (1991). In addition, she works nationally as a consultant to parents' groups, community groups, and teacher unions on issues of school reform. She was awarded the Janet Helms Distinguished Scholar Award in 1994.

Jane Gaskell is a professor and associate dean of Graduate Programs and Research in the Faculty of Education at the University of British Columbia, where she has served in various roles since 1974. She has authored or co-authored papers and books focusing particularly on the sociology of education and the role of women in the education system. Her books include *Gender Matters From School to Work* (1992) and *Gender In/Forms Curriculum* (with John Willinsky, 1995). She has spent the last two years as Chair of the Coordinating Committee, and principal author of the final report of the *Exemplary Schools Project,* for the Canadian Education Association.

Deirdre M. Kelly is an assistant professor in the Department of Educational Studies at the University of British Columbia. Her research interests include school dropouts and pushouts, alternative education, feminist studies, and participatory research methodology. She has published articles in *World Development, The International Encyclopedia of Education, Youth and Society,* and *The American Sociologist,* and is the author of *Last Chance High: How Girls and Boys Drop In and Out of Alternative Schools* (1993). She is currently conducting comparative ethnographic research on two comprehensive high school-based day care programs for teen mothers and their children.

Harvey Krahn is a professor of sociology at the University of Alberta. His research and teaching interests include the sociology of work, school–work transitions, political sociology, and public policy. His publication includes a variety of papers on these subjects and a (co-authored) textbook on the sociology of work in Canada.

Margaret D. LeCompte is an associate professor in the School of Education at the University of Colorado in Boulder. She is co-author of *Giving Up on School* (with Gary Dworkin), *The Way Schools Work* (with Kathleen DeMarrais), *Ethnography and Qualitative Design in Educational Research* (with Judith Preissle) and co-editor of the *Handbook of Qualitative Design in Educational Research* (with Wendy Millroy and Judith Preissle), and author of numerous articles. Her research interests include at risk students, school reform, and research methods.

Nancy Lesko is an associate professor in the Department of Curriculum and Instruction and an adjunct in the Department of Women's Studies at Indiana University in Bloomington. She teaches in the areas of secondary multicultural education and feminist and poststructuralist theories and schooling. She has recently published a review of U.S. policies on school-aged mothers in *Curriculum Inquiry* and guest-edited an issue of *Theory into Practice, Rethinking Middle Grades.* She is currently writing a book that will critically examine conceptions of adolescence, which is tentatively titled *Act Your Age.*

Leslie G. Roman is an associate professor of educational studies at the University of British Columbia. She co-edited *Becoming Feminine: The Politics of Popular Culture* and *Views Beyond the Border Country: Raymond Williams and Cultural Politics.* She has written extensively in cultural studies, feminist theory, antiracist pedagogy, and critical ethnography. She is currently completing two books: *Dangerous Territories: Struggles for Difference and Equality,* co-edited with Linda Eyre, which examines backlash politics in education; and *Transgressive Knowledge,* which compares the resources of poststructural and postcolonial feminism for developing antiracist and antisexist pedagogy.

Kjell Rubenson is a professor of Adult Education and Director of the Centre for Policy Studies in Education at the University of British Columbia. His main research activities are in the fields of sociology of adult education, comparative education, work and education, and lifelong learning.

Julian Tanner is an associate professor of sociology at the University of Toronto, Scarborough Campus. His research and teaching interests include the sociology of youth, deviance, criminology, and the sociology of work. His publications include a variety of papers on these subjects and a forthcoming textbook on deviance and delinquency in Canada.

Index